Indigenous Religious Traditions in Five Minutes

Religion in 5 Minutes

Series Editors
Russell T. McCutcheon
University of Alabama
Aaron W. Hughes
University of Rochester

Volumes in the Religion in 5 Minutes book series are each an opportunity for novice readers to benefit from the expertise of scholars, all addressing common questions about everything from Hinduism and Buddhism to paganism and Indigenous religion. Students and general readers will find here questions that they might ask—What is the oldest religion? Do all religions have scriptures?—all answered in a readable manner. Because each chapter can be read in about five minutes, the books offer ideal supplementary resources in classrooms or an engaging read for those curious about the world around them. And sooner or later, the assumptions entailed in the questions themselves take center stage for the contributors. With recommended readings in each chapter, the Religion in 5 Minutes book series meets readers where they are and invites them to entertain just how fascinating the world might be.

Published

Religion in Five Minutes
Edited by Aaron Hughes and Russell T. McCutcheon

Buddhism in Five Minutes
Edited by Elizabeth J. Harris

Hinduism in Five Minutes
Edited by Steven W. Ramey

Forthcoming

African Diaspora Religions in Five Minutes
Edited by Emily D. Crews and Curtis J. Evans

Ancient Religion in Five Minutes
Edited by Andrew Durdin

Atheism in Five Minutes
Edited by Teemu Taira

Christianity in Five Minutes
Edited by Robyn Faith Walsh

Islam in Five Minutes
Edited by Edith Szanto

Judaism in Five Minutes
Edited by Tim Langille

Pagan Religions in Five Minutes
Edited by Suzanne Owen and Angela Puca

Indigenous Religious Traditions in Five Minutes

Edited by
Molly H. Bassett and Natalie Avalos

SHEFFIELD UK   BRISTOL CT

Published by Equinox Publishing Ltd.

UK: Office 415, The Workstation, 15 Paternoster Row, Sheffield, South Yorkshire S1 2BX

USA: ISD, 70 Enterprise Drive, Bristol, CT 06010

www.equinoxpub.com

First published 2022

British Library Cataloguing-in-Publication Data

A catalogue record for this book is available from the British Library.

ISBN-13   978 1 80050 202 4   (hardback)
          978 1 80050 203 1   (paperback)
          978 1 80050 204 8   (ePDF)
          978 1 80050 249 9   (ePub)

Library of Congress Cataloging-in-Publication Data

Names: Bassett, Molly H., 1980- editor. | Avalos, Natalie, editor.
Title: Indigenous religious traditions in five minutes / edited by Molly Bassett and Natalie Avalos.
Description: Sheffield, South Yorkshire ; Bristol, CT : Equinox Publishing Ltd., 2022. | Series: Religion in 5 minutes | Includes bibliographical references and index. | Summary: "Indigenous Religious Traditions in Five Minutes aims to answer many of the questions that come to mind when we think about the religious lives of Native and Indigenous peoples of the world. Specialists respond to questions in easily accessible language and provide references for further exploration, making this volume useful for personal study or classroom use"-- Provided by publisher.
Identifiers: LCCN 2022009256 (print) | LCCN 2022009257 (ebook) | ISBN 9781800502024 (hardback) | ISBN 9781800502031 (paperback) | ISBN 9781800502048 (epdf) | ISBN 9781800502499 (epub)
Subjects: LCSH: Indigenous peoples--Religion--Miscellanea.
Classification: LCC BL380 .I57 2022 (print) | LCC BL380 (ebook) | DDC 299--dc23/ eng/20220801
LC record available at https://lccn.loc.gov/2022009256
LC ebook record available at https://lccn.loc.gov/2022009257

Typeset by Scribe Inc.

Contents

The Study of Indigenous Religious Traditions

Indigenous Futurity

Preface

When we met via Zoom to discuss what a volume on Indigenous religious traditions might look like, the problem of terminology came up right away. Many scholars in the subfield, Native and non-Native, will tell you that the category of religion is an ill-fitting one—it doesn't readily map onto Native American and Indigenous lifeways. In addition, the way that Indigenous religious traditions have been racialized as failed or faulty epistemologies and Indigenous peoples as "noble savages" has colored the way they are perceived by the general public and in the larger field. These racialized perceptions shaped some of the questions we collected but also how scholars in the subfield chose to respond to them. For example, the question "What is a spirit animal?" suggests that such a thing discretely exists in Indigenous worlds as a universal category. It does not. Instead of answering this question, a scholar explored the question "What does it mean when Indigenous peoples say animals are 'sacred'?" While the series' original volume sought to answer everyday questions that were racially charged—that is, "Why are there so many radical Muslims in the world today?"—we soon realized that we had to forge a careful balance between addressing such questions head on and shifting them completely. The reframing is pedagogical, and we hope readers will read between the lines here to see how.

In addition to thinking about the category of religion, we also talked about how to ensure that the phrase "Indigenous religious traditions" was encompassing and did not rigidly adhere to the boundaries of any set of scholarly subfields. For general readers, it may be surprising to think that the scholars who contribute to this volume might choose to present at different conferences or in different programs of large conferences. Scholars who study Indigenous religious traditions may belong to the Native American and Indigenous Studies Association (NAISA), the American Academy of Religion (AAR), the British Association for the Study of Religions (BASR), the European Association for the Study of Religions (EASR), the Society for the Study of Native American Religious Traditions (SSNART), the American Anthropological Association (AAA), and the American Society for Ethnohistory (ASE). Many of these scholarly societies meet in annual conferences where academics self-sort into subfields to discuss their research interests. For example, in the American Academy of Religion, the Indigenous Religious Traditions Unit takes as its mission exploring the "theoretical, methodological, and conceptual issues in the study of indigenous religious traditions the world over." The Indigenous Religious Traditions Unit may collaborate with other program units related to Indigenous cultures or themes related to them, including African Diaspora Religions, African Religions, Native Traditions in the Americas, and Religions in Latina/o Americas.

As we began inviting colleagues to contribute to this volume, we found that some were eager to take on big questions like "Why does the title of this book use the phrase 'Indigenous religious traditions' rather than 'Indigenous religions'?" while others were hesitant to think of their research as contributing to the study of Indigenous religious traditions. While the volume mostly includes scholars who work squarely in the field of religious studies, we have contributions from scholars whose work primarily sits in Native American and Indigenous studies, history, anthropology, and even area studies. We made a conscious effort to prioritize contributions from Native and Indigenous scholars and scholars of Native/Indigenous descent who think/write about Indigenous religious life, given the ways Native/Indigenous scholars have historically been structurally marginalized or dismissed as "less objective" in the academy. We were also eager to include esteemed elder voices within the subfield, such as Tink Tinker, Davíd Carrasco, Christopher Jocks, and Inés Hernández-Ávila, alongside those of brilliant junior and midcareer scholars. The question of who is Indigenous and who has the right or responsibility to advocate for and/or on behalf of Indigenous communities arises in explicit and implicit ways throughout this volume. Scholars who study Indigenous religious traditions bear a responsibility for clear thinking, ethical action, and transparent positioning in relation to this question, whether they are Indigenous or not.

We decided to organize the volume into four general categories that were resonant with the original yet specific to our subject matter of Indigeneity:

- questions about the subject of Indigeneity itself and its relationship to religion,
- questions that address the actual study of Indigenous religious traditions (including what religious traditions fit in this category),
- questions about Indigenous religious life as a phenomenon (what these lifeways consist of), and
- one final question about the future of Indigenous life (what Native futures look like).

All of the answers are driven by the scholarly study of Indigenous religious traditions with considerable emphasis on the methodological interventions articulated by Native and Indigenous studies. These interventions include acknowledging the racist, colonial legacy of academic work on Indigenous peoples that has interpellated that study and has historically misrepresented or disparaged these lifeways. Most importantly, you'll see the ways contributors, Native and non-Native, work to center the scholarly authority of Indigenous epistemologies when discussing topics ranging from the land, gender, or ceremonial life.

One of the goals of this volume was to trouble the assumptions that a general audience and even other scholars in the field may have of Indigenous peoples and their religious lifeways. We have sought to dispel racist stereotypes and harmful tropes (such as the vanishing Indian—we're still here!) but also illustrate the rich complexity of what Indigenous religious traditions may look like around the world. Many of these short pieces will become instant classics for both their profound analysis but also their experiential wisdom. In sum, we hope this volume brings the dynamic reality of Indigenous life to readers in ways that enrich and inspire, ultimately deepening our collective understanding of what we call religion.

Acknowledgments

We would like to thank our teachers and mentors, especially the late great Inés Talamantez, without which the subfield of Native American religious traditions would not have developed in the way it did. Thank you to the work of Native and Indigenous scholars in the field who have withstood decades of marginalization and have written and spoken their intellectual truth despite it all. Thank you to our Indigenous ancestors who survived so that we could be here now to honor you with this work and these words. Thanks to our families for their support, love, and laughter. We greatly appreciate the assistance of Georgia State University graduate students Nathan Springer and Obie Njoku in preparing the manuscript.

This work is dedicated to the liberation and sovereignty of Native and Indigenous peoples all around the globe. In peace, love, and solidarity.

Molly H. Bassett, Associate Professor and Chair,
Religious Studies Department, Georgia State University

Natalie Avalos, Assistant Professor,
Ethnic Studies Department, University of Colorado, Boulder

Indigeneity and Religion

1

Why does the title of this book use the phrase "Indigenous religious traditions" rather than "Indigenous religions"?

Tisa Wenger

A complete answer to this question would require a whole course on the colonial history of the category of religion and another on the study of Indigenous religious traditions. The short version is that the word "religion" is a product of specific European histories and has never been a comfortable fit for the Indigenous traditions that we're discussing in this book. The phrase "religious traditions" is not a perfect solution, but it signals this categorical misfit and suggests the ongoing, holistic vitality of Indigenous traditions.

Consider Christopher Columbus's comment in his journal about the Arawak people he met in the Bahamas in 1492: "They should be good servants and intelligent, for I observed that they quickly took in what was said to them, and I believe that they would easily be made Christians, as it appeared to me that they had no religion," he wrote. "These people are very simple as regards the use of arms. . . . With fifty men they can all be subjugated and made to do what is required of them."

As Columbus's comment implies, Europeans of his time did not consider "religion" to be a universal human characteristic. Christians in late antiquity had adopted the Latin word *religio*—which in ancient Rome meant to observe one's duties, including the obligations owed to the emperor and the gods—and used it to signify the worship of their one true God. There was only one true religion, Christianity, and Indigenous people had nothing that qualified as such. If it didn't look like Christianity, then it wasn't religion.

Over the centuries, European explorers and imperial officials typically judged Indigenous beliefs and practices not as true religion but as superstition, paganism, or heathenism instead. These comparisons drew on implicitly Christian assumptions about what could be legitimated as religion and, as with Columbus, served to justify the conquest and subordination of Indigenous peoples. These legacies remain very much alive in derogatory stereotypes that still circulate about Indigenous cultures and religious traditions today.

In self-defense, especially where religious freedom is protected by law, Indigenous people have often insisted that their traditions are authentic religions that must be respected and protected as such. The tribal council at Taos Pueblo in New Mexico, for example, responded with outrage to an order from their US Indian agent in 1924 that would have prevented them from holding important tribal initiations. They could never "comply with this order, no matter what the penalty may be," they wrote, "because this order would violate our religion and also destroy it." Eventually, in this case, the agent backed down, and the initiations continued.

Such approaches did not always prevent government suppression and have mostly failed to protect Indigenous sacred lands. Still, building on the work of Native American activist and policy advocate Suzan Shown Harjo (Cheyenne and Hodulgee Muskogee), religious studies scholar Michael McNally explains that even when Native American religious freedom appeals have failed in the courts, the insistence by Native people that their traditions are indeed *religious* have added essential gravitas and drawn valuable public support for their claims.

And yet many Indigenous leaders have remained uncomfortable with the category of religion. This term has no direct equivalent in any Indigenous languages and carries with it a host of alien assumptions. "The language makes no distinction between religion, government, or law," Chief Oren Lyons of the Onondaga Nation once explained. "Tribal customs and religious ordinances are synonymous. All aspects of life are tied in to one totality." A concept of religion that requires Indigenous societies to separate out these aspects of life—and that places an exclusive emphasis on interior spirituality or individual practice and belief—can distort and disarm Indigenous traditions. An individualized and decontextualized concept of *religion* can also detract from Indigenous sovereignty struggles that rest on a collective sense of peoplehood.

Indigenous scholars and activists have tended to prefer the phrase "religious traditions" because it shifts the weight to the noun "traditions," with "religious" as a modifying adjective. To be sure, the word "tradition" carries its own baggage. It can be mistaken to mean that the cultural practices in question are timeless and must remain pure and (mostly) unchanged to be considered authentic. Such a conclusion misconstrues *all* human traditions, which are continually made and remade to meet contemporary needs. Nevertheless, the shift to "religious traditions" offers a useful distance from a category (religion) that has too often imposed a Christian-shaped mold. This shift also implies Lyons's point that there is no "religion" apart from other aspects of Indigenous life—in other words, that every aspect of these traditions is to be respected, holistically, as *religious*.

About the author

Tisa Wenger, professor of American religious history at Yale University, is the author of *We Have a Religion: The 1920s Pueblo Indian Dance Controversy and American Religious Freedom* (University of North Carolina Press, 2009) and *Religious Freedom: The Contested History of an American Ideal* (University of North Carolina Press, 2017). She is coeditor, with Sylvester Johnson, of *Religion and U.S. Empire: Critical New Histories* (New York University Press, 2022).

Suggestions for further reading

In this book
See also chapters 8 (Why is "religion" a problematic category for understanding Indigenous traditions?), 9 (Why is it sometimes risky to present Indigenous traditions as religious?), and 10 (Is "tradition" a useful category?).

Elsewhere
Chidester, David. *Savage Systems: Colonialism and Comparative Religion in Southern Africa*. Charlottesville: University Press of Virginia, 1996.

Dees, Sarah. *The Materialization of Native American Religions: The Smithsonian, Settler Colonialism, and the Study of Indigenous Lifeways*. Lincoln: University of Nebraska Press, forthcoming.

McNally, Michael D. *Defend the Sacred: Native American Religious Freedom beyond the First Amendment*. Princeton, NJ: Princeton University Press, 2020.

Wenger, Tisa. *We Have a Religion: The 1920s Pueblo Indian Dance Controversy and American Religious Freedom*. Chapel Hill: University of North Carolina Press, 2009.

2

What makes a religion an "Indigenous religion"?

Graham Harvey

Two complex words are brought together in the phrase "Indigenous religions." This should be a cause for excitement. We will know more about what religions are when we know more about Indigenous religions. And we will know more about Indigenous worlds and lives when we know more about Indigenous religious traditions.

Both the words "Indigenous" and "religion" are often taken to point to something in the past. They seem to emphasize origins and involve inherited traditions. But receiving a tradition is not the end. People who respect traditions improvise from them, making them fit present reality and create better possibilities for the future. Because thinking about each word, separately and together, aids us in seeing processes, scholars have proposed the more verb-like terms "Indigenizing" and "religioning" to provoke thinking about dynamic relationships.

Some of the key themes of importance when people talk about Indigenous religions are land, kinship, ceremonies, and relationships within larger-than-human communities. While all religions are experienced in particular places (because they are performed with bodily actions and senses), Indigenous religions are often defined by a strong and explicit emphasis on belonging to specific places or locations and to extensive kinship groups (i.e., those involving ancestors and other species). We can, for example, talk about the Lakota, Māori, and Yanomami religions as the religions of both specific people and particular lands. The ceremonies central to Indigenous religions often celebrate, defend, and enhance the territories important to multispecies communities who dwell there. Nonetheless, they are not confined within hard borders. They support people as they travel to new locations, and elements of these religions can be shared with guests, allies, and others. This is part of what enables people from different places to recognize one another as adherents of Indigenous religious traditions.

It is vital to note that many Indigenous people are adherents of religions originating elsewhere. For example, some are Baháʼí, Buddhist, Christian, Hindu, Muslim, or New Age. While this makes these and other religions the "religions of Indigenous people," the phrase "Indigenous religions" usually points to an inheritance from Indigenous ancestors and localities. They can often be recognized because they involve inherited customary actions, songs, clothes, shared foods, and instruments (e.g., drums, tobacco, tattoos, feather fans, and dance moves).

Land and ancestry are broad themes. They can indicate that something might be an Indigenous religion but should not be used as a checklist or test. The Hopi religion is not the same as the Sámi religion, and both differ from the Kanaka Maoli religion. Equally, there are variations among families, clans, and larger communities in the ways in which traditions have evolved. Religions of all kinds vary enormously. They are adaptive to new situations. Indigenous people have survived the onslaught of European colonialism by shaping religious ideas and practices to new realities.

One of the ways in which Indigenous people have adapted is in responding to the term "religion." Many insist that "religion" is the wrong word for their customary ceremonies, stories, and relationships with the larger world. For them, "religion" only suggests beliefs about otherworldly beings or states. Or "religion" might suggest "not practicing what you preach." However, other Indigenous people have objected strongly to European colonizers who claimed that an alleged lack of anything like their Christianity justified conquest and slavery. Taking up the term "religion" in this context involves a rebuttal of the idea that all religions must be like the invaders' Christianity. Instead, religion can be recognized in ceremonies and narratives that encourage locally appropriate relationships with places and their larger-than-human communities.

Students of religion ought to understand that while comparisons can help us understand new (to us) phenomena, they require care. If a community does not have someone like a "priest," perhaps they have a "shaman" or a "medicine person." Turning the tables, we can ask whether the Polynesian term "taboo" might help us understand features of religions elsewhere. Thus, an understanding of Indigenous terms is often vital to a full understanding of these and other religions. Meanwhile, words like "respect" (in Indigenous languages or in translations) are shared by many or all Indigenous religions.

Indigenous religions are vibrant because they are adaptive and relevant to the ever-changing world. They aid Indigenous people in defending traditions, places, and lives, and they encourage celebrations that anticipate the well-being of future generations. They are relevant both when they resist outside influences and when they invite sharing, which might improve the world.

About the author

Graham Harvey is professor of religious studies at the Open University in the United Kingdom. His research largely concerns the "new animism," especially in rituals and protocols through which Indigenous communities engage with the larger-than-human world. He is editor of Routledge's *Vitality of Indigenous Religions* series and Equinox's *Religion and the Senses* series.

Suggestions for further reading

In this book
See also chapters 1 (Why does the title of this book use the phrase "Indigenous religious traditions" rather than "Indigenous religions"?) and 9 (Why is it sometimes risky to present Indigenous traditions as religious?).

Elsewhere
Cox, James L., ed. *Critical Reflections on Indigenous Religions*. New York: Routledge, 2013.

Hartney, Christopher, and Daniel J. Tower, eds. *Religious Categories and the Construction of the Indigenous*. Leiden: Brill, 2016.

Johnson, Greg, and Siv Ellen Kraft, eds. *Handbook of Indigenous Religion(s)*. Leiden: Brill, 2017.

Kraft, Siv Ellen, Bjørn Ola Tafjord, Arkotong Longkumer, Gregory D. Alles, and Greg Johnson. *Indigenous Religion(s): Local Grounds, Global Networks*. London: Routledge, 2020. https://www.taylorfrancis.com/books/e/9781003021513.

Robertson, David, with Bjørn Ola Tafjord and Arkotong Longkumer. "What Do We Mean by Indigenous Religion(s)?" Religious Studies Project, October 2, 2017. Accessed August 10, 2020. https://www.religiousstudiesproject.com/podcast/what-do-we-mean-by-indigenous-religions/.

3
Were all religions at one time "Indigenous"?

Tyler M. Tully

What English-speaking people refer to as "religion" has no equivalent term in most other cultures and languages, yet it is often assumed (and researched) as if it were truly universal. "Indigenous," by contrast, represents a very specific qualifier grounded in particular locations and polities. Asking, then, "Were all religions at one time 'Indigenous'?" seems an apparent contradiction in terms, as it attempts to describe something typical next to an utterly unique designation. On the one hand, "Indigenous" is often defined in opposition to European invasion and settlement, which suggests a rather straightforward description as to what it is not. However, this is not to suggest that "Indigenous" reflects a universal totality such that every non-Eurowestern community practices the same behaviors or adopts the same beliefs—although some Eurowestern categories would describe them as such.

The contemporary discourse on "religion" is an excellent case in point. While non-Indigenous conversations often situate "religion" (and its associated signifiers "belief," "faith," etc.) in a private sense against a public "secular" sphere (i.e., the realm of "science," "politics," "the state," etc.), traditional Indigenous societies do not make such tidy distinctions between actions and ideals, spirit and matter, or even humans and nonhumans. Indeed, as early as the sixteenth and seventeenth centuries, imperial merchant traders sought to increase colonial commerce by cataloging the languages, cartographies, and customs of Europe's *others* but often found Indigenous people had no "religion"—an idea shared as late as the early 1800s with Thomas Jefferson. Even earlier encounters in West African communities caused Portuguese enslavers to coin novel terminologies, such as "fetish," to describe Indigenous traditions and knowledge systems they did not fully comprehend. Added to this are familiar phrases in the study of religion, such as "mana," "animism," "totem," "ancestor worship," "taboo," and the ubiquitous "primitive mentality," all of which contribute to long-standing discourses on civility and barbarity, culture and nature, secularity and religion.

For the greater part of the last two centuries, the academic study of religion—in all of its approaches—demonstrates at least two enduring characteristics: disagreement over methods and a fixation on "primitive" cultures. Indeed, overestimating the latter is a difficult endeavor, as foundational studies in religion from anthropology, sociology, psychology, linguistics, and history attest. Publications in the period between the nineteenth and early twentieth centuries display a strong influence from sociocultural evolution—that is, the theory that all peoples and civilizations demonstrate "superior" or "inferior" forms of advancement when measured along the same timeline. The fathers of modern anthropology, Sir E. B. Tylor (1832–1917), and ethnology, Lewis Henry Morgan (1818–1881)—early advancers of the idea of a basic psychic unity or common mental capacity—searched for religion's origins among what they considered to be vanishing races eclipsed by the march of progress. In linking Indigenous cultures to "neurotics," children, and "savages" in *Totem and Taboo* (1913), psychologist Sigmund Freud (1856–1939) drew inspiration from the groundbreaking book *The Native Tribes of Central Africa* (1899)—an early anthropological work that also inspired phenomenologist of religion Mircea Eliade (1907–1986). Social anthropologist Sir James Frazer (1854–1941) and founder of modern sociology Auguste Comte (1798–1857) held that cultures developed from a "lower" form of superstition to a "higher" state of reason, a notion that influenced Émile Durkheim (1858–1917) and Lucien Lévy-Bruhl (1857–1939), who developed different theories of cognitive evolution and drew on Indigenous societies for evidence.

The Gilded Age of imperial expansion, which was preoccupied with discovering religion's "origins," led scholars to study contemporary "primitive" peoples living on the periphery of European empires as if they exemplified an earlier human condition. While Lévy-Bruhl would later recant his previous statements in the wake of research produced by those arguing against scientific racism, such as physicist turned anthropologist Franz Boas (1858–1942), what Tylor calls "the minimum definition of religion" (1871, 1:383) and what Durkheim refers to as "the essential and permanent aspect of humanity" (1912, 13) describe the role that Indigenous people played as the lowest common denominator for comparison across all people and time periods.

With this background in mind, it is important to note the chronological progression implied in asking, "Were all religions at one time

'Indigenous'?"—as if *at one time*, everyone was "Indigenous" and that all "religions" descend from these origins. However, this risks not only erasing contemporary Indigenous communities and their unique and political relationships with particular locations; it also suggests a timeline of regression or romanticism such that present Indigenous communities inhere something timeless that moderns do not. Instead of trafficking in the same old colonial tropes, perhaps a better question might be, *Why don't we call non-Indigenous religions "invasive" as a norm?*

About the author

Tyler M. Tully is a doctoral candidate in religion and the Arthur Peacocke Graduate Scholar in Theology and Science at Oxford University. As a fifth-generation Oklahoman of settler and Native (Chickasaw) descent, Tully's interdisciplinary research and teaching engage intersecting entanglements among religion, race, gender, science, and colonialism.

Suggestions for further reading

In this book
See also chapters 2 (What makes a religion an "Indigenous religion"?) and 4 (What does "Indigenous" mean for the study of religion?).

Elsewhere

Bieder, Robert E. *Science Encounters the Indian, 1820–1880: The Early Years of American Ethnology.* Norman: University of Oklahoma Press, 1989.

Chidester, David. *Savage Systems: Colonialism and Comparative Religion in Southern Africa.* Charlottesville: University Press of Virginia, 1996.

Fitzgerald, Timothy. *Discourse on Civility and Barbarity.* Oxford: Oxford University Press, 2010.

Kraft, Siv Ellen. *Handbook of Indigenous Religion(s).* Leiden: Brill, 2017.

Masuzawa, Tomoko. *The Invention of World Religions: Or, How European Universalism Was Preserved in the Language of Pluralism.* Chicago: University of Chicago Press, 2005.

4

What does "Indigenous" mean for the study of religion?

Tyler M. Tully

Once upon a time, scholars studying religion divided the world into four parts that happened to correspond with types or levels of civilized advancement. European Christianity stood atop this list, while Jews and "Mohammedans" of North Africa and the Middle East occupied a separate and secondary stratum. The "ancient religions" of the Far East represented another genre of polytheism, while the "savages" of "pagan" Africa and the Americas, who practiced animism or nature worship, made up the remainder. Thus geographies, religions, and cultures overlapped at this time to define different "nations" or races, which were all measured along the same timeline. *Sociocultural evolution*, in other words, determined a universal hierarchy in which Eurowesterners occupied the most advanced stages of civilization while "preliterate" and "primitive" peoples stood on the opposite side of the spectrum.

Today, most people associate the study of religion with the modern academic discipline of "religious studies," which sprang up across North American universities during the 1960s–1970s. However, research on religion is actually much older and extends from a variety of academic fields, including anthropology, linguistics, sociology, psychology, ethnography, and history. For nearly 150 years prior to the arrival of "religious studies," scholars of religion looked for its origin among "preliterate," "basic," or "tribal" societies living on the peripheries of European empires. During this formative period of research, scholars were motivated to quickly capture information, as the reigning theory of the time held that tribal cultures would soon become extinct when confronted with the unstoppable onset of modern civilization.

Although Eurowestern scholars at this time employed different approaches to their research, most relied on data gathered from "Native informants"—that is, tribal members that were paid, coerced, or freely offered information concerning their own cultures and communities. On very rare occasions, Native informants were recognized as amateur scholars. More common was the practice of mediating all data about tribal societies through Eurowestern "experts" who did not see "primitive" peoples as capable of critically gathering, assessing, or fully explaining their own traditions and ceremonies in an unbiased manner. In addition to the sociocultural theory of evolution, which saw some people as more or less advanced than others by racial and geographic comparison, that early scholars of religion did not see Natives as valid producers of knowledge is perhaps the next most popular hallmark of this unfortunate era.

With the advent of the US civil rights era, American Indian, Chicano, Mexican American, Native Alaskan, and Hawaiian student activists organized for greater representation and inclusion in academic institutions across North America. In the face of hundreds of years of discrimination and organized colonial violence against their Native people and persons, these scholars desired that their communities be taken seriously as valid producers of academic knowledge. It was during this period that organizations such as the Native American and Indigenous Studies Association (NAISA) and Latin American Studies Association (LASA) came into being.

Terms such as "primitive" and "savage" have rightly fallen out of usage in recent decades given their obvious overlap with Anglo-Saxon supremacy and race science. Indigeneity, however, is not reducible to race or even phenotype, as some Indigenous communities—such as the Sámi of Lapland in northern Scandinavia—reflect. Other traditional ways of belonging in North American Indigenous nations involve long-standing histories of adoption regardless of one's color. According to the United Nations, Indigenous peoples inhere the right to self-identify as such given the histories of imperialism that sought to remove, assimilate, and erase them. What is popularly understood as "Indigenous sovereignty" therefore involves the right of Indigenous communities to determine their own membership criteria.

Today, scholars, legal agencies, and nongovernmental organizations describe "Indigenous" peoples according to their location and proximity to colonial invasion. A people group is "Indigenous," in other words, if they have a long-standing relationship to a particular place prior to the arrival of European colonization. While this obviously shares some overlap with nonwhite racialization—that is, though the great majority of "Indigenous" non-Europeans around the globe are racialized as not-white—Indigeneity itself depends on a community's relationship to place prior to European contact rather than color or creed.

About the author

Tyler M. Tully is a doctoral candidate in Religion and the Arthur Peacocke Graduate Scholar in Theology and Science at Oxford University. As a fifth-generation Oklahoman of settler and Native (Chickasaw) descent, Tyler's interdisciplinary research and teaching engage intersecting entanglements among religion, race, gender, science, and colonialism.

Suggestions for further reading

In this book
See also chapters 2 (What makes a religion an "Indigenous religion"?) and 8 (Why is "religion" a problematic category for understanding Indigenous traditions?).

Elsewhere

Chidester, David. *Empire of Religion: Imperialism and Comparative Religion*. Chicago: University of Chicago Press, 2014.

Masuzawa, Tomoko. *The Invention of World Religions: Or, How European Universalism Was Preserved in the Language of Pluralism*. Chicago: University of Chicago Press, 2005.

Smith, William Robertson, and Robert A. Segal. *Religion of the Semites: The Fundamental Institutions*. New York: Routledge, 2017.

Tafjord, Bjørn Ola. "Indigenous Religion(s) as an Analytical Category." *Method & Theory in the Study of Religion* 25(3) (2013): 221–243.

UN General Assembly, Resolution 61/295, United Nations Declaration on the Rights of Indigenous Peoples, *UN Wash* 12 (September 13, 2007): 1–18, https://www.un.org/development/desa/indigenouspeoples/wp-content/uploads/sites/19/2018/11/UNDRIP_E_web.pdf.

5

Are Indigenous religions only those practiced by Indigenous people?

Angela Puca

In an attempt to delineate what might be the characteristics of an Indigenous religion, James Cox identifies three main ones. The first is a focus on ancestors, which is found in beliefs, rituals, and social practices and makes kinship relations important. The second trait is the identification with one specific geographical area. This implies that their rituals and practices are not universally applicable but rather contingent on the place within which they were developed and that have generated their own specific cosmology. Key is also the means of transmission, for knowledge and practices are passed on orally rather than via books. For Cox, Indigenous religions are those practiced by Indigenous people, but this assimilation of elements of one into the other and vice versa is not as clear-cut as language may lead us to believe and has been challenged by more recent scholarship.

The category of Indigenous people is a political classification aimed at identifying, protecting, and guaranteeing the rights of the people—now a minority—who inhabited a territory before its mass colonization occurred. According to the International Labour Organization and the United Nations, Indigenous people are those who are original or first peoples of a place where they have been colonized. This category seems to be solely applicable to those countries where a massive wave of colonization occurred in a short period of time and on such a large scale as to starkly demarcate a distinction between the before and after, the outsiders and the Native people, the colonizer and the colonized. Consequently, the category of Indigenous people is an extremely useful political classification that is contingent on specific geographical areas and subject to the legislation of the country taken into consideration.

However, the category of Indigenous people—as geographically contingent and politically charged—appears insufficient by itself to understand what Indigeneity is when it comes to religion. If Indigenous religions are those practiced by Indigenous people, would Christianity be an Indigenous religion when it becomes the dominant one within such communities? And what about Indigenous beliefs and rituals practiced by people who are not, or no longer, Indigenous?

Lumping together Indigenous religions and Indigenous people risks impairing or influencing the understanding of both and flattening all the nuances derived from their own fields of expression. For instance, since the definition of Indigenous people is a political classification, contingent on a specific place and its legislation, keeping the people entangled in the religion might compromise a full grasp on what an Indigenous religion is in its own right due to it being dependent on one government's law. This would hinder the appreciation of possible underlying patterns across Indigenous religions from different countries while, similarly, limiting the perception of Indigenous people as having to engage in a specific set of beliefs.

A European Indigenous practice may still exhibit traits associated with Indigenous religions, such as the connection to the land, the centrality of kinship relations, and a community-centered approach. Even if we are to include as a trait that of being "colonized," there is still the chance to encounter a cultural translation of such an element. As my fieldwork with the Italian tradition of *Segnature* showed, there can be religious minorities forced to adapt and remain quietly underground due to a dominant religious and cultural system that opposes their existence. This tradition is the label I employed for the vernacular healing practice of the *Segnature*, a term that refers to magical gestures and words used by its initiates that have gone through a syncretization with Catholicism.

The minority living within a dominant culture, when it comes to religion, might become a system of practices not accepted by a domineering sociotheoretical framework that classifies them as "the Other" from the norm. For instance, the predominant paradigm in Western society endorses a preassumed rationalism that dictates what is real (the measurable, repeatable, and standardized) and what is not. As a consequence, those vernacular healers who cure illnesses are seen as delusional because the "reality" of those practices is denied. When the latter trait is found alongside a connection to the land and its spirits, a community-serving approach, and the oral transmission of knowledge, it becomes clear how disentangling Indigenous religions from Indigenous people allows one to keep the question open on whether such a religious tradition may classify as Indigenous.

The conversation on what constitutes an Indigenous religion is still ongoing within academic circles, and I argue, along with other scholars, that decoupling the category from that of Indigenous people would help the inquiry on the two groups, allowing for a more nuanced, accurate, and contextual understanding of both.

About the author

Dr. Angela Puca is currently lecturing at Leeds Trinity University and holds a PhD on Indigenous and transcultural shamanism in Italy, awarded by the University of Leeds. Her research interests include magic, shamanism and the concept of Indigeneity, witchcraft, paganism, and esotericism. In addition, she hosts a YouTube channel called Angela's Symposium to divulge the academic study of such topics to a wider audience.

Suggestions for further reading

In this book
See also chapters 2 (What makes a religion an "Indigenous religion"?) and 3 (Were all religions at one time "Indigenous"?).

Elsewhere
Cox, J. L. *From Primitive to Indigenous: The Academic Study of Indigenous Religions*. London: Ashgate, 2007.

Kraft, S. E., B. O. Tafjord, A. Longkumer, G. D. Alles, and G. Johnson, eds. *Indigenous Religion(s): Local Grounds, Global Networks* (1st edition). Abingdon, UK: Routledge, 2020.

Owen, S. "Druidry and the Definition of Indigenous Religion." In *Critical Reflections on Indigenous Religions*, edited by J. L. Cox, 81–92. London: Routledge, 2013.

Puca, A. "The Tradition of Segnature: Underground Indigenous Practices in Italy." *Journal of the Irish Society for the Academic Study of Religions* 7 (2019): 104–123.

6

How can spiritual traditions create Indigenous traditions in new places?

Ras Michael Brown

Africans enslaved in the Americas were violently displaced from the environments that oriented their religious cultures. In addition to the many physical and emotional forms of suffering they endured in captivity, they had to find ways to re-create their spiritual identities and remap their spiritual geographies while exiled to new landscapes of oppression. Doing so entailed processes of *becoming* spiritually Indigenous that drew from ancestral concepts and practices long established in West-Central and West African societies. These processes in turn inspired the elaboration of novel expressions of spiritual Indigeneity in numerous African diasporic religions.

But how could someone *become* Indigenous? After all, the label "Indigenous" presumes a state of already being anchored in place or an identity embedded in a lineage that has continuously inhabited an area for as long as anyone remembers. West-Central and West African societies often explained their histories through stories of migration that featured historical/mythical ancestors who either reached an accord with or vanquished the original inhabitants, often depicted as distinct kinds of humans or as other-than-human beings (usually animals or local spirits). Indigenous spiritual power was especially potent, even necessary, and could only be accessed through Indigenous spiritual authorities. How could this problem be resolved for newcomers, who were not firstcomers and lacked this Indigeneity? They had to *become* Indigenous through alliances with Indigenous beings and the acquisition of status as spiritually Indigenous people.

Spiritual identities and geographies in many African and African diasporic religious cultures have relied on relationships with entities that we can call "nature spirits." We may better understand these entities as "Native spirits" because people often attributed to them the qualities of Indigeneity conceived of as primordial forces and substances embodied in awe-inspiring and formidable features of the natural environment, such as waterfalls, springs, natural pools, and remarkably shaped stones. They did not simply exist *on* the land within its formations. They were *of* the land as emanations of the life and energy that animated ecologies in their seen and unseen dimensions. More important for communities of people, they were revered as "guardians of the land" that ensured ecological vitality through abundant rains, animals, and plants at the same time that they protected the procreativity of humans living in their domains. By forging connections with Native/nature spirits, people obtained sacred approbation to build their communities and attained spiritual Indigeneity in new surroundings.

One of the most notable methods for establishing these connections was the process of consecrating people to Native/nature spirits through initiation associations, sometimes mischaracterized as "secret societies." Though initiation associations had different names and variations in their practices, they typically culminated in the consecration of initiates to a patron spirit through ritual death and rebirth.

In some associations, initiates even emerged as Native/nature spirits, as seen in the *kimpasi* association in Kongo-Angola from the seventeenth century and into the twentieth century. After an extended period of training and ordeals in the kimpasi camp located deep in the wilderness, initiates experienced "*nkita* death" and were then resurrected to become "nkita peo-ple" (nkita was the association's Native/nature spirit). With their new status, nkita people could intervene with nkita power to restore their communities in times of distress.

During the same period, Kongo-Angolan communities focused their notions about "guardians of the land" on Native/nature beings they called *simbi* that supported not only communities but also individuals unmoored from precious kinship and place ties. Simbi conveyed vulnerable and mar-ginal people into their natural abodes and returned them empowered with new knowledge, abilities, and status. Simbi thus provided the most direct tether to Indigeneity by reinforcing (sometimes even replacing) fragile blood/lineage kinship with identity rooted in the land. And because simbi (and similar beings) were native to natural environments everywhere, captive Africans encountered them in the Americas along with the spirits connected to the Indigenous people already present on those lands. So no matter how far African descendants were sent away from their homes, families, and the graves of their ancestors, simbi and other Native/nature spirits could be accessed to enable them to regain their spiritual identities as people of the land.

Creating Indigenous traditions in new places was thus integral to the historical development of West-Central and West African religious cultures as well as the diasporic scions cultivated from them. Indeed, the imperative of Indigeneity in African contexts took on added urgency as captive Africans were dispersed throughout the Atlantic world from the mid-fifteenth century through the mid-nineteenth century. Just as we find many manifestations of Kongo-Angolan simbi and nkita in the Americas, we see similar meanings and purposes connected to the wide range of nature-based entities in the African diasporic religions of Brazil, Haiti, Cuba, and elsewhere. African newcomers and their American-born descendants could rely on their guardian Native/nature spirits to become reoriented as spiritually Indigenous people and sustain their communities displaced by the violence of captivity.

About the author

Ras Michael Brown is an associate professor in the Department of History at Georgia State University. His research and teaching interests engage the long historical development of religions and cultures in the African diaspora. He has written numerous articles on early African/American communities and their spiritual cultures, and his book *African-Atlantic Cultures and the South Carolina Lowcountry* (Cambridge University Press, 2012) was honored as the inaugural recipient of the Albert J. Raboteau Prize for the Best Book in Africana Religions in 2013.

Suggestions for further reading

In this book
See also chapter 44 (If Native American religious traditions are place based, how do "urban Indians" practice their religion?).

Elsewhere
Brown, Ras Michael. *African-Atlantic Cultures and the South Carolina Lowcountry*. New York: Cambridge University Press, 2012.

Fu-Kiau, A. kia Bunseki-Lumanisa. *N'Kongo ye Nza Yakun'Zungidila: Nza-Kôngo (le mukongo et le monde qui l'entourait)*. Kinshasa, Zaire [DRC]: Office National de la Recherche et de Développement, 1968.

Fu-Kiau, K. kia Bunseki. *"Simba Simbi": Hold Up That Which Holds You Up*. Pittsburgh, PA: Dorrance, 2006.

Klieman, Kairn A. *"The Pygmies Were Our Compass": Bantu and Batwa in the History of West Central Africa, Early Times to c. 1900 C.E.* Portsmouth, NH: Heinemann, 2003.

7

Why do some Indigenous people insist that what they practice is not religion?

Chris Jocks

I earned my PhD in religious studies from the University of California, Santa Barbara, under the direction of the late and beloved Mescalero Apache scholar Inés Talamantez. Inés's graduate students were trained to navigate complex domains of thought, language, relationship, and action in our own Indigenous homelands as well as others'. We learned the conceptual and analytical tools of religious studies; we also learned to Indigenize them. So I was not surprised when I began to encounter Indigenous people who scoffed at my degree, informing me that "our traditional ways are not religion." I was not offended; there are useful lessons to be learned from this criticism, which operates on multiple levels.

One version of the argument is that "our traditions are a way of life, not something we do for a couple of hours a week." This is certainly true for many Indigenous practitioners, but it is also true for people like the Amish or members of Christian or Buddhist monastic orders. In fact, the most devout practitioners of almost any religion would insist that their practice is also a way of life. So this critique is actually directed not at religion itself but at modern congregants for whom a perfunctory observance is sufficient.

Another version is that Indigenous practices are spiritual rather than religious. This goes deeper. Recent polls indicate that an increasing portion, perhaps a majority now, of the general public in the United States consider themselves spiritual rather than religious. When asked what they mean by this, most reference a sense of spiritual presence or energy that is personally accessible and unfettered by institutions, mandated beliefs, or formalistic rituals. Individual experiences are indeed a time-honored component of most Indigenous traditions—think of the sweat lodge in its various versions or the experience of individuals in a peyote meeting—but these are always embedded in collective ritual practices, some extremely ancient. Getting up to make offerings at sunrise is a highly individualized practice for many Native people, but in most cases, such practices are intended to complement and inform—not replace—collective observances that sometimes actually *are* mandated.

One can go even deeper with this Indigenous sense of incongruity with the term "religion." It could be that the religion it rejects is any religion founded on individual salvation because this atomizes individuals and thus trivializes the core value of Indigenous life: relationship, or more specifically, kinship. There is more. Since the Enlightenment, many established religions based on individual salvation have also come to accept and accommodate the European scientific tradition of a physical universe devoid of spirit. Many churches profit from this accommodation, which offends another key premise of Indigenous traditions. As Native people, we attend not just to a circle of relatives that includes human and other beings but also to what in English we have to call spirits—beings or entities that are close to us as they animate and sometimes exist within physical forms and laws.

Within sight of my home is a mountain held sacred by thirteen Indigenous nations. Powerful entities live upon or within this mountain. It is a source of strength, protection, knowledge, and healing. Thanks to laws that privilege profit over spirit, laws based on the European vision of a material universe devoid of spirit, this mountain is being desecrated by a private business operating with government permits on land the United States claims to own. Two hundred thirty miles south, Apache people have been battling since 2015 to protect another sacred place. Oak Flat is threatened with complete obliteration by another profit-making scheme, this one involving a giant block-cave copper mine. Profits would go to Rio Tinto, the international mining company that recently destroyed one of the oldest sites of human habitation in Australia, a site revered and loved by Indigenous people there.

A universe suffused with relationship, made intelligible to human beings in specific places through gifts of language and gesture and reciprocity over generations by spiritual beings within the natural/physical world, is a universe that cannot be found in the face of religions that were forced on Indigenous people by missionaries in the service of conquest. This is why so many Indigenous people today refuse to put on the term "religion." More intellectual definitions of religion that could encompass all these alternatives, including Indigenous ones, are flights of fancy to Native people who have paid dearly the cost of religious conquest—and continue to pay to this very day.

About the author

Chris Jocks, Kahnawà:ke Mohawk, is senior lecturer in Applied Indigenous Studies at Northern Arizona University. He earned his PhD in Religious Studies under the direction of Inés Talamantez at the University of California, Santa Barbara, in 1994. His work includes publications on the conceptual incongruity between Indigenous and settler state societies and nations, as manifest in law, religion, and social practices. He is also engaged with local Indigenous community advocacy in northern Arizona.

Suggestions for further reading

In this book
See also chapters 1 (Why does the title of this book use the phrase "Indigenous religious traditions" rather than "Indigenous religions"?) and 9 (Why is it sometimes risky to present Indigenous traditions as religious?).

Elsewhere
Jocks, Chris. "Restoring Congruity: Indigenous Lives and Religious Freedom in the United States and Canada." In *Traditional, National, and International Law and Indigenous Communities*, edited by Marianne O. Nielsen and Karen Jarratt-Snider, 81–103. Tucson: University of Arizona Press, 2020.

Nelson, Melissa K., ed. *Original Instructions: Indigenous Teachings for a Sustainable Future*. Rochester, VT: Bear, 2008.

Wenger, Tisa. *We Have a Religion: The 1920s Pueblo Indian Dance Controversy and American Religious Freedom*. Chapel Hill: University of North Carolina Press, 2009.

8
Why is "religion" a problematic category for understanding Indigenous traditions?

Philip P. Arnold

Location matters. I am a historian of religions living in Onondaga Nation Territory, the heartland and capital of the Haudenosaunee (Iroquois) Confederacy. Onondaga is one of three Haudenosaunee nations that is recognized for their precolonial matrilineal clan system of governance (the "Longhouse tradition"). They retain the same sovereign status represented in the first international treaties made with the United States, which also established the United States as a new international power. The Haudenosaunee are unique because they refused to accept "guardianship" of the United States through the Bureau of Indian Affairs. Collaborative work with the Haudenosaunee and their aversion to the category of "religion" have forced me to reconsider the word. They insist they practice not religion but a way of life based on the development of a "good mind" that is rooted in gratitude for the gifts of life. This is expressed through art, dance, ceremonies, food, and diplomacy. The term "values" better describes these reciprocal aspects of Indigeneity, while the term "religion" has come to represent world domination.

Since first contact, religion has been used as a weapon against Indigenous peoples. In the fifteenth century, papal bulls mandated that Christian discoverers seize non-Christian bodies, lands, and property. The Doctrine of Discovery (DoD) is the religious foundation upon which Christian supremacy was established to justify the taking of land. Columbus's voyages ushered forth the Age of Discovery and legitimized horrendous acts of violence as the means to establishing a New World order. The DoD continues as a legal principle used by state governments and multinational corporations today against Indigenous peoples around the world.

Values, however, enable a consideration of Indigenous traditions at a deeper level by asking, for example, what it means to be human and how we are related to the natural world. Indigenous values are closely held ethical and moral systems that have the potential to guide individuals and nations. Haudenosaunee values expressed in the Great Law of Peace deeply impressed Benjamin Franklin and other "Founding Fathers" throughout the eighteenth century. At various times, Haudenosaunee "chiefs" ("royaner," "men of the 'good mind'") taught the colonists ancient values that had been delivered by the Great Peacemaker over one thousand years earlier. Throughout the nineteenth century, Haudenosaunee clan mothers (female title holders who select the royaner) influenced early suffragists in Upstate New York. Haudenosaunee influences on Western democracy and the women's movement are two examples of how Indigenous values transformed the world.

Values are also directly involved with economic relationships that define how a society or nation determines the relative worth of material life. Values are set in our symbolic monetary economy over and against like things. There is a reason why capitalist and Indigenous values systems clash so often. Values define how a society understands its relationship with the natural world. For example, Indigenous values relate to land as a relative (Mother Earth, Pachamama, etc.) to which one belongs. This stands in stark contrast with how a capitalistic society views land as real estate or private property—that which is seen as the bedrock of human freedom. Values that are understood to be an economy of relationships, however, reveal how human beings are personally and culturally embedded in the material world—what has been called the "materiality of religion." As historian of religions Charles H. Long has pointed out about the work of Mircea Eliade, all religions are oriented to specific places deemed sacred and associated with mountains, rocks, bodies of water, trees, and so on. Essentially, the origins of religion are Indigenous.

In 2013, my wife (Sandy Bigtree, Mohawk) and I formed an educational collaborative with local colleges and universities to write the narrative for the Skä·noñh—Great Law of Peace Center, located on Onondaga Lake near Syracuse, New York. We repurposed what was formerly a Jesuit fortified mission site. The Skä·noñh Center now tells the Haudenosaunee story that over one thousand years ago, the Peacemaker, Hiawatha, and Jikonseseh (the Mother of Clans) convinced Tadodaho (a feared sorcerer and cannibal) to turn from war and accept the "Great Binding Peace." The center focuses on Haudenosaunee values, which start with Skä·noñh—or a peace that can only be attained when human beings are in proper relationship with the natural world. As a result of this collaborative work, we formed the Indigenous Values Initiative, which also supports the American Indian Law Alliance and their vital work at the United Nations on behalf of Indigenous rights. We also hold yearly educational events around the DoD and lacrosse.

Words matter. Methodological shifts enable new possibilities for collaborative scholarship. Changing the category of Indigenous "religions" to "values" allows academics to engage in a more equitable and authentic dialogue that may reveal new possibilities that lead us toward a more viable future.

About the author

Philip P. Arnold is associate professor and chair of the Religion Department; core faculty in Native American and Indigenous studies, Syracuse University; and founding director of the Skä·noñh—Great Law of Peace Center. His books are *Eating Landscape: Aztec and European Occupation of Tlalocan* (University Press of Colorado, 1999); *The Gift of Sports: Indigenous Ceremonial Dimensions of the Games We Love* (Cognella, 2012); and *Urgency of Indigenous Values and the Future of Religion* (Syracuse University Press, 2023). He established the Doctrine of Discovery Study Group (www.doctrineofdiscovery.org) and the Indigenous Values Initiative (www.indigenousvalues.org).

Suggestions for further reading

In this book
See also chapters 7 (Why do some Indigenous people insist that what they practice is not religion?) and 9 (Why is it sometimes risky to present Indigenous traditions as religious?).

Elsewhere

Arnold, Philip P. *The Gift of Sports: Indigenous Ceremonial Dimensions of the Games We Love*. San Diego, CA: Cognella, 2012.

Basic Call to Consciousness. Rooseveltown, NY: Akwesasne Notes, 1978.

Eliade, Mircea. *The Myth of the Eternal Return*. Translated by Willard R. Trask. New York: Harper, 1954.

Long, Charles H. *Significations: Signs, Symbols, and Images in the Interpretation of Religion*. Aurora: Davies, 1999.

Neighbors of the Onondaga Nation. *Neighbor to Neighbor, Nation to Nation: Readings about the Relationship of the Onondaga Nation with Central New York, USA*. Syracuse, NY: Syracuse Peace Council, Indigenous Values Initiative, 2014.

9

Why is it sometimes risky to present Indigenous traditions as religious?

Bjørn Ola Tafjord

To classify Indigenous traditions as religious may be treacherous because, globally, there are billions of people—Christians, Muslims, Buddhists, Hindus, and adherents of other religions—who think of Indigenous religious traditions as idolatry, false, or primitive. In addition, numerous non-religious people dismiss Indigenous religious traditions as superstition or irrationality. Many of these people find it appropriate to try rectifying or eliminating traditions that they cannot make conform to their own religious or secular world views, which they see as superior.

When Indigenous traditions come across as religious, some are ready to take direct action against them. Christian missionaries are one example. Historically, missionizing has been about demonizing or demoting select parts of Indigenous traditions and replacing them with Christianity. Indigenous religious traditions are still today among the main targets of missionaries and preachers, especially in Africa, Asia, and Latin America, much like they were during the heyday of European colonialism. The number of missionaries and preachers and their resources are actually larger than ever before. (To start grasping the scope of ongoing worldwide missionizing, visit the websites of the Evangelical Lausanne movement.) In some parts of Africa and Asia, where Muslims are the majority, and in particular where radical reformists have taken power, it may be fatal to present Indigenous traditions as religious. Even if practitioners of Indigenous traditions themselves often conceive of what they do as Islamic, reformists may judge them differently. Anyone whom reformists associate with illicit religious deviation is at risk of persecution. (Remember the Yazidis and the atrocities of ISIS in Iraq and Syria in 2014.) Also Buddhist and Hindu nationalists (for instance, in Myanmar and India) target

Indigenous religious traditions and their practitioners with the ambition to change and align them with particular versions of Buddhism and Hinduism. Meanwhile, many atheist educators (for example, in China) try to undermine anything they consider religious. Around the world, states as well as nongovernmental organizations, some of them secular, others religious, administer programs aiming at educating and developing Indigenous communities while construing Indigenous religious traditions as obstacles to enlightenment, progress, and deliverance. (My home country, Norway, sponsors such projects run by missionary organizations working in Africa, Asia, and Latin America.)

In other words, to religionize Indigenous traditions may be tantamount to exposing practices, artifacts, places, and practitioners to attacks from people and institutions who, for divergent ideological reasons, depreciate or disavow Indigenous religions. Yet we should acknowledge how, lately, in some Western contexts, it has proven politically and socially constructive for Indigenous people to invoke Indigenous religiosity in order to convey urgency and more-than-human community (e.g., in the protests against the building of an oil pipeline across Lakota territory at Standing Rock in the United States between 2016 and 2017). However, for activists, religionists, and students in liberal democracies, where religion and Indigenous peoples are subjects of special human rights (at least formally, even if not always in reality), it can sometimes be difficult to comprehend how the legal, political, social, and religious conditions are significantly different elsewhere. Instead of prompting protection, claims about Indigenous traditions being religious are regularly rendering them vulnerable to repression wherever religious reformists or zealous secularists are in power. Labels like "animism" or "shamanism" and other stereotypical naming of Indigenous religions have the same effect.

Many Indigenous people therefore prefer to present their own traditions in other terms. Members of the Bribri in Talamanca, Costa Rica, opt for words like "knowledge," "law," "history," "medicine," "art," "science," or, more generally, "culture" and "tradition"—words that connote reason, reliability, and creativity but not religiosity. Such conceptual choices are about more than clever strategies to disarm adversaries. Many Indigenous people genuinely mean that the term "religion" does not capture the essence of their complex traditions. To explain their practices and ideas, pedagogically, to one another or to outsiders, they prefer other concepts that they consider more accurate. Many Bribris have warned me that we risk misunderstanding Indigenous traditions if we call them religious.

When representatives of an Indigenous community do not refer to their own traditions as religious, then it is usually not advisable for us as students or scholars to do so either due to the exposure and the misunderstandings that it might engender. We influence how our audiences understand the people and the practices we describe. It is thus a matter of academic ethics to do our best to minimize the risk of having our work serve as warrant for those who are targeting religious Indigenous traditions to convert or destroy them.

About the author

Bjørn Ola Tafjord is professor of the study of religions at the University of Bergen, Norway, and principal investigator of the collaborative research project the Governmateriality of Indigenous Religions (GOVMAT).

Suggestions for further reading

In this book
See also chapters 1 (Why does the title of this book use the phrase "Indigenous religious traditions" rather than "Indigenous religions"?), 2 (What makes a religion an "Indigenous religion"?), and 8 (Why is "religion" a problematic category for understanding Indigenous traditions?).

Elsewhere
de la Cadena, Marisol. *Earth Beings: Ecologies of Practice across Andean Worlds*. Durham, NC: Duke University Press, 2015.

Tafjord, Bjørn Ola. "Scales, Translations and Siding Effects: Uses of *Indígena* and *Religión* in Talamanca and Beyond." In *Religious Categories and the Construction of the Indigenous*, edited by C. Hartney and D. J. Tower, 138–177. Leiden: Brill, 2016. https://doi.org/10.1163/9789004328983_009.

10
Is "tradition" a useful category?

Greg Johnson

Whether or not "tradition" is a useful category, it most certainly gets used in a variety of ways, some of them highly consequential for Indigenous communities.

Perhaps the most common use of tradition, whether in popular culture, academic, or legal contexts, is to connote authenticity as a function of durability over time. Something is traditional because it has persisted while other things have changed. Framed thus, tradition carries a high value for many Indigenous communities, and traditional leaders are esteemed accordingly. In particular, ritual and myth are often sites of the self-conscious preservation and perpetuation of tradition in this sense. But even here we should note that all traditions show evidence of innovation and accommodation. Such dynamics are best understood as facets of tradition rather than corrosive forces against it, a theme we will return to below.

Things construed as traditional often carry a metonymic load, meaning that they stand for a larger entity. For example, think of how a traditional Lakota headdress can signify "Plains Indian" in the popular imagination. This mechanism points us to the symbolic capacity of "tradition," which can be expansive or restrictive and reductive, as when that same image of a headdress signals to some audiences that it stands for an object and people from the past that are frozen there. All too often this is how discourses of tradition as authenticity get twisted by non-Natives: things and people deemed "traditional" are really real but from a different time. The profoundly harsh consequence of tradition being captured in this manner is that anything from contemporary Native communities that does not resemble fetishized symbols of tradition may be denigrated as inauthentic and diminished. Vertiginously, then, tradition here functions as a trap of sorts. One extension of this dynamic is that symbols of tradition (let's imagine the headdress again) can be readily alienated from cultural contexts and appropriated for use and abuse by people and institutions with no connection whatsoever to the object, whether they be institutions or sports fans.

Let's briefly consider how some of these dynamics of tradition play out in legal contexts for Native people. In the United States and Canada, for example, space for Indigenous appeals to tradition has in recent decades been built into a variety of laws and policies concerned with such things as repatriation and burial protection, arts and crafts authentication, and various forms of subsistence rights protection. In these cases, "tradition" flags cultural knowledge and practices, often based on religious claims, that warrant legal standing and may potentially contribute to legal protections. On the face of it, this trend reverses centuries of discrimination against Native peoples and their traditions, and many benefits from such laws and policies have redounded to communities as a result. However, the same dynamic we noted above has at times been evident in legal contexts. Namely, "tradition" can backfire, becoming a hostile category to Native interests. Lawyers and judges, for example, may fail to recognize living Indigenous peoples as meaningfully traditional because they do not adequately resemble familiar instances of frozen tradition. In such cases, the law protects tradition in principle but fails to see or protect it in practice. Another way tradition can be a counterproductive category is when laws distinguish between "traditional" and "contemporary" practices, the former receiving protection but the latter not. Functionally, this way of parsing tradition may yield protection of things from the past, but it does not—categorically—extend protections to people in the present, setting up yet another time trap by which Native people are caught by non-Native perceptions of what "tradition" should look and sound like. Imagine a dispute over a ceremonial space, for example, and picture the frustration of a Native community when the judge finds the testimony of an archaeologist more relevant than that of a ritual practitioner.

A way out of this bind is to think of tradition as a process, not a product. Traditions are dynamic, flexible, and sometimes radically innovative. Generally speaking, most people seem to recognize this about traditions such as Christianity and Judaism, so it shouldn't be such a leap to see it elsewhere. My point isn't that traditions are only about change. They entail continuity insofar as tradition is an ongoing process of culturally directed change. Here we have an example of why studying categories matters: tradition is a category of promise and perils. If thought about with critical care and used in ways that honor the ongoing lives of tradition in action, it can yet do good work.

About the author

Greg Johnson teaches at the University of California, Santa Barbara, where he is a professor in the Department of Religious Studies and director of the Walter H. Capps Center for the Study of Ethics, Religion, and Public Life. His research focuses on the intersection of religion and law in Indigenous contexts, with particular attention to repatriation, burial protection, and sacred land claims.

Suggestions for further reading

In this book
See also chapters 1 (Why does the title of this book use the phrase "Indigenous religious traditions" rather than "Indigenous religions"?), 8 (Why is "religion" a problematic category for understanding Indigenous traditions?), and 9 (Why is it sometimes risky to present Indigenous traditions as religious?).

Elsewhere
Hobsbawm, Eric, and Terrence Ranger, eds. *The Invention of Tradition.* Cambridge: Cambridge University Press, 2012.

Nohelani Teves, Stephanie. *Defiant Indigeneity: The Politics of Hawaiian Performance.* Chapel Hill: University of North Carolina Press, 2018.

11
What skill sets do students and scholars use to understand Indigenous religious traditions?

Molly H. Bassett

As the chapters in this volume demonstrate, the religious traditions of Indigenous peoples are interwoven into Native groups' histories, everyday lives, ceremonies, and celebrations. While someone could make a similar claim about many different cultures, Indigenous peoples' ongoing subjection to colonialism invites us to interrogate the intellectual frameworks, theories, and methods we bring to research focused on Indigenous cultures. Our reflection on our own positionality and epistemologies might lead us to develop skill sets and approaches that incorporate multiple voices, perspectives, and knowledges (along with a healthy amount of humility). Many of the contributors to this volume—both Indigenous and non-Indigenous scholars—have taken winding pathways through various professions, personal encounters, and academic fields to arrive at the chapters they have contributed to this collection. I am deeply appreciative of every contributor. From the first author who agreed to write to the last chapter we received, each shares a perspective from which I have learned, as will many other readers.

Students and scholars of Indigenous religious traditions take circuitous and direct paths in their learning. Most people first encounter Indigenous religious traditions in popular culture and in primary and secondary education about Native peoples. Some colleges and universities include departments dedicated to the study of Native and Indigenous cultures, while others expect departments like ethnic studies, anthropology, Africana studies, or religious studies to teach students about Indigenous cultures. While some students first encounter Indigenous religious traditions in a classroom, many begin understanding Indigenous religious traditions through less formal study. Perhaps a book like this one will lead a reader from a chapter to a suggested reading and into a deeper engagement with an Indigenous religious tradition. As you read this volume, you will encounter contributors who identify as Indigenous and non-Indigenous and whose training reflects a variety of academic disciplines.

Indigenous and non-Indigenous scholars who study Indigenous religious traditions may (or may not) be trained in the study of religions, and they likely draw on a carefully considered selection of linguistic training, legal studies, visual and material culture, archaeological materials, ethnohistories, and literature. This work can occur in a traditional institution of higher learning, like a college or university, and/or in community contexts. For Indigenous scholars, knowledge of their own culture and other cultures may form the basis of their research and give rise to the questions they explore. Many Indigenous and non-Indigenous scholars dedicate years to acquiring familiarity with, if not fluency in, Native languages and develop relationships with Indigenous scholars and community members.

Collaborations abound in the study of Indigenous religious traditions. A number of the non-Indigenous contributors to this volume regularly collaborate with Indigenous research partners or groups. Collaborations have not always been the norm, however. While there are many ways to respectfully study human cultures and acknowledge the violence of contact and colonialism, there are an equal (if not greater) number of ways to perpetuate colonialist mentalities. As with antiracist teaching, teaching using decolonizing methodologies involves, as Audra Simpson and Andrea Smith have written, "engag[ing] the historical and political context that defines truth . . . [because] epistemologies have material consequences."

There are canonical voices in the study of Indigenous cultures, including Linda Tuhiwai Smith, Vine Deloria Jr., and Victor Montejo, among others (many of whom you'll find "suggested" throughout this volume). Each contributor to this volume could list dozens of thinkers who have helped them craft their own skill set. I name teachers (Rudy Busto, Jeanette Favrot Peterson, Davíd Carrasco, Delfina de la Cruz, Sabina de la Cruz, Abelardo de la Cruz, John Sullivan, and Charles Lloyd), writers (Gabriel García Marquez, Leslie Marmon Silko, Louise Erdrich, and Joy Harjo), and researchers (Robin Kimmerer, Henry Louis Gates Jr., Marisol de la Cadena, Tim Ingold, and Alfred Gell).

What skill set do I use in my own research on Mexica-Aztec religious traditions? I have learned to triangulate sources so that when one record—say the alphabetic record—is incomplete, I can turn to visual and material culture. Developing this skill set involved learning to read and communicate in other languages, including Spanish and Nahuatl. (Nahuatl is an Indigenous language spoken by approximately two million Nahuas in Mexico; the Mexica-Aztecs spoke an older version of Nahuatl.) It also involved developing literacy in other academic disciplines, including art history and anthropology. My skill set includes critiques of theories and methods that perpetuate colonialist visions or versions of Indigenous religious traditions, including the "world religions" model and narratives that privilege non-Indigenous cultures. I developed this skill set to research questions I had about Mesoamerican religions and to teach students decolonial approaches to the study of religions.

My skill set and approaches are not perfect. Like you will, I have learned *so much* from the contributors to this volume. If you're curious about the skill sets students and scholars of Indigenous religious traditions use, I encourage you to turn the page and keep reading.

About the author

Molly H. Bassett is an associate professor and chair in the Department of Religious Studies at Georgia State University. She published *The Fate of Earthly Things* with the University of Texas Press in 2015. Her current book project explores bundles as theory and method in the study of Mesoamerican religions. A fourth-generation Appalachian, she lives in Atlanta, Georgia, with her spouse, kids, and animal companions.

Suggestions for further reading

In this book
See also chapters 35 (How do archaeologists study religion in the Indigenous past?) and 12 (Why study Indigenous religious traditions?).

Elsewhere
Cadena, Marisol de la. *Earth Beings: Ecologies of Practice across Andean Worlds.* Durham, NC: Duke University Press, 2015.

Carrasco, David. *City of Sacrifice: The Aztec Empire and the Role of Violence in Civilization.* Boston: Beacon, 1999.

The Florentine Codex: An Encyclopedia of the Nahua World in Sixteenth-Century Mexico. Edited by Jeanette Favrot Peterson and Kevin Terraciano. Austin: University of Texas Press, 2019.

Simpson, Audra, and Andrea Smith, eds. *Theorizing Native Studies.* Durham, NC: Duke University Press, 2014.

Witherspoon, Gary. *Language and Art in the Navajo Universe.* Ann Arbor: University of Michigan Press, 1977.

12

Why study Indigenous religious traditions?

Graham Harvey

It may seem simplistic to say that we should study Indigenous religious traditions *because they exist*. However, more is at stake than the assertion that every religion deserves inclusion in our studies. Studying Indigenous religious traditions not only brings more information into view, more facts to learn about, but also raises important and exciting critical themes and issues for discussion.

Scholars have paid remarkably little attention to Indigenous religious traditions. In some religious studies departments, such traditions might only be mentioned when research by anthropologists is introduced. This misses out on studying a large number of ways in which people make sense of the world. Meanwhile, some Indigenous studies colleagues seem nervous about the word "religion," perhaps because they are unfamiliar with recent developments in studies of religion. To many people, "religion" suggests organized and hierarchical institutions encouraging belief in unseen beings, realms, or realities. Perhaps "religion" suggests odd rituals with little connection to everyday life—as in the criticism often leveled against religious people that they do not live up to the ideals they preach. Whether or not this criticism is ever deserved, the study of religion is now increasingly interested in "lived religion," or "what people actually do." For example, rather than asking what people believe about life after death, researchers might ask what foods people share or avoid. They are more interested in religious lives than in what leaders and texts declare to be "the truth." This important development encourages a richer engagement with religions, including Indigenous religious traditions.

Until recently, most academic teaching about religions has focused on a small group of traditions and particularly emphasized the ideas or beliefs taught by religious leaders and texts. The addition of so-called new religious movements to the curriculum has improved matters not only by reaching beyond what used to be called "world religions" (i.e., Buddhism, Christianity, Hinduism, Islam, Judaism, and sometimes Sikhism and Shinto) but also by asking more sociological questions. This trend improved understanding of the ways in which religious people join with or keep distant from others. More importantly, it focused attention on change and diversity—common processes in all religions but ignored when the only question was "What does this religion teach?"

In recent decades, scholars of religion have realized that there are many Indigenous religious traditions and that these provide new perspectives that demand and reward attention. It would take a large book just to list the variety of Indigenous traditions that exist among the Indigenous nations of every inhabited continent, each of them more or less distinct from those of even neighboring communities. Topics that are already at the heart of religious studies (and other disciplines) are given fresh information for consideration. These include ritual or ceremony, stories or mythologies, rites of passage (e.g., namings, marriages, funerals), initiation, sacredness, and taboos. Discussions of religious leadership and social structures have been enriched by including shamans, medicine people, and healers. The growing interest in ecological matters has gained from a consideration of Indigenous emphases on place, belonging, and world renewal but also from the particular impact of climate change on Indigenous communities.

Beyond widening perspectives on existing debates, new themes have been generated by increasing scholarly interest in matters of importance to Indigenous people. These include justice, sovereignty, and activism. The growing use of terms like "ontology" and "relationality" points to inspiring thinking about what makes people human and what makes someone a better person. While such debates challenge common assumptions developed within European colonialism, they do not always acknowledge the influence of Indigenous knowledge holders. The necessity of advancing more ethical ways of doing scholarly work is another good reason for learning from (not just about) Indigenous traditions.

To conclude, if Indigenous religious traditions are not studied, then we are not really seeking to understand all of life. We miss out on some vibrant and exciting ideas and practices that could significantly improve our engagement with all religions. And we are not open to new thoughts or challenges. We need to build on an awareness that Indigenous people have important perspectives on the issues that continue to shape the cultural, ecological, and political world. Indigenous religious traditions, braided into the ideas and practices arising from historical and contemporary Indigenous experiences, invite and improve vibrant conversations among students in all disciplines.

About the author

Graham Harvey is professor of religious studies at the Open University in the United Kingdom. His research largely concerns the "new animism," especially in rituals and protocols through which Indigenous communities engage with the larger-than-human world. He is editor of Routledge's Vitality of Indigenous Religions series and Equinox's Religion and the Senses series.

Suggestions for further reading

In this book
See also chapters 30 (Is an academic approach to Indigenous religions innately colonizing?) and 15 (Why are Indigenous African and Afrodiasporic religions relevant to you?).

Elsewhere
Cox, James L., ed. *Critical Reflections on Indigenous Religions*. New York: Routledge, 2013.

Hartney, Christopher, and Daniel J. Tower, eds. *Religious Categories and the Construction of the Indigenous*. Leiden: Brill, 2016.

Kraft, Siv Ellen, Bjørn Ola Tafjord, Arkotong Longkumer, Gregory D. Alles, and Greg Johnson. *Indigenous Religion(s): Local Grounds, Global Networks*. London: Routledge, 2020. https://www.taylorfrancis.com/books/e/9781003021513.

Olupona, Jacob K., ed. *Beyond Primitivism: Indigenous Religious Traditions and Modernity*. New York: Routledge, 2004.

13

What is the origin of common stereotypes of Native American religious life?

Sarah Dees

Someone who is unfamiliar with Native American religions may likely have picked up some ideas about them through the media. If pressed, they might be able to name stereotypical examples: a rain dance, peace pipes, or Plains Indian tipis. Where did these ideas come from, and how have they circulated so widely? Representations of Native traditions have long circulated in governmental, religious, scientific, and popular realms via official reports, surveys, travel narratives, museums, art, literature, and movies. Through these varied forms, descriptive and visual representations have shaped non-Natives' perspectives of Native religions. One of the most influential vehicles for stereotypical depictions of Native traditions in recent history, films in the Western genre, was influenced by earlier forms of media. While representations furthered in popular media may offer non-Natives a glimpse of a culture with which they are unfamiliar, these depictions are often distorted and may not accurately present traditions in the ways that Indigenous practitioners would want them to be represented.

When considering representations of Native American religions, it is important to consider *who* has produced a representation and *why*—what purpose it was meant to serve. Some of the earliest non-Native representations of Indigenous traditions were in the form of official documentation produced by European invaders and missionaries. As the United States took root and expanded, efforts at documenting and representing Native Americans continued. During their official expedition on behalf of the US government from 1801 to 1803, Lewis and Clark and members of their party took many notes and drawings, which they shared with leaders in Washington. This information was valuable to the government, but the mainstream American public was interested in Native people as well.

DEES—WHY DO WE STEREOTYPE NATIVE RELIGIOUS LIFE?   41

Beginning in the 1830s, artist George Catlin (1796–1892) embarked on numerous trips throughout what is now the American West, eventually producing hundreds of portraits and paintings that included depictions of dances and ceremonies. Catlin publicly displayed these works in the United States and Europe, speaking with visitors about his experiences. The photographer Edward Curtis captured portraits of Native Americans as he traveled throughout the West beginning in the early nineteenth century. The public was interested in these types of expeditions, and written accounts published in popular newspapers and magazines circulated among a broad public audience.

Museums have been another site where the mainstream public has been exposed to representations of Native American traditions. Non-Natives collected physical artifacts during their travels, some of which they displayed publicly. Dioramas of Native American cultures and traditions portrayed scenes or ceremonies, and displays have included sacred and significant objects. Importantly, historical exhibits, books, and art presenting features of Native cultures did not simply offer an objective account of features of Native American religious life. They often tried to convey some sort of "argument" about Native religions. Critics have suggested Catlin's paintings were exaggerated to make Native ceremonies seem "wilder." Edward Curtis famously edited his well-known photographs, removing technology that people regularly used in order to craft images of Native peoples as inherently premodern.

Ideas about Native traditions have been prominent in popular media, from novels to movies. Books such as James Fenimore Cooper's 1826 novel *The Last of the Mohicans* described features of Native cultures, along with tragic narratives that suggested Native Americans were in decline. These tropes were reproduced in the Western movie genre, a form of media that represents perhaps the single most influential in shaping ideas of Native traditions. In these films, generally set in the nineteenth century in the American West, Native people were depicted as either "peaceful" or "savage." Generally, they portrayed Plains Indians, circulating stereotypes of antagonistic Indian warriors on horseback.

While the influence of non-Native representations on mainstream American thought looms large, there is a long history of Native Americans who have represented their traditions on their own terms. Writers such as Charles Eastman, Gertrude Bonnin, and Francis La Flesche have shared their perspectives on religion and culture. One of the goals of the Red Power movement of the 1970s and later efforts for Indigenous sovereignty has been self-representation. It is important to consider how communities wish to be represented. When thinking about a representation, viewers should consider the following: When was this image (or movie, or display, etc.) created? Who made it and under what circumstances? Who funded it? What does it "argue"? Did the individuals or communities who are represented play a role in creating the image? What is the greater context of the display? These questions are especially pertinent with regard to representations of Native American religions.

About the author

Sarah Dees is an assistant professor of religious studies at Iowa State University. Her first book, a history of Smithsonian research on Native American religions, will be published by the University of Nebraska Press.

Suggestions for further reading

In this book
See also chapters 28 (What moral responsibilities do scholars and students have in studying Indigenous religions?) and 39 (Was the Washington R*dskins cultural appropriation?).

Elsewhere
Bataille, Gretchen M. *Native American Representations: First Encounters, Distorted Images, and Literary Appropriations*. Lincoln: University of Nebraska Press, 2001.

Garroutte, Eva May. *Real Indians: Identity and the Survival of Native America*. Berkeley: University of California Press, 2003.

Reclaiming Native Truth. "Compilation of All Research from the Reclaiming Native Truth Project." https://www.firstnations.org/publications/compilation-of-all-research-from-the-reclaiming-native-truth-project/.

14

How do ideas about race shape understandings of Native American religious life?

Sarah Dees

What's the difference between the categories of "religion" and "race"? When I pose this question to my students, they often suggest that individuals can choose to join a particular religion, while race is a marker of biological identity—something that one cannot choose. However, historically, these categories were not as distinct as this simple division would suggest. Understandings of biological, cultural, and spiritual differences have shaped encounters between Native Americans and non-Natives. Religious ideologies influenced Europeans' interactions with Native Americans during their earliest incursions into what are today the Americas. Likewise, ideas about race and racial differences have affected outsiders' perceptions of Native American religious traditions. While scholars today recognize that "race" (like "religion") is a constructed category with meanings that have changed over time, the social forces that created and maintained these ideas continue to operate.

Ideas about the nature of religious and racial differences developed concomitantly over time and were sharpened through the process of colonialism. Some scholars highlight the nineteenth century as the key era in which scientific racism and the vocabulary of race developed; however, ideas about essential, inherited human differences had already circulated for centuries by that point. During the medieval era, notions of difference were articulated on the basis of biological characteristics as well as culture and religion. These notions were heightened by the Muslim expansion into Europe and the ensuing Christian Crusades and Reconquista. The history of religious warring in Europe and the Mediterranean world served as a foundation for European Christians' encounters with Indigenous peoples and traditions. As Europeans explored distant regions and began to colonize parts of what are today the Americas, Africa, and Asia, they theorized the original inhabitants of these lands. Enlightenment thinkers including Carl Linnaeus sorted human groups into divisions based on phenotype and geography. Europeans also noted cultural differences. They used the terms "pagans" or "heathens" to describe Native Americans, drawing on a religious category—someone who is not a Christian—to refer to a distinct cultural or political group.

During the nineteenth century, Euro-American thinkers drew on science to reinforce their ideas about essential, inherited human differences. Religions factored into theories of difference as well. In works of comparative religion, theologians described Indigenous traditions as "primitive," distinguishing them from so-called "civilized" or "enlightened" religions. Often, "comparative" works from this era advanced ideas of Christian supremacy. Racial ideas were often implicit—if not explicit—in these discussions, the repercussions of which went beyond the realm of theory. Federal Indian agents pointed to Native American religious traditions as signs that Native Americans were "uncivilized" and culturally inferior to Euro-Americans. Through the process of assimilation, which they claimed would "elevate" Native Americans, agents of the US government in the nineteenth century targeted Native American cultures. The supposedly secular US government pointed to religious traditions as evidence of the need for assimilation and called for Native people to convert to Christianity. Modern conceptions of "race" were not only about biology but also about psychology, spirituality, and culture.

Today, scientists agree that race is a constructed category—people are all one species. However, while race may be an illusion or a construct, the effects of racism are very real. Ideas about racial differences still permeate culture and social interactions and laws, which are unevenly applied. According to a 2018 study, two-thirds of Americans polled did not believe that Native Americans face racial discrimination. Members of Native communities have suggested that a general lack of awareness and understanding of Native American history and culture and US settler colonialism has contributed to discrimination. In effect, this profound lack of awareness about the ongoing presence of Indigenous peoples is a new form of racism. This "invisibility" translates to difficulties for practitioners of Indigenous religions as well. Lack of understanding about Native traditions, paired with structures meant to protect "Western" religions, has created difficulties in legally protecting Native traditions.

About the author

Sarah Dees is an assistant professor of religious studies at Iowa State University. Her first book, a history of Smithsonian research on Native American religions, will be published by the University of Nebraska Press.

Suggestions for further reading

In this book
See also chapters 3 (Were all religions at one time "Indigenous"?), 38 (What is the deal with cultural appropriation?), and 40 (What is decolonization, and what does it have to do with Indigenous religious traditions?).

Elsewhere
Boyarin, Jonathan. *The Unconverted Self: Jews, Indians, and the Identity of Christian Europe*. Chicago: University of Chicago Press, 2019.

Mauro, Hayes Peter. *Messianic Fulfillments: Staging Indigenous Salvation in America*. Lincoln: University of Nebraska Press, 2019.

Nagle, Rebecca. "Invisibility Is the Modern Form of Racism against Native Americans." *Teen Vogue*, October 23, 2018. https://www.teenvogue.com/story/racism-against-native-americans.

15

Why are Indigenous African and Afrodiasporic religions relevant to you?

Ayodeji Ogunnaike and Oludamini Ogunnaike

Indigenous African religious traditions are often not well known in so-called Western societies, and the image presented of Afrodiasporic traditions like Haitian Vodou is usually othering, prejudicial, and sinister. Furthermore, because Indigenous religions are usually closely associated with specific geographical and cultural contexts, these traditions are often not the first port of call for students of religion. However, because African religious traditions are so practically oriented, they primarily seek to address universal human and cosmological conditions and issues and thus have important wisdom and insight to share with all people across time and space. In fact, the development of Afrodiasporic religious traditions during and after the Atlantic slave trade demonstrates not only how mobile these traditions are but also how they empowered an incredibly diverse group of people to survive and overcome some of the most inhumane circumstances and challenges imaginable.

African and Afrodiasporic religious traditions are highly relevant in all settings because, technically speaking, they are not quite "religions" in the modern, Western sense of the term. Most African languages do not have a direct translation for the world "religion," and what we might identify as religious activity is inextricable from all other aspects of life like family identity, occupation, medicine, or the arts. Most deities are not individual parts of abstract belief systems but concrete realities. For example, Ogun—the Yoruba deity (orișa) of war, justice, and the hunt—simply *is* justice and the iron implements used in war, hunting, agriculture, or even transportation. As a result, any and all interactions with metal and technology are Ogun rituals and fall within his domain. In this way, *everyone* engages with Ogun on a daily basis, and Ogun's rituals, myths, and iconography help all people do so in ways that are as beneficial as possible. There is no part of life that is not explained and governed by some such spiritual force, and as new domains of life emerge, the traditions are flexible enough to incorporate them. Practitioners of African and Afrodiasporic traditions make their ritual knowledge and ancestral wisdom available even to those who do not actively practice their traditions, and they understand their service to a Supreme Deity and/or lesser spirits as assisting in putting the world back in order. A prominent example is the tradition of Ifa divination, which uses mythical archetypes, proverbs, and poems to explain the root causes of whatever issue a client might have and present its solution. When our undergraduate students have worked with Ifa diviners, Ifa has helped them make important business decisions, heal familial psychological trauma, and even restore order to romantic relationships! Although Ifa enjoys a high international profile, similar roles are played by diviners all over Africa and its diaspora, including South African Sangomas or Manbos of Haitian Vodou.

Because there is no division between the sacred and secular or even the natural and supernatural in their cosmologies, African and Afrodiasporic religious traditions offer their own unique relational and sacralized understanding of what in the West would be called the environment or "nature." Given our current ecological crisis, many practitioners and students of African and Afrodiasporic traditions have turned to them to assert more positive ritual processes and orientations that can address the issue by helping humans see and relate to the Divine in our physical world and critique our current exploitative and degrading relationship with the environment.

Just as these traditions offer deep knowledge about our external world, they also possess remarkable insights into our internal, personal worlds, offering opportunities to know ourselves and how we should live on a deeper level. Most lineages and individual practitioners have one or a small number of tutelary deities, ancestors, or other spirits who function like sacred "parents" or patron saints that govern most aspects of their lives. Gaining experiential knowledge about the nature, talents, shortcomings, and symbols of these spiritual powers through their mythology, dances, songs, ritual objects, initiation, and sometimes even bodily possession brings practitioners to greater self-actualization and knowledge of themselves. Without engaging in the ritual practices of specific traditions, our students enjoy discovering which deities or spirits seem to govern their lives and personalities and the practical wisdom that comes with this knowledge.

In conclusion, the number of reasons why African and Afrodiasporic religions are relevant to all people is as large as the number of issues in our world and the people who wrestle with them. Although they draw on Indigenous philosophical, spiritual, and cultural bodies of knowledge, they are flexible enough to speak to all circumstances and offer wisdom even to those who are not actively involved in their practice.

About the authors

Ayodeji Ogunnaike is an assistant professor of Africana studies at Bowdoin College whose research is centered on the Yoruba tradition of Ifa divination and orature but also includes Islam and Christianity in African and Afrodiasporic religions, particularly Brazilian Candomblé.

Oludamini Ogunnaike is an assistant professor of African religious thought and democracy at the University of Virginia whose research focuses on the intellectual and aesthetic dimensions of West African Islamic traditions, particularly Sufism, and Yoruba orişa traditions, particularly Ifa.

Suggestions for further reading

In this book
See also chapters 6 (How can spiritual traditions create Indigenous traditions in new places?), 12 (Why study Indigenous religious traditions?), and 62 (Is Voudou dangerous?).

Elsewhere
Abimbola, 'Wande, and Ivor Wilks. *Ifá Will Mend Our Broken World: Thoughts on Yoruba Religion and Culture in Africa and the Diaspora.* Roxbury, MA: Aim, 1997.

Fernandez Olmos, Margarite, and Lizabeth Paravisini-Gebert. *Creole Religions of the Caribbean: An Introduction from Vodou and Santeria to Obeah and Espiritismo* (2nd edition). New York: New York University Press, 2011.

Ogunnaike, Ayodeji. "Oyinbo Ọmọ Asogun Dere: An Analysis of Racial Injustice, Gun Violence, and Sexual Assault, in America through a Traditional Yoruba Perspective." *Journal of Interreligious Studies* 23 (2018): 103–126.

Olupona, Jacob. *African Religions: A Very Short Introduction.* New York: Oxford University Press, 2014.

16
What makes Vodou an Indigenous tradition?

James Padilioni Jr.

Within a Vodou world view, the earth is a grounding source of resonant power. As the word "Vodou" translates to "spirit," it also communicates the broad notion of ritual obligation that all humans have toward the ancestral lineages from whence their life has sprung. Not only the affective memories of their ancestors' turmoils of soul and triumphs of spirit but the very floral, faunal, and fungal life-forms that perpetually support the human community's full vitality—the macro- and micronutrients that power the metabolic, material forms of their bodies and the chemicals that compose them, the phosphorus, calcium, magnesium, and all those physical elements whose celestial heritage witnessed the birth of the cosmos itself.

Generations of living and dying in one location create layered landscape ecologies of commemoration. Cemeteries form sites of pilgrimage when Vodou practitioners follow ritual obligations to libate the gravesites of their ancestors. But the spirits and ancestors of Vodou are not dead in an absent sense; they are agentive beings with multiple cycles of afterlife, and over time, these spirits may transfer the presence of their soul energy into natural formations like waterfalls, trees, caves, and other topographical features of the earth. Moreover, Vodou temples are often deliberately constructed with bare earthen floors that, where possible, are centered around the trunk of a large tree that grows deep into the sacred land of Ginen—Guinea/Africa—the name Vodou practitioners call the otherworldly realms. Thus, the practice of Vodou focuses devotees' awareness upon the physical conditions of impermanence, rendering the entire plane of matter a memento mori that complements the Adamic premise of Biblical myth: "For you are dust, and to dust you shall return" (Genesis 3:19).

The geographic dislocation imposed upon Indigenous Africans, stolen from their worlds of meaning and transported to the Americas, only amplified Vodou practitioners' desire to return to Ginen upon one's death.

The transatlantic slave trade was a sacrilegious event that depopulated communities and disappeared priests and priestesses, creating a dearth of ritual knowledge that left sacred landscape sites unattended. This genocide of sacral life was tragically mirrored on the other side of the Atlantic Ocean, as those same enslaving European settler-colonists were working to conquer societies of American first peoples, whose land and natural resources they pilfered for mercantilist aspirations of political-economic domination.

These forced encounters engendered a clandestine relationship between Indigenous Americans and Indigenous Africans, who saw in each other a reflection of their mutual entrapment. Running away together to the hills, swamps, gullies, and mountainsides of the American plantation zone, fugitive Africans and insurgent Americans forged maroon communities, bonded to each other through initiatory oaths performed at pre-Columbian ritual sites of spiritual power. Through the legacy of these Afro-Amerindian alliances, many traditions of African diasporic Vodou have assumed a shared custodial relationship over the sacred landscapes of the Americas.

Perhaps the most vivid example of such Indigenous solidarity is Haiti, the world's first, independent Black republic. While under French rule, the colony of Saint-Domingue, as it was then known, was the Bourbon family's richest American holding, as the more than eight hundred thousand captive Africans enslaved within the western half of Hispaniola produced nearly 40 percent of Europe's imported sugar and 60 percent of its coffee. But it was during a Vodou ceremony, thickly set within the Bois Caïman, a swampy outpost along the northern coast (Plaine-du-Nord) dubbed "Alligator Woods," that the priestly duo of Dutty Boukman and Cécile Fatiman consecrated to Spirit their tactical plans for a massive, multipronged African insurrection. The ensuing August 1791 uprising continued unabated for nearly thirteen years until Revolutionary leader Jean-Jacques Dessalines officially declared the independence of the former colony in 1804. But in choosing a dignified appellation for this new beacon of the Black Americas, the liberated Africans of Saint-Domingue eagerly restored the land to its rightful Taíno name, Ayiti, the "rugged, mountainous land" whose valiant anticolonial struggles map across the very countryside.

If Indigeneity refers, literally, to "that which the earth generates of itself," then land sovereignty and ecological sustainability are preeminent political concerns for the intergenerational practice of Indigenous Vodou. As we journey deeper into these Anthropocenic times of amplifying, catastrophic climate change, we must reevaluate Vodou traditions as a store bank of Indigenous Afro-Amerindian perspectives toward sacred ecology, whose rites of obligation and libation bind us to the land and to one another and offer us fresh insight for creating sustainable, planetary futures.

About the author

James Padilioni Jr. is visiting assistant professor of religion at Swarthmore College. His research and teaching foreground is African diasporic ritual cultures, ontology and critical race theory of Blackness, and deep ecology studies, with a particular focus on Afro-Latinx folk Catholicism, herbalism and pharmacopeia, and spirit ecstasy traditions. James also cohosts the *Always Already* critical theory podcast (alwaysalreadypodcast .wordpress.com).

Suggestions for further reading

In this book
See also chapters 18 (Is Vodou [Voodoo] a religion?), 19 (Is Voudou an American religion or an Indigenous religion?), and 62 (Is Voudou dangerous?).

Elsewhere
Danticat, Edwidge. *After the Dance: A Walk through Carnival in Jacmel, Haiti*. New York: Vintage, 2015.

Geggus, David. "The Naming of Haiti." *New West Indian Guide / Nieuwe West-Indische Gids* 71(1–2) (1997): 43–68.

Tarter, Andrew. "Trees in Vodou: An Arbori-cultural Exploration." *Journal for the Study of Religion, Nature, and Culture* 9(1) (2015): 87–112.

17
What is the difference between Vodou, Voudou, and Voodoo?

Emily Suzanne Clark

I know this is not a dictionary, but this is more than an etymology lesson. This short chapter thinks about some similarities and differences between Haitian Vodou, New Orleans Voudou, and New Orleans Voodoo. These are not the only religious traditions of the African diaspora worth comparing, but limiting our scope to these related traditions provides focus. All three words, "Vodou," "Voudou," and "Voodoo," originate from the Fòn-Ewè word *vodun*, which translates to "god." The Fòn-Ewè language group is part of a larger collection of dialects and cultural traditions centered on the Gulf of Guinea along the West African coast. Sometimes referred to as Yorùbáland, Europeans heavily colonized this region and enslaved and sold many people. Religious traditions and understandings of the world across Yorùbáland, though with differences, would be familiar to their neighbors. Separated from their homes and the larger community, enslaved Africans in the Americas could learn from the religious traditions of their ancestors and their fellow enslaved men and women. In terms of the African diaspora, vodun became, as one scholar has put it, "Africa *reblended*."

The term "reblended" is illustrative of syncretism. Syncretism refers to a cultural process in which practices and ideas from multiple cultures mix together to create a new one. The tradition called Haitian Vodou blended religious traditions across Yorùbáland along with some ideas and practices from Catholicism, all within the contextual frame of slavery and colonialism. Spirit possession by the gods, or the *lwas*, empowered Vodou practitioners and connected them back to their homeland. When the lwas possess a person, African spirits become physically present there on the Caribbean island.

New Orleans Voudou is another syncretic religious tradition of the African diaspora. Voudou has a similar historical "origin" as Haitian Vodou: adaptions of African traditions in the American context of slavery. Like in Haiti, Voudouists in New Orleans believe in a network of spirits with both African and Catholic influence. Vodou and Voudou both feature a main god with lower spirits, called the loa/lwa in Vodou and referred to as spirits in Voudou. There are differences across their spiritual pantheons but a number of similarities too. Voudou and Voodoo refer to the same tradition in New Orleans, but the different spellings draw our attention to a similar dynamic as that between Vodou and Voudou. In New Orleans, the francophone spelling of Voudou was more common before the turn of the twentieth century, when the Americanized spelling of Voodoo became more popular. The Americanization of the spelling reflected larger changes in the city's cultural and religious traditions. For example, African American Protestantism became another force of influence on Voodoo, especially Black Pentecostalism and its gifts of the Holy Spirit, such as glossolalia. Glossolalia, more commonly referred to as speaking in tongues, would be familiar to a tradition with spirit possession.

Syncretism is clearly at work in all these traditions. Voudou becomes Voodoo as new religious ideas and practices are brought to New Orleans, and the shifting in spelling reflects this. None of these spellings are absolute. With immigration across the Caribbean, both historically and today, there are practitioners of Haitian Vodou in New Orleans. There are practitioners of New Orleans Voudou who use all those spellings—Vodou, Voudou, and Voodoo—interchangeably. Capitalization also varies. The traditions are distinctive but also translatable and recognizable across time, space, and community. This is indicative of many African diasporic religions. They are adaptable and can change with context.

The situational nature of these traditions also has implications for the study of religion. Syncretism, though an incredibly helpful theory, introduces a bit of a problem. Arguing that syncretic religions are ones that have blended other religions can suggest that there are some "pure" religions that exist elsewhere. If Haitian Vodou is syncretic, does that mean that French Catholicism and African vodun are purer? The quick answer is no, and that points to a larger dynamic in the study of religion. There is no pure, "undiluted" religion anywhere. Religion is always messy and deeply entangled in everyday life. The syncretism behind Vodou, Voudou, and Voodoo encourages us to embrace that messiness and pay attention to process and context.

About the author

Emily Suzanne Clark is associate professor of religious studies at Gonzaga University, where she teaches undergraduate courses in American religions. She is the author of *A Luminous Brotherhood: Afro-Creole Spiritualism in Nineteenth-Century New Orleans* (University of North Carolina Press, 2016) and coeditor of *Race and New Religious Movements: A Documentary Reader* (Bloomsbury, 2019). She has also published on New Orleans Voudou, Jesuit missions in the Pacific Northwest, and the Moorish Science Temple.

Suggestions for further reading

In this book
See also chapters 18 (Is Vodou [Voodoo] a religion?), 21 (Is Adivasi religion different from Hinduism?), and 62 (Is Voudou dangerous?).

Elsewhere
Alasdair, Pettinger. "From Vaudoux to Voodoo." *Forum of Modern Language Studies* 40(4) (2004): 415–425.

Fandrich, Ina J. "Yoruba Influences on Haitian Vodou and New Orleans Voodoo." *Journal of Black Studies* 37 (2007): 775–791.

Matory, J. Lorand. *Black Atlantic Religion: Tradition, Transnationalism, and Matriarchy in the Afro-Brazilian Candomblé*. Princeton, NJ: Princeton University Press, 2005.

Thompson, Robert Farris. *Flash of the Spirit: African & Afro-American Art and Philosophy*. New York: Vintage, 1984.

18
Is Vodou (Voodoo) a religion?

James Padilioni Jr.

The word "vodun" translates to "spirit" in the Fon, Ewe, and Gbe languages spoken in the historic Kingdoms of Oyo (ca. 1300–1896) and Dahomey (ca. 1600–1906), today located within the West African nations of Ghana, Togo, Benin, and Nigeria. Through trade relations and migration patterns, these kingdoms created a shared religious culture focused on Mawu-Lisa, the androgynous creator deity (demiurge) with two poles of personality: Mawu, the feminine principle embodied by the moon, and Lisa, the masculine principle embodied by the sun. Mawu-Lisa's power diffuses throughout the cosmos, with the various vodun spirits acting as conduits of cosmic power upon the earth plane.

During the transatlantic slave trade of the sixteenth through the nineteenth centuries, over twelve million ethnic Africans, including many from Dahomey and Oyo, were taken captive and transported to diverse locales across the Americas. In the French Caribbean, this ritual tradition came to be called *Vodou*, as Africans enslaved by Catholic masters worked out a set of correspondences that related the iconography of popular folk saints with the personalities of the Vodou spirits, now called *lwa* (from the French *loi*, "law, principle"). Spurred by the Haitian Revolution (1791–1804), Vodou practitioners further scattered throughout the Caribbean and the Gulf Coast basin, creating a broad Vodou-Conjure zone with local variants and spellings, including *Vodou* in Haiti; *Vodú / La Veintiuna División* in the Dominican Republic; *Voudou* and *Voodoo* in Louisiana and New Orleans; *Hoodoo-Conjure* of the southeast Atlantic Coast and Chesapeake Basin of the United States; and *Sanse* in Puerto Rico. Vodou also shares similarities with *Obeah* in Jamaica and the Anglophone Caribbean and is embedded within traditions of Cuban *brujería*, Brazilian *Macumba-Quimbanda*, and Mexican and Central American *curanderismo*. *Voodoo* also refers to stereotypical "Hollywood" (mis)representations of this broad tradition throughout the Atlantic littoral.

Within Haitian Vodou, the most prominent of the American traditions, the Mawu-Lisa concept of an all-powerful creator deity is recon-
ceived as *Bondye* (from French *Bon Dieu*, meaning "good God"). The lwa
spirits manifest the power of Bondye in material forms, either natural
landscape features or human-created amulet-like assemblages of intermixed natural and fabricated materials, known diversely as *gris-gris*, a
mojo or *mojo hand*, a *wanga/ouanga*, or *Paket kongo*. When practitioners
fashion these talismans as anthropomorphic figures, what results is the
infamously misunderstood "Voodoo doll" of popular culture lore.

Contrary to Christian missionary accounts, Vodou is not a Satanic cult,
nor does it engage in so-called devil worship. While animal sacrifice—
however visceral its bloody appearance—features within some Vodou
rites, these sacrifices are never performed out of sadistic intentions but
function as a form of invocation and propitiation (ritual offering) to the
lwa spirits, not unlike the related Judaic and Islamic practices of *Korban*
and *Qurbani*, respectively, the slaughtering of a goat or ram during holy
day feasts.

Healing and wellness are the core aspects of all Vodou practices. As
Vodou holds to a holistic understanding of health, sickness and affliction
may manifest in any domains of life—physical, spiritual, social, psychic,
political, and so on—and migrate across to the others. The first premise
of a Vodou cosmos is material impermanence set against the incessant
recycling of soul energy in a move not unlike Dharmic traditions. Practitioners of Vodou seek out protection and empowerment against the
vagaries of life, using ritual performance to serve the spirits (*sevi lwa*) and
call upon ancestors, spirit guides, guardian angels, and the lwa who hold
custodianship over aspects of human life. Vodou ceremonies are fundamentally opportunities for healing that feature a constellation of drum
rhythms, vocal calls and responses, dance routines, food items, and other
sensory-perceptive elements that become energized and "well heated"
(*bien echoufe*) throughout the duration of the event. This ritual heat allows
spirits to mount the bodies of their devotees. Thus entranced, the *oungan*
(priest) or *mambo* (priestess), as a spirit medium, yields the use of their
body to the spirit, who then is able to communicate knowledge (*konesans*)
to humans from the heavenly realms. These rituals intend to create an
equilibrium (*balans*) of spiritual energy capable of generating health and
wellness within the community.

If one definition of *religion* etymologically relates to the Latin *religare*,
which connotes the idea of binding and tying things together through
oaths, then the practice of Vodou is eminently religious. The Vodou cosmos tethers together the living and dead, material and ethereal, the lwa,

humans, animals, and the arrayed forces of nature, in a constellation of mutual obligation with *Bondye* that cannot be forfeited or dispatched, so long as the earth endures.

About the author

James Padilioni Jr. is visiting assistant professor of religion at Swarthmore College. His research and teaching foreground is African diasporic ritual cultures, ontology and critical race theory of Blackness, and deep ecology studies, with a particular focus on Afro-Latinx folk Catholicism, herbalism and pharmacopeia, and spirit ecstasy traditions. James also cohosts the *Always Already* critical theory podcast (alwaysalreadypodcast .wordpress.com).

Suggestions for further reading

In this book
See also chapters 2 (What makes a religion an "Indigenous religion"?), 16 (What makes Vodou an Indigenous tradition?), and 17 (What is the difference between Vodou, Voudou, and Voodoo?).

Elsewhere
Hurston, Zora Neale. *Tell My Horse: Voodoo and Life in Haiti and Jamaica.* New York: Harper Perennial, 2009.

Michel, Claudine, and Patrick Bellegarde-Smith. *Vodou in Haitian Life and Culture: Invisible Powers.* New York: Palgrave Macmillan, 2006.

Roberts, Kodi A. *Voodoo and Power: The Politics of Religion in New Orleans, 1881–1940.* Baton Rouge: Louisiana State University, 2015.

19

Is Voudou an American religion or an Indigenous religion?

Emily Suzanne Clark

This question requires either less than a minute or well over a hundred minutes; five minutes is a difficult yet still useful compromise. Voudou is both an American religion and an Indigenous religion, and we learn a lot from considering it to be both. The categories of Indigenous religion and American religion are easy and difficult to define. The simple approach would be to conclude that all religions are Indigenous to somewhere, so all religions are Indigenous, and an American religion is one that is practiced in the Americas. The difficult method considers what those classifications mean in general and what those classifications mean for an African diasporic religion.

The category of Indigenous religion is one that this entire volume considers. The typical "world religions" paradigm includes the major religions that have spread across the world—like Christianity, Islam, Buddhism, Hinduism, and Judaism—and then collapses those numerically smaller traditions that seem contextually specific to the category of Indigenous religion. These are often religious traditions of Australian aboriginal peoples, Native American and First Nations tribes, and many religious traditions from Africa. It's a complicated category composed of a variety of religions that dominant scholarship deems not important enough to earn their own "world religions" category. Typically, in a "world religions" paradigm, an Indigenous religion is one that is clearly connected to the place it originated. This makes it distinctive from a transportable—or as Vine Deloria Jr. put it, a missionary—religion that is picked up and moved elsewhere. Those "portable" religions get the category of "world religions." However, it is worthwhile to consider voluntary versus forced movement. While this is a bit of a simplification, portable religions are often brought by immigrants who choose to leave their original homes. Enslaved peoples and colonized peoples practice Indigenous religions. It would seem like power dynamics have something to do with how scholars categorize a world religion versus an Indigenous one.

American religion is also a difficult category to define. It reminds me of a greased pig, a tradition common to the Texas fairs of my childhood where children chase a pig covered in Vaseline. The firmer your grip around a greased pig, the more it slips through your grasp. Many scholars of American religions would define it as any religious tradition that is either shaped by the Americas or shapes the cultures or politics of the Americas. By this definition, there is a wide variety of religions that fit the mold. However, much to the chagrin of many college professors, some people consider Wikipedia an authority on the topic. While it has since been updated, in August 2019, the entry for "History of Religion in the United States" began with "The history of religion in the United States began with European settlers," which erased untold years of Indigenous religious history. This idea was mirrored in nineteenth- and twentieth-century scholarly works on what was an American religion; it was white Protestant Christianity. While research on American religion has troubled that definition, its historical roots hold significance. American religions are the religions of those with political and social power, which historically has meant white Protestantism. However, like Indigenous religion, that definition reveals a power dynamic.

If we consider Voudou, a religious tradition of the African diaspora that began to develop in New Orleans in the 1700s, to be both an Indigenous religion and an American religion, we realize two important things. Categorizing Voudou as both emphasizes what is meant by those terms. For Indigenous religion, it means recognizing that the historical, social, and cultural context of a place deeply shapes the religions that are practiced there. Being a religion forged in the context of slavery and white supremacy in Louisiana, there is no way that Voudou could not be shaped by or in turn shape its cultural context. Elements of it are unique to that context. Additionally, to consider Voudou an American religion means recognizing that same dynamic as being influenced by the context of the United States as a nation-state—that is, a country shaped by understandings of citizenship and a religion that *belongs* in the United States. Any religion Indigenous to the United States is an American religion.

About the author

Emily Suzanne Clark is associate professor of religious studies at Gonzaga University, where she teaches undergraduate courses in American religions. She is the author of *A Luminous Brotherhood: Afro-Creole*

Spiritualism in Nineteenth-Century New Orleans (University of North Carolina Press, 2016) and coeditor of *Race and New Religious Movements: A Documentary Reader* (Bloomsbury, 2019). She has also published on New Orleans Voudou, Jesuit missions in the Pacific Northwest, and the Moorish Science Temple.

Suggestions for further reading

In this book
See also chapters 17 (What is the difference between Vodou, Voudou, and Voodoo?), 62 (Is Voudou dangerous?), and 22 (Is Shinto an Indigenous religion?).

Elsewhere
Clark, Emily Suzanne. "Nineteenth-Century New Orleans Voudou: An American Religion." *American Religion* 2(1) (2020): 131–155.

Deloria, Vine, Jr. "Is Religion Possible? An Evaluation of Present Efforts to Revive Traditional Tribal Religions." *Wicazo Sa Review* 8(1) (Spring 1992): 35–39.

Fandrich, Ina J. "Yoruba Influences on Haitian Vodou and New Orleans Voodoo." *Journal of Black Studies* 37 (2007): 775–791.

Morrow Long, Carolyn. *A New Orleans Voudou Priestess: The Legend and Reality of Marie Laveau*. Gainesville: University Press of Florida, 2006.

20
Is Adivasi religion the same as Hinduism?

William Elison

Adivasis—literally "original inhabitants" in Hindi and other Indic languages—are India's Indigenous communities. They are colloquially known in Indian English as "tribals." According to the latest official population figures—those of the 2011 Census of India—they make up 8.9 percent of the national total of 1.2 billion.

Some people who fall within the category have adopted it, on an individual or community level, as a matter of self-identification. Others have not. The term "Adivasi" is extremely elastic, encompassing the Indigenous populations of islands in the Indian Ocean, most of the citizens of India's northeastern border states, high-profile groups like the Banjaras (exoticized in Bollywood movies as "Gypsies"), and marginalized demographics across rural and even urban India. Like Hindu castes, these are distinct communities whose bounds are drawn and maintained by the norm of endogamy (marriage and reproduction within the group). And as with Scheduled Castes, the former "Untouchables"—whose condition of historical and structural disadvantage is recognized by the government with inclusion on lists, or "schedules," attached to the constitutions of India's states—tribal identity is also a matter of official certification. "Scheduled Tribe," or ST, is often used as a synonym for "tribal" by officials, journalists, and activists.

What does this all have to do with religion? To approach this question, it's helpful to have a sense of how Indian government policy builds on colonial antecedents and how the idea of "tribe" devised by British administrators builds, in turn, on the texts and teachings of classical Hinduism. Scholars in my field owe a debt to Nicholas Dirks for showing the deep investment of the colonial regime in a project of anthropological classification: pigeonholing the empire's subjects within categories of caste and tribe. If you lived in British India, and you weren't marked down as a member of a caste, you probably belonged to a tribe. The Schedules mentioned above of disadvantaged castes and tribes eligible for reparatory government policies are in fact one legacy of this system.

So what's the difference between a caste and a tribe? Where the state is concerned, tribes are made up of people who are, in a word, peripheral. At the social level, they stand outside of the Hindu caste hierarchy. And at the spatial level, they are located in wilderness areas outside the agricultural base of caste society. Records often refer to "remote tribes." This was not an official designation, but there were in fact formal categories conceived around this attribution of distance or peripherality: "forest tribe," "hill tribe," "nomadic tribe." Temporal distance is inscribed in "early tribe," which the postcolonial government has amended to "primitive tribe."

The construction of tribes as separate from but adjacent to castes can be traced through thousands of years of Hindu thought. In much of the classical corpus—epic and mythological literature, taxonomic *shastra* knowledge—that was historically dominated and disseminated by Brahmins, a place is reserved for tribal communities outside the pale of civilization. (And per this tradition, for "civilization," you can read "caste society.") Tribals are wild people, jungle people, who inhabit the forest alongside other antisocial beings: beasts, hermits, and outlaws. Importantly, however, the forest is lawless but not godless; it is often counterpoised in Sanskrit literature to the complicated and ultimately corrupt lifestyle of the city. Again, in Brahminical writings, the forest people are savages. But the tradition makes room for noble savages as well as benighted ones.

Now let's fast-forward to the present. It's precisely this double-sided characterization—ignorant yet spiritually pure—that defines the popularly held view of tribals among today's Hindu Right. Imperfectly assimilated junior partners, they are already-almost-Hindus, Hindus in the rough. Contemporary right-wing leaders seek to cement this bond with Adivasi populations through proselytization. In the highly volatile context of Hindu majoritarian politics, the chief competition they see is with Christian churches, whose missionizing work (begun in colonial times) has brought about a strong Christian affiliation among the ST populations of India's far northeast.

Nowadays, politicians have done their best to make "conversion" of this sort a dirty word. And thus when Hindu groups pursue their own mission-izing, they define their purpose as *ghar wapsi*, which means "return home." Return, that is, to the ultimate source of all authentically Indian spiritual paths. Return where you already belonged. To the *sanatana dharma*, the eternal religion given voice in the Vedas, its essence kept pure ever since under the stewardship of priests, monastics, and saints (most of whom do happen, at the end of the day, to be Brahmin by caste).

About the author

William Elison is associate professor of religious studies at the University of California, Santa Barbara. An ethnographer and historian, he specializes in the religions of modern South Asia. He is the author of *The Neighborhood of Gods: The Sacred and the Visible at the Margins of Mumbai* (University of Chicago Press, 2018) and is currently at work on a short history of Mumbai for Cambridge University Press.

Suggestions for further reading

In this book
See also chapters 17 (What is the difference between Vodou, Voudou, and Voodoo?) and 21 (Is Adivasi religion different from Hinduism?).

Elsewhere
Dirks, Nicholas B. *Castes of Mind: Colonialism and the Making of Modern India*. Princeton, NJ: Princeton University Press, 2001.

Middleton, Townsend. *The Demands of Recognition: State Ethnography and Ethnopolitics in Darjeeling*. Stanford, CA: Stanford University Press, 2016.

Singh, Bhrigupati. *Poverty and the Quest for Life: Spiritual and Material Striving in Rural India*. Chicago: University of Chicago Press, 2015.

21

Is Adivasi religion different from Hinduism?

William Elison

What do Adivasis themselves have to say all about this? Their diversity notwithstanding, tribal peoples living in interdependency with the broader society tend to follow beliefs and practices that share key features with the observances of peasant-caste and Scheduled Caste Hindus. Among these communities, cultic practices center on deities that are identified with, and encountered in, special spaces. By this I mean special kinds of spaces: villages, individual dwellings, bodies of water. And I also mean specific locations: *this* crossroads, *this* threshold, *this* sacred mountain. Contact between human beings and these local deities—who are recognized as intrinsic members of the village community—generally involves mediation via spirit possession or other visionary experiences. Among the human members of each village, there will be special kinds of people, and of course specific individuals, who will have more credibility as mediums than others.

Some things about these local cults fit right into the right-wing blueprint for a Hindu India. In his foundational manifesto of 1923, *Hindutva—Who Is a Hindu?*, V. D. Savarkar, the movement's house intellectual, drew up a nontheistic formulation that collapses religion onto nation: Hindu identity = racial inheritance + spiritual bond to the national territory. His is a Hindu recasting of *Blut und Boden*—"Blood and Soil"—a bedrock principle of radical nationalism. And note that by the terms of this equation, Adivasis, with their myriad sacred sites, are already essentially Hindu on both counts. For the fascist Savarkar, proselytization was needed only to the degree that it could awaken tribals to the consciousness of this essential spirit, giving them the tools to realize their natural genius in the words and ideas of the Sanskrit inheritance. (To be sure, the image of Brahmin trusteeship does tend to linger here in the background.) Adivasis attracted to assimilation along these lines don't have to contend with the degree of stigma that confronts Scheduled Caste groups, whose aspiration to upward mobility is often denounced as uppity or worse. (In this connection, if familiarity breeds contempt, the tendency of upper-caste people to exoticize Adivasis works to relative advantage.) Over the past decades of right-wing ascendancy in India, some of Hindu fascism's most enthusiastic foot soldiers have come from tribal communities.

And yet there are other aspects of the cults of tribal deities that don't sit well with Hindu nationalists. Or with other proselytizing organizations, even if their politics are on the gentler side. Spirit possession—widespread though it may be among Hindus, especially people from nonelite castes—is considered something of an embarrassment by the voices that dominate in public. It's dismissed as a residual or backward practice. Other elements targeted by modernizers from inside as well as outside tribal communities include the use of alcohol in religious contexts (or in others) and animal sacrifice. A group that seeks integration as a caste in good standing with other Hindu castes will typically move to cast aside these features. They are, precisely, marks of the "tribal": emblems of barbarism that cost us respect in the eyes of others, sites of pollution that stain us and impede our progress.

My own fieldwork interlocutors come from the Warli community, whose territorial claims include forested areas increasingly threatened by absorption within Mumbai's urban sprawl. I know modern-minded Warli leaders who urge the rejection of booze and much else that distinguishes the observances of their tribal religion from those of modern mainstream Hinduism. At the same time, they are anti-integrationist—committed to Adivasi particularity and autonomy. One point where it's important to draw a hard line is the renaming of deities. To follow the nesting logic of Brahminical Hinduism, in which specific local deities are identified as manifestations or avatars of the gods of the translocal Sanskritic tradition, who in turn, in the final analysis, are discrete aspects of an ultimate godhead, this theological concession, they understand, is also a territorial concession.

What will become of Warli claims to the forests of northern Maharashtra, whose tribal geography is marked out with sacred sites? If once we open up the sacred to Hindus, will not the sites themselves be taken over? And if our territorial gods are not unique and Indigenous—what becomes of our own identity as human indigenes? My activist friend Prashant—an atheist as far as his personal convictions are concerned—makes the rounds of tribal shrines in the area. He reminds the villagers to be mindful of land rights when outsiders ask the names of the gods worshipped there. "You don't tell them 'Ganesh,' 'Durga,'" he coaches them. "Make sure you say, 'Hirva,' 'Naran' . . ."

About the author

William Elison is associate professor of religious studies at the University of California, Santa Barbara. An ethnographer and historian, he specializes in the religions of modern South Asia. He is the author of *The Neighborhood of Gods: The Sacred and the Visible at the Margins of Mumbai* (University of Chicago Press, 2018) and is currently at work on a short history of Mumbai for Cambridge University Press.

Suggestions for further reading

In this book
See also chapters 20 (Is Adivasi religion the same as Hinduism?) and 17 (What is the difference between Vodou, Voudou, and Voodoo?).

Elsewhere
Savarkar, Vinayak Damodar. *Hindutva—Who Is a Hindu?* 1923. Reprint, Bombay: Veer Savarkar Prakashan, 1969.

Sundar, Nandini. *Subalterns and Sovereigns: An Anthropological History of Bastar* (2nd edition). Delhi: Oxford University Press, 2007.

Vitebsky, Piers. *Living without the Dead: Loss and Redemption in a Jungle Cosmos*. Chicago: University of Chicago Press, 2017.

22
Is Shinto an Indigenous religion?

Emily B. Simpson

The Association of Shinto Shrines, an administrative organization that oversees the majority of Shinto shrines in Japan, states online that "Shinto is the indigenous faith of Japan." But is Shinto truly an Indigenous tradition? Is Shinto even a religion?

The mythology of Shinto centers on the landscape of Japan, from the origin myth of the creator gods Izanagi and his wife, Izanami, dipping a spear in the primordial sea and letting drops of brine fall to create the Japanese archipelago to the highly localized origin stories of particular shrines and their *kami* (deities) in regional histories and institutional documents. Indeed, Shinto's reputation as a nature religion derives in part from the concept that kami either are themselves natural phenomena or can manifest in them, from Mt. Fuji to individual trees and rocks at particular Shinto shrines. Yet this also means that regional differences in kami and associated rituals are considerable. Shrines, rituals, and *matsuri* (celebratory festivals meant to both worship and entertain the kami) look and feel quite different depending on where they are and what they are meant to represent and achieve. This is partially because Shinto lacks many of the hallmarks of most global religions: a founder, an ethical code, and a definitive sacred text.

As is also true of many Indigenous traditions, the idea of Shinto as an ancient tradition passed down to today with little alteration or outside influence ignores key historical realities. First, religious and philosophical traditions from the Asian continent—Buddhism, Daoism, and Confucianism—have profoundly impacted the development of Shinto. Indeed, no written records from before the introduction of continental culture in Japan exist. Even the central Shinto mythologies were written after religious traditions from India, China, and Korea had been in Japan for centuries. Scholars debate when Shinto became an organized religion: some consider the rise of the imperial court, its official mythologies and rituals in the eighth century, including the first documented use of the word "Shinto," to be its starting point. Others think Shinto really emerged far later, when the first independent Shinto schools emerged in the thirteenth and fourteenth centuries.

In fact, Shinto may have become a unified, organized religion only in the modern period, when the government co-opted Shinto as the state creed. Shinto was chosen precisely because it was perceived as Indigenous rather than foreign, and most of the discernibly foreign elements were removed or deemphasized. As part of Japan's drive to rapidly modernize and compete with Western powers, "State Shinto" emerged in the late nineteenth and early twentieth centuries. State Shinto emphasized loyalty and veneration toward the emperor by standardizing shrine rituals, practices, and architecture. Significantly, Shinto observances were defined as a patriotic duty rather than religious practices. The Japanese constitution of 1889 granted freedom of religious choice to Japanese subjects while mandating participation in Shinto ceremonies as the *duty* of Japanese subjects and *not* religious in nature. Shinto's relationship with the Japanese empire is perhaps best demonstrated by the building of Shinto shrines—and suppression of other religious traditions—in Japanese territories. Thus, Shinto was reclaimed as an Indigenous tradition and used to suppress other Indigenous traditions both at home and abroad.

While State Shinto was outlawed and dismantled after Japan's defeat in World War II in 1945, this version of Shinto had a profound effect on how Shinto operates today. First off, many core practices within Shinto, including Shinto weddings, date from this period. Second, many Japanese today continue to view Shinto not as a religion but rather as a set of customs and traditions unique to Japanese culture. Finally, Shinto's earlier associations, borrowings, and hybridization with other religious traditions are generally forgotten in favor of considering it a wholly Indigenous tradition or, as the Association of Shinto Shrines puts it, "faith." Although Shinto is by no means unusual in borrowing elements from other religious traditions, its supposed "Indigeneity" is at least partially the creation of an ultranationalist state.

Thus, we might say that Shinto is defined by a series of paradoxes. It is often labeled a world or global religion, even though it has a minimal presence outside Japan (especially as shrines in Japan's wartime territories have all been dismantled). It is Indigenous to Japan, but it adopted multiple elements from other traditions, and its former relationship with ultranationalism has also made it a tool of oppression. Finally, Shinto's status as a religion at all is complicated by the elements it lacks and by its previous "official" definition as a nonreligion.

About the author

Dr. Emily B. Simpson received her PhD from the University of California at Santa Barbara in 2019 and is a fellow at Harvard University. Her research centers on reinterpretations of the legend of Empress Jingū, a third-century empress appearing in early Japanese chronicles, within various Buddhist and Shinto traditions and within women's cults. Her book project, entitled *Crafting a Goddess: Divinization and Womanhood in Late Medieval and Early Modern Narratives of Empress Jingū*, explores how diverse religious institutions divinized Empress Jingū, focusing on her martial and shamanic deeds, her motherhood and pregnancy, or her connections to maritime communities.

Suggestions for further reading

In this book
See also chapters 2 (What makes a religion an "Indigenous religion"?) and 19 (Is Voudou an American religion or an Indigenous religion?).

Elsewhere
Breen, John, and Mark Teeuwen. *A New History of Shinto*. Chichester, West Sussex: Wiley-Blackwell, 2010.

Hardacre, Helen. *Shinto: A History*. Oxford: Oxford University Press, 2017.

Minoru, Sonoda. *The World of Shinto: Reflections of a Shinto Priest*. Tokyo: International Foundation of Shinto, 2002.

Reader, Ian. *Shinto: Simple Guides*. London: Kuperard, 2008.

23
Do Chicanos practice Indigenous religious traditions?

Rudy Busto

Chicano identity is bound to the political and cultural activism of the 1960s and early 1970s by Mexican-descent Americans rejecting assimilation into American society. The Chicano Movement, initiated as a coalition of several distinct local movements, coalesced at the end of the 1960s. As Mexicans, Chicanos inherited the legacy of the *mestizaje* ideal that interpreted Mexico's history and destiny as the result of the biological and cultural blending of Iberia with Indigenous Mexican, primarily Aztec/ Nahua peoples. Emphasizing an Aztec heritage of empire and masculine heroism, the Chicano Movement's eventual turn to cultural nationalism as a foundation for their politics derives from the 1969 manifesto El Plan Espiritual de Aztlán. El Plan based its call to Chicano self-determination by appealing to the mythological place of Aztec origin, Aztlán, located somewhere north of the Aztec city-state Tenochtitlan (Mexico City) and presumably in the territory Mexico lost to the United States in the 1848 Treaty of Guadalupe Hidalgo. Aztlán focused the Chicano movement, inspiring political goals, rooting communal and personal identities, and unleashing the production of poetry, fiction, plays, and a distinctive graphics art tradition.

This renaissance of the Indigenous also offered an attractive alternative to Roman Catholicism, whose historical neglect and policies had relegated Mexican Americans to poor examples of American Catholicism. In this spiritual vacuum, some Chicanos joined Indigenous Mexican *danza* traditions, bringing into the American public the spectacle of feathered and caped dance troupes accompanied by drumming, the blowing of conch-shell horns, the use of rattles, and wafting *copal* offerings. For members of these *Azteca danza* troupes, dancing is the act of prayer, and their involvement may include instruction in revitalized forms of Indigenous philosophy, training in ethical daily comportment, and puberty rite of passage ceremonies to instill Indigenous values and pride. The reception of Aztec dancing at powwows continues to be mixed; some Native Americans find solidarity with danzantes, while others reject what they regard as the appropriation of Indigenous culture by Mexican Americans.

While the cultural nationalism of the Chicano movement celebrated the glories of the Aztec empire, critics pointed out failings and blind spots in the ideology owing to the rush to embrace an idealized Aztec past, including the overreading of the theory of mestizaje, an unrelenting sexism, and the inability of the movement to extend beyond the reach of college and university students and Chicano studies programs. Movement intellectuals appealed to the work of Mexican philosopher Jose Vasconcelos, whose 1929 *La raza cósmica* argued that Latin America would serve as the crucible for the forging of a "cosmic" fifth race out of the world's races. Movement Chicanos ignored the hispanophilic tendency in Vasconcelos's theory and narrowed the idea of the amalgamation of world races down to the commingling of the Indigenous with the European. Vasconcelos's text thus served as an intellectual legitimation for movement indigenists who interpreted the text to fit their agenda.

The publication of Gloria Anzaldúa's *Borderlands / La Frontera: The New Mestiza* in 1987 was the culmination of decades of growing dissent and reaction against the machismo of the Chicano movement. As the movement glorified the "Four Horsemen of the Chicano Movement" (César Chavez, Rodolfo "Corky" Gonzales, José Angel Gutiérrez, and Reies Lopez Tijerina), it justified the secondary role of women by reinforcing cultural (Catholic) norms of motherhood, purity, and service to the family. Anzaldúa's book announced an unrepentant and assertive Chicana Indigeneity that overturned the masculinist and heteronormative claims of the movement and Mexican culture itself. She reinterpreted Aztec culture and religion, infusing her spirituality with feminist goddess theory, Jung, and an Afro-Caribbean spirit possession experience of the Aztec goddess Coatlicue. *Borderlands / La Frontera*'s devastating assault on the Indigeneity of the Chicano movement catalyzed subsequent generations of Mexican-descent activists and intellectuals to whom Anzaldúa calls to thrive on the borders of nation-states, cultures, sexuality, and gender.

In the twenty-first century, Chicano Indigeneity is a widespread identity. It is, however, not uniformly understood and practiced. Many first-generation Chicano activists entered the university to build Chicano studies programs and continued to promote a distinct identity apart from, but in alliance with, other Latinos. Chicano cultural nationalism survived through the end of the last century in the student organization MEChA (Movimiento Estudiantil Chicano de Aztlán), where many first-generation

Mexican-descent college students were drawn to the movement's politics. Outside the university, Indigeneity in Mexican-descent communities continues to be most visible in the ubiquitous Aztec dancing at public events. In the domestic sphere, Indigenous healing practices, foodways, and vocabulary continue as they have for generations.

About the author

Rudy V. Busto is associate professor of religious studies at the University of California, Santa Barbara. His teaching and research focus on religion and race, particularly Latinx and Asian American traditions.

Suggestions for further reading

In this book

See also chapters 36 (Why reconstruct precolonial Indigenous religions in the Americas?) and 37 (Are Aztec dancers practicing a religion?).

Elsewhere

Anzaldúa, Gloria. *Borderlands / La Frontera: The New Mestiza* (4th edition). San Francisco: Aunt Lute, 2012.

de la Torre, Renée, and Cristina Gutiérrez Zúñiga. "Chicano Spirituality in the Construction of an Imagined Nation: Aztlán." *Social Compass* 60(2) (June 2013): 218–235.

Forbes, Jack. *Aztecas del Norte: The Chicanos of Aztlan.* Greenwich, CT: Fawcett, 1973.

Gallegos, Bernardo P. "Whose Lady of Guadalupe? Indigenous Performances, Latina/o Identities, and the Postcolonial Project." *Journal of Latinos and Education* 1(3) (2002): 177–191.

Moraga, Cherríe. "Codex Xeri: El Momento Historico." In *The Chicano Codices: Encountering Art of the Americas*, edited by Patricia Deher, 20–22. San Francisco: Mexican Museum, 1992.

24
Is Neo-Paganism an Indigenous religious tradition?

Abel R. Gomez

The rising visibility of global Indigenous issues following the ceremonial encampments at Standing Rock and the growing popularity of Neo-Pagan religions in the United States may cause some to ask about the relationship between Indigenous and Neo-Pagan religions. Both kinds of religions revere the natural world, honor various cycles of celestial bodies, and seek to live in balance with the human and more-than-human worlds. In this chapter, we will explore the relationship between Neo-Pagan and Indigenous religions by looking at Wicca, the most popular form of Neo-Pagan religion in North America.

Neo-Pagan (new or contemporary pagan) religions are incredibly diverse and include varying forms of revived practices with roots from ancient Europe, Egypt, the Middle East, and elsewhere. Wicca is the most well-known revival of such practices as well as the most visible form of religious witchcraft. Practitioners self-identify as Wiccans and/or witches and often trace their spiritual lineage to the ancient peoples of western Europe. A highly diverse religious system, Wicca often centers on practices that align with eight seasonal shifts called Sabbats, ritual celebrations of the moon called Esbats, and magical practices such as divination, healing, and spell casting. Wicca is typically characterized by the veneration of a Goddess connected to the earth and moon and a God connected to the sun and the hunt, though this varies considerably across groups. The birth, growth, death, and rebirth of the God are often tied directly to the earthly cycles celebrated in the eight Sabbat rituals. Some Wiccans are formally initiated members of small religious congregations called covens, while others may practice alone.

The revival of Wicca is often attributed to a British civil servant named Gerald Gardner who published the book *Witchcraft Today* in 1954, claiming to be an initiate of one of the last remaining covens. According to

Gardner, witchcraft was a strain of the old Indigenous religion of the British Isles, with a more ancient history tied to the Stone Age. In practice, the system that Gardner popularized was a blend of older European symbols and traditions with elements of European esotericism such as ceremonial magic. Following the spread of Wicca to the United States in the 1960s, it also blended with political movements, especially feminism and environmentalism. It has since become one of the fastest-growing religions, which has also incorporated influences from many sources, including Asia and the psychology movement as well as the specific mythological and ritual structures of a given practitioner's ancestry.

Several prominent American Wiccan leaders, like Scott Cunningham, Starhawk, and Phyliss Curott, have suggested similarities between Wicca and Indigenous religions. Such leaders have undoubtedly been influenced by the work of anthropologist turned spiritual leader Michael Harner. Harner popularized "core shamanism," a series of techniques synthesized from diverse Indigenous practices that allow practitioners to enter altered states of consciousness to journey to unseen worlds and converse with spiritual allies. Some Wiccans see engagement with these practices as reclaiming the essential roots of their spiritual traditions. For some Native Americans, such practice by non-Native peoples is a violent appropriation and reduction of Indigenous spirituality.

While some Wiccans view their practice as "nature based" and see a kinship with Indigenous peoples, there are important differences. Many scholars define Indigenous religions as communal and place-based traditions into which people are born and that are shaped by experiences of colonization, racism, and the defense of ancestral lands. If this is the case, Wicca and similar Neo-Pagan religions would not be Indigenous. Though some Wiccans see themselves as spiritual descendants of women killed during the European witch burnings, their persecution is not the same as colonization. Furthermore, in the United States, where the majority of Wiccans are white and middle class, their access to open spaces to practice this nature-based religion is a direct result of the ongoing colonial occupation of Indigenous lands. It is also true that there are a growing number of Wiccans who are Black, Indigenous, and/or other people of mixed race or color who blend European-based practices of Wicca with those of their own cultural heritage.

Neo-Pagans and Indigenous religious leaders sometimes engage in cultural exchange on local levels as well as in larger transnational contexts, such as the World's Parliament of Religions. Shared concerns about the future of the planet and their responsibility to steward the earth are religious values that offer a bridge between these groups of traditions that have distinct histories and relationships to colonialism and land.

About the author

Abel R. Gomez is an assistant professor of Native American and Indigenous spiritual traditions in the Religion Department at Texas Christian University. He holds a PhD from the Religion Department at Syracuse University. His research focus is on sacred sites, decolonization, and Indigenous survival among the Ohlone peoples of the San Francisco–Monterey region.

Suggestions for further reading

In this book
See also chapters 2 (What makes a religion an "Indigenous religion"?), 5 (Are Indigenous religions only those practiced by Indigenous people?), and 22 (Is Shinto an Indigenous religion?).

Elsewhere
Adler, Margot. *Drawing Down the Moon: Witches, Druids, Goddess-Worshippers, and Other Pagans in America*. New York: Penguin Books, 2010.

Berger, Helen. *A Community of Witches: Contemporary Neo-Paganism and Witchcraft in the United States*. Columbia: University of South Carolina Press, 1999.

Hutton, Ronald. *The Triumph of the Moon: A History of Modern Pagan Witchcraft*. New York: Oxford University Press, 2019.

Magliocco, Sabina. *Witching Culture: Folklore and Neo-Paganism in America*. Philadelphia: University of Pennsylvania Press, 2004.

25

Are Indigenous people who adapt or alter their rituals and traditions (either by choice or by historical necessity) less authentic than their ancestors?

Kelsey Dayle John

In short, no. To understand why, it is important to think about what it means to be authentic and who decides who is authentic and who is not. Most of the time, the word "authentic" is used by non-Indigenous people to measure an Indigenous person's position on an imaginative scale of authenticity from "real Indian" to "assimilated Indian." However, this measurement scale has a problematic history.

Dakota historian Philip Deloria uses a concept called the "noble savage," which helps explain the problem with the authentic. The "noble savage" describes a sentiment where settlers both "despise and are infatuated with" Native Americans. Fascination mixes with fear to cause hatred, and the two cannot be separated. The noble savage is fascinating for every part of their life, including their religious practices, but they are hated for being the antithesis of the settler-colonial narrative. Settler colonialism is the idea that the entire settlement and colonization of the Americas is based on the continual erasure and removal of Indian persons. (Think: the land cannot be "open for settlement" if Native religions tell about Native peoples' relationship with the land since the beginning of time.) This means Native people are physically in the way, and their religions (which fundamentally emanate from the land and connect them to the land) are a relational barrier that keeps them "in the way." However, the fascination often masks the fear and hatred in what Eve Tuck and Wayne K. Yang call *a settler move to innocence*, or a way of eliminating the guilt settlers feel about colonialism.

"Authentic" is a word connected to the "noble savage" concept. The more "authentic" an Indian is, the more fascinating they become. As the fascination increases, so does the hatred. Academic research and media representations contribute to the portrayal of Natives as "fascinating" in cultural items like cowboy and Indian movies, anthropological research on tribal ceremonies, and the collection of Native artifacts. Often these objects/texts are judged for their "authenticity" but are rarely judged in relationship to promoting tribal sovereignty. This judgment is connected to a Western linear view of progress where a person starts as authentic, untouched, or traditional and moves toward being civilized and assimilated. In the settlement and colonization of the Americas, removing Indians was justified because it was seen as progress, or a movement toward more technology, more money, and more civilization. Assimilation policies inflicted on Indigenous communities (like forced removals from ancestral lands and residential boarding schools) were aimed to erase authenticity and traditional practices. This is how the system was designed, to "kill the Indian and save the man"—a phrase used by Andrew Jackson and the theme of his administration's Indian policies.

The word "authenticity" is just like the phrase "noble savage," where Indians are both hated and admired for being "authentic"; settlers desire to preserve Native authenticity while simultaneously ridding them of it. For example, Native appropriations are abundant in mascots, fashion, and rituals (things like teepees, the former Washington Redskins' mascot, and the fad of burning sage), but what does not come with these appropriations is an increased awareness of tribal sovereignty or a critical view of settler colonialism.

Imagine, if there was never violent settler colonization, if there was never land theft or policies aimed at eradicating Indigenous religions, there would have never been a scale measuring "authentic to assimilated." Sure, there would have been changes and adaptations in religion, culture, language, and ceremonies. Indigenous persons were/are not static people. They can grow, change, adopt, adapt, borrow, and so on. The main difference is that prior to settler colonialism, changes and adaptations were not enforced through mass policies of assimilation that targeted every aspect of Indigenous life, including religious practices. For example, Indigenous peoples were only granted legal protection of religious practice in 1978 under the American Indian Religious Freedom Act. Prior to this, many traditional ceremonies and rituals were considered to be illegal.

Usually the word "authenticity" is a veiled form of judgment about where to position an Indigenous person on a colonial scale of how "assimilated" they are. If it comes from a Non-Native person, what credentials do they have to decide what is authentic and what is not? If it comes from a Native person, why would they position their own relatives on a scale that was meant to erase their community and way of life?

Of course, rituals and traditions have been altered by necessity to survive policies of assimilation and cultural genocide, and they have been altered by choice. But both alterations should be seen as acts of what Minnesota Chippewa scholar Gerald Vizenor calls survivance: not simply surviving assimilation but fostering "an active sense of presence over absence." As Indigenous persons change and adapt, it's important to remember that most Indigenous world views understand progress to be cyclical not linear. So even when Indigenous persons make choices to return to the "old ways," they're not moving backward on a linear scale; they're coming full circle.

About the author

Kelsey Dayle John (Diné) is an assistant professor with a joint appointment in gender and women's studies and American Indian studies. She holds a PhD in Cultural Foundations of Education from Syracuse University. Her work is centered on animal relationalities, particularly horse/human relationships, as ways of knowing, healing, and decolonizing education. Alongside her work in Indigenous animal studies, Kelsey's research interests also include Indigenous feminisms, decolonizing methodologies, and tribal colleges and universities.

Suggestions for further reading

In this book
See also chapters 2 (What makes a religion an "Indigenous religion"?) and 3 (Were all religions at one time "Indigenous"?).

Elsewhere
Deloria, Philip J. *Playing Indian*. New Haven: Yale University Press, 1998.

Pevar, Steven. L. *The Rights of Indians and Tribes*. Oxford: Oxford University Press, 2012.

Tuck, Eve, and Wayne K. Yang. "Decolonization Is Not a Metaphor." *Decolonization: Indigeneity, Education & Society* 1(1) (2012): 1–40.

Vizenor, Gerald, ed. *Survivance: Narratives of Native Presence*. Lincoln: University of Nebraska Press, 2008.

26

Can I convert to or practice an Indigenous religious tradition if I am not an Indigenous person?

Donnie Begay

It would depend mostly on which Indigenous religious tradition the non-Indigenous person wishes to obtain and practice. Everybody is able to join Indigenous social gatherings, such as powwows, feasts, potlatches (originated in Alaska), and other similar events. A non-Indigenous person engaging in the actual religious aspect of Indigenous traditions and religion would most likely be met with apprehension. There are several reasons for this apprehension.

First, so much has already been taken away from Indigenous people by non-Indigenous people. Only after the American Indian Religious Freedom Act of 1978 could Indigenous people openly and freely practice their religious traditions. Before the Religious Freedom Act, Indigenous people who practiced their religious traditions could be fined or incarcerated. Even before the Religious Freedom Act, outside organizations such as the Boy Scouts of America had already appropriated much of Native American culture for their personal use, such as the incorporation of Native American images in their handbooks.

Second, the ceremonies and religious traditions are often handed down by Indigenous people's ancestors in specific situations, such as when they need help, need to regain balance and harmony, or need assistance knowing where to move to have a better life. Those stories are sacred and often kept only within that people group. These stories and teachings are heavily guarded and not openly discussed, especially with anthropologists, ethnographers, and missionaries. Access to sacred places of religious traditions is closely guarded, and places like the Pueblo kiva are only for the men who are initiated. These kivas are closed even to the women of the tribe. However, Frank Cushing, an American anthropologist and ethnologist, once gained access to a Zuni kiva by holding a young Zuni man at knifepoint. Perhaps this is the reason most of the Pueblos do not allow outsiders into their village during their religious events.

Third, conversion is another foreign concept to Indigenous peoples because Indigenous people gain their identity from their family and relatives and their relation to the land, creation, and the Creator. The thought of converting to some other tribe or nation would be tantamount to betrayal and losing one's identity. If a non-Indigenous person wishes to convert or practice Indigenous religious traditions, then they will be asked about their intentions. For what reason do they want to convert? For Indigenous people, the purpose and reasons for doing their religious traditions are to be healed and to restore balance and harmony to one's life. How Indigenous people go about healing and restoring balance and harmony comes from their own teachings and stories. If a non-Indigenous person seeks healing, then they will be asked why they have not gone to their people and learned how they found healing from the stories, ceremonies, and teachings of their ancestors. Indigenous religious traditions are believed to be handed down by the Creator or by one of his/her messengers (similar to angels or prophets in Christianity) for Indigenous people—and some tribes would say for them alone. Indigenous religious traditions are considered sacred; they are not for show or to freely give to the world. To make them available to anyone and everyone would reduce their sacredness to a commodity, hence possibly losing their healing and restorative power.

About the author

Yá'át'ééh, **Donnie Begay** lives in Albuquerque, New Mexico, and is married to Renee, who is from Zuni Pueblo. They have three daughters: Natalia, Kaya, and Peri. Donnie is Navajo and grew up on the Navajo reservation. He is born into his mother's clan, Honágháahnii (One-Who-Walks-Around), and born for his father's clan, Kinyaa'áanii (Towering House People). He graduated from New Mexico State University with a BA in business administration, graduated from George Fox University (now Portland Seminary) with an MA in intercultural studies, and is working on his PhD from the University of Divinity in Australia.

Suggestions for further reading

In this book
See also chapters 5 (Are Indigenous religions only those practiced by Indigenous people?) and 38 (What is the deal with cultural appropriation?).

Elsewhere
Deloria, Vine, Jr. *God Is Red: A Native View of Religion.* Golden, CO: Fulcrum, 2003.

Fixico, Donald. *The American Indian Mind in a Linear World: American Indian Studies and Traditional Knowledge.* New York: Routledge, 2003.

Tinker, George E. *Missionary Conquest: The Gospel and Native American Cultural Genocide.* Minneapolis, MN: Fortress, 1993.

Twiss, Richard. *One Church, Many Tribes.* Bloomington, MN: Chosen, 2000.

27

Can non-Indigenous religious traditions become Indigenous?

Bjørn Ola Tafjord

Yes, in several ways. Today, most Indigenous people adhere to a religion that has historical origins in another community and another geographical region. Indigenous people are Christians, Muslims, Buddhists, or members of other proselytizing religions and consider this part of their own Indigenous identities, communities, and cultures. So if "becoming Indigenous" means being appropriated by Indigenous people and "non-Indigenous" means having historical origins elsewhere, then there are countless examples of non-Indigenous religious traditions becoming Indigenous. Moreover, many Indigenous people have embraced religious traditions from other Indigenous communities and rerooted them in their own community. The examples of non-Indigenous religious traditions becoming Indigenous thus multiply when "Indigenous" is understood as referring to a specific local community for whom anybody and anything from any other community—also from other communities who might self-identify as Indigenous—are foreign, exogenous, or "non-Indigenous."

In Talamanca, Costa Rica, some members of the Indigenous Bribri community consider the Bahá'í Faith their Indigenous religion. They know well the history of the Bahá'í Faith's founding in a Muslim community in the Middle East in the mid-nineteenth century and stories of how foreigners have introduced it in Talamanca from the 1960s onward. But this does not prevent many of them from understanding it as a continuation, a confirmation, and even an enhancement of their own Indigenous traditions. In addition to emphasizing how, nowadays, the Bahá'í Faith is the religion of Indigenous peoples all across the world and thus an aspect of a global Indigenous community, Bribri Bahá'ís present their religion as Indigenous in the narrowest sense: as special and integral to the entire history of the Bribri. They achieve this by reinterpreting Sibö, who, according to traditional Talamancan accounts, was a protagonist in the creation of the human world and the first human beings, a lawmaker, and the educator of the first generation of Bribris. Casting Sibö as not only one among many predecessors of Bahá'u'lláh—the latest of God's messengers to humankind, the successor of Mohammed, and the founder of a new era according to Bahá'í doctrine—but also the very first messenger from the one and only God, sent especially to the Bribri, they give their own Indigenous community a unique position in both the history of humankind and the history of divine revelation. Thereby, the Bribri become the first Bahá'ís—and thus the Bahá'í Faith becomes Indigenous to the Bribri.

Religious narratives also serve to accommodate Indigenous traditions vis-à-vis the different Christianities that missionaries have brought to Talamanca over the past century. Some Catholic Bribris compare certain parts of their Indigenous traditions to the old religion of Israel, the one described in the Old Testament. They argue that all ancient religions became superseded through God's intervention in the world with Jesus Christ and the subsequent spread of Catholic Christianity. Although they denounce some Indigenous traditions as superstitious and redefine many more as cultural but not religious practices, they do maintain and acclaim numerous Indigenous traditions as pillars of Bribri Catholicism and as the legitimation of what Bribris have always known and done. They understand Catholicism as universally Indigenous—and some Indigenous traditions as Catholicism.

Bribris who are Evangelicals, Pentecostals, Seventh-day Adventists, or Jehovah's Witnesses preach a clearer break with the Indigenous traditions that they consider false or diabolic. However, a wide range of Indigenous traditions that they classify as cultural but nonreligious are spared from such condemnation and practiced alongside or even as part of their Christianity. Members of these churches say that their religion is the only true religion for Indigenous people and all other people alike. They see it as the only appropriate Indigenous religion.

Then there is the influence of African traditions in Talamanca that were brought over mainly but not only by people emigrating from Jamaica. Some of these traditions—certain funeral rituals, for instance—are regarded as partly religious and partly Indigenous by their Bribri practitioners. More recently, non-Indigenous scholars, teachers, and tourists as well as the internet have brought new Indigenous religious traditions to Talamanca, especially ideas and practices of shamanism and animism, concepts that historically were foreign to the Bribri. Last but not least, we must not forget the continuous exchanges between Bribris and various neighboring Indigenous peoples—for example, through intermarriage, migration, and political cooperation, prompting copious inclusions of other Indigenous traditions in the Bribri repertoires of both religious and nonreligious Indigenous traditions.

The concept of religion itself has gone from non-Indigenous to Indigenous in Talamanca. The inherent dynamism of Indigenous traditions has made many of them resilient in enduring encounters with colonial forces over centuries.

About the author

Bjørn Ola Tafjord is professor of the study of religions at the University of Bergen, Norway, and principal investigator of the collaborative research project the Governmateriality of Indigenous Religions (GOVMAT).

Suggestions for further reading

In this book
See also chapters 1 (Why does the title of this book use the phrase "Indigenous religious traditions" rather than "Indigenous religions"?) and 8 (Why is "religion" a problematic category for understanding Indigenous traditions?).

Elsewhere
Kraft, Siv Ellen, Bjørn Ola Tafjord, Arkotong Longkumer, Gregory D. Alles, and Greg Johnson. *Indigenous Religion(s): Local Grounds, Global Networks.* London: Routledge, 2020. https://www.taylorfrancis.com/books/e/9781003021513.

Tafjord, Bjørn Ola. "How Talking about Indigenous Religion May Change Things: An Example from Talamanca." *Numen* 63(5–6) (2016): 548–575. https://doi.org/10.1163/15685276-12341438.

The Study of Indigenous Religious Traditions

28
What moral responsibilities do scholars and students have in studying Indigenous religions?

Afe Adogame

The historiography of Indigenous religions and Indigenous peoples has been burdened by a colonizing provenance, power, and perspective that has contributed to the evolution and development of the study from obscurity into mainstream academic inquiry. To what extent do scholars and students pay attention to ethics in research, especially working among Indigenous people in addition to vulnerable, marginalized, and gendered communities? What ethical challenges and dilemmas do scholars and students face in studying Indigenous religions?

In decolonizing the study of Indigenous religions, scholars and students should aim to privilege Indigenous voices in telling their own stories, histories, and narratives through their own cosmological imaginaries and how this is shaped by people they encounter and who live around them. At the same time, scholars and students of Indigenous religions and peoples need to pay attention to how they negotiate emic-etic dynamics and the insider-outsider enigma. They must consider cultural and ethical responsibilities by recognizing their positionality as well as their social, cultural, and epistemic locationality. This entails opening to the cultural, religious, and social universe of Indigenous peoples so that each respective phenomenon opens to the scholar and student in turn. This helps uncover multiple layers of hegemony at the intersection of gender, age, ethnic, racial, religious, economic, political, cultural, and social identities. One of the ideas of intersectionality is for individuals, groups, and communities to self-identify.

Structural positioning is instrumental in reconfiguring the inventiveness of Indigenous religious imaginaries. Caution is needed in (re)telling the (his)tory of Indigenous peoples and meaning-making subjectivities.

Self-reflexivity helps avoid essentializing Indigenous cosmologies and religious cultures. Indigenous religious traditions are the majority of the world's religions. They not only deserve but demand to be studied. Most often, defining an Indigenous religion from its belief system is putting it upside down. Social structures and cultural traditions are infused with a spirituality that cannot be easily separated from the rest of the community's life. The perception of religion as a phenomenon separate from culture is not a suitable reflection of the embedded nature of "religion" in Indigenous cultures. Religions, societies, and cultures are hardly static and unchanging; they are dynamic and constantly in flux.

The religions of these Indigenous peoples are far from having any monolithic structure. A common denominator of the respective traditions is the affinities and dynamism that their historical specificities, cosmological systems, and ritual dimensions exemplify. Indigenous religions encompass phenomena that are primarily defined in terms of their orality, world views, and ritual orientation toward specific geocultural landscapes. As predominantly oral cultures, these traditions are not characterized by any historical foundation; their histories, beliefs, and practices are encoded in and transmitted through oral traditions, myths, legends, art, paintings, sculpture, music, songs, and dances transgenerationally. There is not a rigid dichotomy between sacred and mundane domains, as these spaces are fluid and interconnected.

Indigenous societies range from those who were significantly exposed in their past and contemporary histories to the colonizing activities of other societies, largely Euro-American. Another commonality of Indigenous religions is their encounter with colonial history and influence and the growth and spread of religions such as Christianity, Islam, Buddhism, and Hinduism. This historical continuity may consist of the continuation for an extended period, reaching into the present, of factors that include occupation of ancestral lands, common ancestry, culture in general or specific manifestations, and language. Common challenges faced by Indigenous peoples include linguistic preservation, land rights, environmental degradation, exploitation of natural resources, political autonomy, and the preservation of religious and cultural identities. Systemic pressures of colonial experience have worked to eradicate, suppress, or erode Indigenous religious traditions.

Indigenous religions and peoples deserve empathetic understanding rather than sympathy in unpacking how they make sense of their lifeways. This entails the scholar and student's social, cultural, and epistemic reflexivity in the intricate process of reinterpreting Indigenous epistemologies. The cultural and moral responsibility of a scholar and student toward

Indigenous religions and peoples also involves finding a delicate balance in conducting and analyzing research in a culturally appropriate way and exploring alternative Indigenous methods and methodologies that resonate with the cultural and epistemological nuances of Indigenous peoples. Decolonizing methodologies bring together several critical, Indigenous, transformative, liberation, feminist, and critical methodologies, and several innovative and creative research methods have gained traction. Decolonizing methodologies contribute to decolonizing knowledge production, but it is also important to pay attention to any potential limitations. It is against this backdrop that moral responsibilities become expedient in studying Indigenous religions. We must be reflexive about the methods we employ, the theories we utilize, the very concepts we embrace, and the conclusions we engender.

About the author

Afe Adogame is the Maxwell M. Upson Professor of Religion and Society, Princeton Theological Seminary, New Jersey, United States. His research focuses on interrogating new dynamics of religious experiences and expressions in Africa and the African diaspora. Relevant book publications include *Alternative Voices: A Plurality Approach for Religious Studies* (2013) and *African Traditions in the Study of Religion, Diaspora, and Gendered Societies* (2013). He is coeditor of the Routledge series Vitality of Indigenous Religions, editor in chief of *AASR E-journal of Religion in Africa and Its Diaspora*, and deputy editor of *Journal of Religion in Africa* (Brill).

Suggestions for further reading

In this book

See also chapters 30 (Is an academic approach to Indigenous religions innately colonizing?), 34 (Why does it matter how we translate religious concepts in Indigenous traditions?), and 40 (What is decolonization, and what does it have to do with Indigenous religious traditions?).

Elsewhere

Adogame, A. *Indigeneity in African Religions: Oza Worldviews, Cosmologies and Religious Cultures*. London: Bloomsbury Academic, 2021.

Chilisa, B. *Indigenous Research Methodologies* (2nd edition). London: Sage, 2019.

Contending Modernities. "Decoloniality and the Study of Religion." https://contendingmodernities.nd.edu/decoloniality/introdecolonial/.

Olupona, J. K. *African Religions: A Very Short Introduction.* Oxford: Oxford University Press, 2014.

Smith, L. T. *Decolonizing Methodologies: Research and Indigenous Peoples* (2nd edition). London: Zed, 2012.

29
Why is repatriation a religious issue for many Native communities?

Greg Johnson

What is repatriation? In the sense used here, it refers to the return of Indigenous objects, including human remains, from non-Native entities, such as museums and universities, to Native communities. This is a significant issue due to the massive number of Indigenous objects that were alienating during global colonial expansion from the sixteenth to the nineteenth centuries. This era coincided with the emergence of institutionalized museums and early forms of physical anthropology, representatives of whom removed massive quantities of objects and remains from Native communities and archaeological sites, including from settings of military struggle and other contexts of profound duress. In such settings, the ability to stage resistance to such heinous acts was significantly and structurally curtailed. The loss and trauma experienced by Native communities cannot be overstated.

In the past several decades, some nation-state and international bodies have recognized this legacy of historical human rights abuses and have enacted redressive legislation and policies with direct input from Indigenous communities. For example, the United States passed the federal Native American Graves Protection and Repatriation Act in 1990, and in 2007, the United Nations issued its Declaration on the Rights of Indigenous Peoples, which has robust language concerning repatriation. The result has been a major movement of human remains and cultural objects back to Indigenous communities in recent years. In an otherwise dimly lit political climate, with land reparations still off the map and daily evidence of ongoing racism, the repatriation movement stands as an imperfect but heartening example of settler governments and institutions engaging Indigenous concerns in a focused and ethical manner. In these ways, repatriation is clearly a historical and legal issue. In what ways is it also a religious issue?

Repatriation is a religious issue for many Native communities because certain objects bind them to their identities, relatives, and places. In a manner largely unfamiliar to settler ontologies, for many Native communities, the nexus of ancestors, place, and cosmos is lodged in certain kinds of objects that exert a claim upon the communities for proper care. Human remains and ritual objects in particular call forth such obligations. If absent from the community, they must be returned. If damaged or otherwise neglected, they must be ministered to. Sometimes this entails returning them to a condition approximating their former cultural use, often in ceremonial settings. Other times, this means facilitating the passage of the object to a new state. In the case of human remains, usually understood to be powerful ancestors, bones are often reinterred or otherwise sequestered. In all cases, the purpose of repatriation is to restore relationships and heal cultural ruptures. Healing in this mode is ultimately religious insofar as it seeks to reconnect severed bonds that hold the community steady in time and space.

For scholars and students of Indigenous religions, repatriation is exciting to study because it combines witnessing human rights processes in action with the chance to observe real-time religious navigation as communities map new futures for traditional objects. To see a religious object returned to ceremonial use after decades or even centuries is emotionally moving and potently instructive about the dynamics of cultural resilience and change. Manifestly, any object returned to its community after an absence is not being returned to the community just as it was. Museum "preservation" has the uncanny result of freezing time for the object. No such mechanism has been available to communities (the harsh effects of stereotypes notwithstanding), with the result that all Indigenous repatriations require sophisticated and deeply involved forms of ritual time travel, as it were, in order to bring the state of the community into alignment with the state of the object and vice versa. In other words, repatriation is religious twice over. In the first instance, it is driven by religious commitments to fundamental relationships that undergird the universe for the community. In the second instance, all repatriations require cultural technologies and strategies to bridge temporal and ontological divides, a kind of work best described as religious.

Another religious aspect of repatriation is found in the way each return enacts and builds upon Indigenous sovereignty. Usually understood in narrowly political frames, sovereignty in many Native contexts is also religious because it extends from mere this-worldly political autonomy to fulfill responsibilities to relatives—including objects—across time and space. As Native communities seek to rebuild forms of sovereignty in the wake of changes wrought by settler states, restoring ancestral foundations through repatriation is often a core strategy and priority.

About the author

Greg Johnson teaches at the University of California, Santa Barbara, where he is a professor in the Department of Religious Studies and director of the Walter H. Capps Center for the Study of Ethics, Religion, and Public Life. His research focuses on the intersection of religion and law in Indigenous contexts, with particular attention to repatriation, burial protection, and sacred land claims.

Suggestions for further reading

In this book
See also chapters 36 (Why reconstruct precolonial Indigenous religions in the Americas?) and 40 (What is decolonization, and what does it have to do with Indigenous religious traditions?).

Elsewhere
Ayau, Edward Halealoha, and Ty Kāwika Tengan. "Ka Huaka'i O Nā 'Ōiwi: The Journey Home." In *The Dead and Their Possession: Repatriation in Principle, Policy and Practice*, edited by Cressida Fforde, Jane Hubert, and Paul Turnbull, 171–189. London: Routledge, 2002.

Fine-Dare, Kathleen. *Grave Injustice: The American Indian Repatriation Movement*. Lincoln: University of Nebraska Press, 2002.

Johnson, Greg. "Indigenous Objects after NAGPRA: In and Out of Circulation." In *The Wiley Blackwell Companion to Religion and Materiality*, edited by Vasudha Narayanan. Hoboken, NJ: Wiley Blackwell, 2020.

30

Is an academic approach to Indigenous religions innately colonizing?

Afe Adogame

The historical trajectory of the study of Indigenous peoples and their religions has evolved through several phases, each involving different purposes and points of view. There are perhaps two major overlapping epochs. First is the period when Indigenous peoples and their religions were studied as "object"—that is, exclusively by non-Indigenous scholars and observers. The second, as "subject," is when the Indigenous peoples and their religions had begun to be studied, and increasingly so, by Indigenous, "Native" scholars who paid more attention to Indigenous histories, narratives, and epistemologies by employing Indigenous research methods and methodologies.

The provenance and shaping of the academic study of religion as a disciplinary field of study have deep imprints and roots in European imperialism and colonial history. Most accounts produced during the study phase of Indigenous peoples as "objects" were useful to the extent to which they served as an "information bank" upon which later scholars depended. This era produced a barrage of opprobrious labels—including animism, fetishism, idolatry, primitivism, totemism, superstition, heathenism, and magic—to designate Indigenous religions. While these essentially pejorative labels have been employed by non-Indigenous peoples to represent Indigenous peoples and their religious lifeworlds, their acceptance and rejection have political and strategic implications that need to be contextually understood. These incongruous terms stamped Indigenous religions with the appearance of sameness and primitiveness and a stigma of inferiority, especially in comparison with Islam and Christianity.

One legacy of the colonial experiment is that it bequeathed an academic approach to Indigenous religions that was inherently colonizing, a perspective that is now in dire need of decolonizing and deconstructing. The phenomena of Indigenous religions pose interesting, complex problems of conceptual description and interpretation. In fact, Indigenous languages have no equivalent synonym for "religion." The very category of religion itself is a Western academic construct, involving both misconceptions and changing perceptions, that hardly does justice to the complexity of Indigenous religious epistemologies. Indigenous religions and Indigenous peoples became a "representation of the Other," a certain bias in Western scholarship to study and define Indigenous religious traditions from within the boundaries of the so-called world religions. The problem is not simply that of the misrepresentation of cultural and religious experiences; it is also an expression of power over the "Other."

Euro-American scholars dominated the academic study of Indigenous religions, impinged their methodologies, and brought their thought patterns, world views, and epistemologies to bear. Within this critical historical milieu, the colonial and missionary machineries invented ways of knowing and meaning-making that anchored and facilitated processes of subjugation, exploitation, and expropriation. Alien forms of reasoning were entrenched while also laying claims to a "civilizing mission." The "European" knowledge introduced into Indigenous societies came on a collision course with Indigenous knowledge systems in a spate of ideological contestation, culminating in a bricolage of knowledge. The knowledge funneled through the colonial process took center stage, assuming a dominant epistemology that marginalized and almost silenced alternative world views and conceptualizations of the universe. Such a hegemonic way of knowing and meaning-making was even presumed to turn Indigenous epistemologies on their heads.

Legacies of the European Enlightenment filtered thought patterns that legitimized tropes of Otherness and binaries of difference espoused as tradition versus modernity, primitive versus civilized, superiority versus inferiority complex into the very fabric of the dominant knowledge. This dominant knowledge was transforming but also entrapping. The contestation that ensued in the production of knowledge produced a chasm of epistemological richness and bankruptcy at the same time. Indigenous epistemologies hardly witnessed their obituary in the face of the knowledge encounter that ensued. This scenario produced multiple discourses and theories of knowledge, and through this, knowledge production is continually negotiated in ways that result in the reification of some meaning-making systems, the invention of others, and kind of "hybridized" epistemologies.

Western scholarship has contributed significantly to the understanding of Indigenous histories, religious cultures, knowledge systems, and lifeways, but it has also paved a path to obscurity and public misunderstanding. Thus, explaining Indigenous political, social, cultural, and religious lifeworlds in Western categories can offer some useful insights, just as it could be obscuring. Therefore, the challenge for Indigenous, Native scholars to take a vantage position in contesting dominant epistemologies, knowledge (re)production utilizing Indigenous methodologies is a pertinent one indeed. An academic approach to Indigenous religions helps shape how we read, teach, and think about colonization and decolonization on the one hand but also how we attempt to decolonize and reinstitutionalize Indigenous religions as an important academic and cultural field of study on the other.

About the author

Afe Adogame is the Maxwell M. Upson Professor of Religion and Society, Princeton Theological Seminary, New Jersey, United States. His research focuses on interrogating new dynamics of religious experiences and expressions in Africa and the African diaspora. Relevant book publications include *Alternative Voices: A Plurality Approach for Religious Studies* (2013) and *African Traditions in the Study of Religion, Diaspora, and Gendered Societies* (2013). He is coeditor of the Routledge series *Vitality of Indigenous Religions*, editor in chief of *AASR E-journal of Religion in Africa and Its Diaspora*, and deputy editor of *Journal of Religion in Africa* (Brill).

Suggestions for further reading

In this book
See also chapters 12 (Why study Indigenous religious traditions?), 28 (What moral responsibilities do scholars and students have in studying Indigenous religions?), and 40 (What is decolonization, and what does it have to do with Indigenous religious traditions?).

Elsewhere
Adogame, A. *Indigeneity in African Religions: Oza Worldviews, Cosmologies and Religious Cultures*. London: Bloomsbury Academic, 2021.

Chidester, D. *Empire of Religion: Imperialism and Comparative Religion*. Chicago: University of Chicago Press, 2013.

Nye, Malory. "Decolonizing the Study of Religion." *Open Library of Humanities* 5(1) (2019): 1–45. https://doi.org/10.16995/olh.421.

Platvoet, J., J. Cox, and J. K. Olupona, eds. *The Study of Religions in Africa: Past, Present and Prospects*. Cambridge: Roots & Branches, 1996.

Smith, L. T. *Decolonizing Methodologies: Research and Indigenous Peoples* (2nd edition). London: Zed, 2012.

31
Can we still use the term "shamanism"?

Emily B. Simpson

The term "shamanism" is difficult to define. Originating from the Tungus language group in Siberia, the term "shaman" referred to those who journeyed to the spirit world and shared the information they acquired with their communities. While scholars and practitioners continue to redefine the term, the idea of shamans connecting to the world of supernatural entities is fairly constant. Shamanism differs from the phenomenon of spirit possession, in which supernatural entities take over and speak through an individual. In contrast, shamans enter a trance state of their own volition and skill, either through an innate capacity or after considerable training. Whether shamans travel to another realm or invite spiritual entities into their minds and bodies and communicate on their behalf, shamans connect with these entities and control the process.

Shamanism and spirit possession also differ considerably in the traditions to which they are applied. Spirit possession has been identified and located within Indigenous traditions as well as specific (and often marginal) sects within Christianity, Judaism, and Islam. Shamanism, on the other hand, is almost universally identified in non-Western Indigenous traditions. This derives in part from the popularization of the term and its use within a history of religions framework. Most famously, Mircea Eliade wrote about shamanism in the 1950s as "an archaic technique of ecstasy." He differentiated shamans from other religious practitioners, such as priests or healers, based on their ability to enter a trance. Eliade saw shamanism as a worldwide phenomenon alongside other -*isms*, including "animism" and "polytheism," and as constituting more primitive forms of religion than the so-called world religions.

This Western-centric and ethnocentric "othering" of shamanism is one reason the term is problematic today. One other major reason for discarding "shamanism" is that it lumps religious practitioners from highly disparate traditions into one category, which is further complicated by the variety of definitions of shamanism in use. Scholars have attempted to narrow the definition by prioritizing and defining aspects like the trance state, the nature of communication with supernatural entities, or the initiation process. Nonetheless, many scholars today question the validity of labeling such a wide range of practitioners as shamans. For instance, the Inuit *angakkuq*, who travels to the underworld to pacify the sea goddess Sedna when community taboos have been broken, and the *sangoma* of South Africa, who summons and channels ancestral spirits, are both categorized as shamans.

Yet there are scholars and religious practitioners who continue to use the term. For both groups, "shaman" provides a convenient and recognizable category in English in cases where the Indigenous language has several discrete terms for similar phenomena. Noted anthropologist Laurel Kendall, in her work on Korean shamanism, uses the term "shaman" because there are multiple Korean terms for these practitioners, and the most common of these is derogatory. Furthermore, in recent years, some Indigenous practitioners have begun to call themselves shamans, either because "shaman" lacks the perceived cultural baggage of traditional terms (which may include gender and racial stereotypes) or because "shaman" allows them to attract a larger clientele in our increasingly global and digital world. These include the sangoma mentioned earlier as well as several independent spiritual healers in Japan today.

Aside from Indigenous groups rebranding their practices as shamanism, there is also a new spirituality movement known as "neoshamanism." Like the closely related New Age movement, neoshamanism responds to a shift away from institutional religions toward a greater focus on the individual while drawing on ancient mythologies or traditional shamanic practices. Accordingly, various groups have utilized shamanism as a framework through which to reconnect to nature and cultural heritage. However, these "neoshamans" are often criticized for engaging in cultural appropriation. In order to avoid this, some "neoshamans" adopt the term "shamanic practitioner" instead. Yet though "shamanic practitioner" may suggest distance from the term "shaman," it still relies on the root word for recognition and thus does not truly "get away" from the problems associated with shamanism.

"Shamanism" is thus a highly loaded term that often serves to over-generalize and erase the unique features of specific Indigenous groups and their communications with supernatural entities. At the same time, shamanism does provide a framework for comparative work on a specific set of religious practices, and the fact that it is adopted by both new religious movements and traditional practitioners demonstrates that it retains a certain resonance and utility. Yet issues of cultural appropriation, ethnocentrism, and perceptions of "shamanic" practices as "primitive" continue to affect the idea of shamanism and its applicability as a conceptual category.

About the author

Dr. Emily B. Simpson received her PhD from the University of California at Santa Barbara in 2019 and is a fellow at Harvard University. Her research centers on reinterpretations of the legend of Empress Jingū, a third-century empress appearing in early Japanese chronicles, within various Buddhist and Shinto traditions and within women's cults. Her book project, entitled *Crafting a Goddess: Divinization and Womanhood in Late Medieval and Early Modern Narratives of Empress Jingū*, explores how diverse religious institutions divinized Empress Jingū, focusing on her martial and shamanic deeds, her motherhood and pregnancy, or her connections to maritime communities.

Suggestions for further reading

In this book
See also chapters 32 (Do Native peoples have shamans?) and 34 (Why does it matter how we translate religious concepts in Indigenous traditions?).

Elsewhere
Eliade, Mircea. *Shamanism: Archaic Techniques of Ecstasy*. Vol. 76. Princeton, NJ: Princeton University Press, 2020.

Kehoe, Alice Beck. *Shamans and Religion: An Anthropological Exploration in Critical Thinking*. Long Grove, IL: Waveland, 2000.

Kendall, Laurel. *Shamans, Nostalgias, and the IMF: South Korean Popular Religion in Motion*. Mānoa Valley: University of Hawaii Press, 2009.

Townsend, Joan B. "Core Shamanism and Neo-shamanism." In *Shamanism: An Encyclopedia of World Beliefs, Practices, and Culture*, edited by Mariko Namba Walter and Eva Jane Neumann Fridman, 49–57. Santa Barbara, CA: ABC-CLIO, 2004.

32
Do Native peoples have shamans?

Edward Anthony Polanco

The short answer is no. This might jar the reader. The long answer is much more complicated, and it is perhaps why many have opted to use "shaman" when referring to Native healers or ritual specialists. The term "shaman" comes from Siberia, stemming from the Tungusic word *šamán* (pronounced "sharman"). In its local context, the word *šamán* signifies a community leader selected and trained to interact with non-human life forces to heal and rectify wrongs. Native tribes, nations, and communities have people that operate under similar parameters. So then why are they not shamans?

Indigenous communities in the Americas have rich and diverse healing practices and practitioners. These practices bear a resemblance to shamanism or shamans, but they have their own names, nuances, and contexts. Some academics and laypeople use the term "shaman" for Native healers as a euphemism for witch doctor, *curandero*, folk healer, medicine man or woman, and so on. While it is also imperative to avoid these terms (because they privilege Western medicine and culture), the word "shaman" is an inadequate alternative. Much like it is best to use specific names for peoples when possible, instead of the broad and reductive umbrella terms "Natives" or "Indians," it is no different for Native healers. For instance, Cherokees call their healers *didanowiski*, the Lakota have the *pejuta wicasa*, and the Diné refer to their healers as *hataaɬii*. Nahuas from Mexico once used the term *tiçitl* for their healers and now use *tepahtiani*, and Nahuas from El Salvador use the term *tapajtiani*. The Quechua peoples in the Andes refer to some healers as *jambij*, while the Yucatec Maya have the *h'men*. It is tempting to use the term "shaman" for all Native communities and lump them into a monolithic group, but that would conceal the nuances in their practices and beliefs.

Like shamans in Asia, Native healers often traverse Western conceptions of medicine (i.e., healing), religion, and perhaps even sorcery. *Titiçih* and *tiçiyotl* (Nahua healing knowledge from sixteenth- and seventeenth-century Central Mexico) provide a useful case study. Titiçih were men and women that practiced tiçiyotl to maintain their communities in *pactinemiliztli* (balance and health) and cure *cocoliztli* (illness). Female titiçih exclusively handled birth attendance and tended to deal with illnesses among children. Both male and female titiçih treated adults with their extensive knowledge of plants, animals, minerals, and rocks.

Titiçih not only helped people heal broken bones and stomach aches but also fixed broken relationships and heartaches. They often diagnosed illnesses by engaging entheogenic plants (substances that release a life force within) such as *ololiuhqui* (*Turbina corymbosa*), *teonacatl* (*Paneolus campanulatus L. var. sphinctrinus*), *piciyetl* (*Nicotiana rustica*), and in some cases, *peyotl* (*Lophophora williamsii*). When consumed, these items released the nonhuman force they contain inside, allowing titiçih to converse with them and receive information about their patient's illness and their cures. Starting in the late sixteenth century, the Catholic Church in New Spain (present-day Mexico, Central America, and the US Southwest) began persecuting titiçih—along with healing specialists from other Mesoamerican communities—and framing them as a threat to Native people's conversion to Christianity. Though many Nahua communities throughout Mexico and El Salvador continue to have healing specialists, Spaniards stomped the word *tiçitl* out of use, and modern *tepahtiani* or *tapajtiani* no longer wield the prestige or social capital their ancestors had. While it is tempting to call Nahua healers "shamans" and their practices "shamanism," these terms obfuscate their intricacies and social value.

Using the terms "shaman" and "shamanism" for any group outside of Asia is a colonizing act that reduces the value and details of the Tungusic people and whatever group the term is applied to. We must decolonize Native healing practices and knowledge, and the first and most basic step is to give each culture and people the respect of using the terms they use. Furthermore, like other aspects of culture, healing has adapted to changing needs. Indigenous healing has not become less effective or obsolete; Western perceptions and constructions have attempted to degrade its value. Using terms like "shaman" or terms that present healing specialists as dipolar opposites to "civilized" and "modern" medicine (i.e., curandero, witch doctor, medicine man or woman) colonize and reduce Indigenous healers and their beliefs. No, Native peoples have never had and do not have shamans; they have *tapajtiani, tepahtiani, didanowiski, pejuta wicasa, hataaʃii, jambij,* and *h'men,* among many others. Each of these specialists has unique practices and knowledge linked to their cultural history and cosmovision.

About the author

Dr. Edward Anthony Polanco is an assistant professor in the Department of History at Virginia Tech. He was born in Los Angeles, California, and his family and ancestors are from Kuskatan (Western El Salvador). His academic interests include Native peoples, Latin America, gender, religion, and healing. His main expertise is healing and gender in the Nahua world (Mexico and El Salvador).

Suggestions for further reading

In this book
See also chapters 31 (Can we still use the term "shamanism"?) and 34 (Why does it matter how we translate religious concepts in Indigenous traditions?).

Elsewhere
DuBois, Thomas A. *An Introduction to Shamanism*. Cambridge: Cambridge University Press, 2009.

Huber, Brad R., and Alan R. Sandstrom. *Mesoamerican Healers* (1st edition). Austin: University of Texas Press, 2001.

Kelton, Paul. *Cherokee Medicine, Colonial Germs: An Indigenous Nation's Fight against Smallpox, 1518–1824*. Vol. 11. Norman: University of Oklahoma Press, 2015.

Klein, Cecelia F., Eulogio Guzmán, Elisa C. Mandell, and Maya Stanfield-Mazzi. "The Role of Shamanism in Mesoamerican Art: A Reassessment." *Current Anthropology* 43(3) (2002): 383–419.

33
What is animism?

Graham Harvey

"Animism" is a term that is increasingly used to label the understanding that the world is a community of related beings, all of whom are encouraged to practice locally appropriate forms of respect. The term is related to words like "animated." It derives from the Latin word *anima*, which has been translated as "soul" or "spirit" and conveys ideas about what distinguishes dead objects from living beings. People in all cultures make such distinctions, but even within a single group, people do not all agree on who or what should be in each category. Also, people's ideas change. We should, therefore, be careful not to assume that cultures are fixed or uniform. In fact, there are several different uses of the term "animism"—each telling us as much about the people who use the word as it does about the people they apply it to.

In the nineteenth century, Edward Tylor, the first professor of anthropology at Oxford University, used "animism" to sum up his theory about religion. All religions, he claimed, are defined by a "belief in spirits." He had collected information from colonial officials and Christian missionaries but also from attending Spiritualist séances and from his own journey through Mexico. In 1871, he presented his interpretation in a two-volume work called *Primitive Culture*. The title already indicates something about his approach, but it is important to note that Tylor was thinking about all religions. He insisted that every religion was rooted in an interesting but flawed interpretation of both unusual and common experiences. He thought that people who did not understand what causes lightning came up with a theory that deities or other spirits were involved. He said that people who had dreams about deceased relatives interpreted them as visits from ancestors or other spirits. He anticipated that such religious interpretations of experiences would be replaced by properly scientific or rational explanations. So "animism" was Tylor's quick way of encapsulating his theory and definition of religion.

Tylor's ideas were soon challenged, and they are largely rejected now. They are only mentioned, as here, as historical background. However, a weak version of Tylor's use survives as a way in which some people distinguish between specific religions. They speak, for example, about the presence in West Africa of Christianity, Islam, and animism. "Animism" is used here to refer to traditional African religions but emphasizes a claim that some people believe in "spirits" rather than the deity of Christians or Muslims. Such comparisons are rarely helpful as ways to understand or engage with people's real-life experiences, practices, or ideas.

Everything so far might suggest that the term "animism" should be rejected. However, in the last few decades, a new use has become important. It is summarized in the opening sentence above. Sometimes this is called the "new animism"—not because there is anything new in seeking to participate respectfully in the community of the larger-than-human world. Indeed, this is a widespread Indigenous theme. This animism is "new" as a scholarly approach, in contrast to that of Tylor. It is closely allied to debates called the "new materialism" and the "ontological turn." In all these, the key question is not how to distinguish animate beings from inanimate objects (as Tylor might have said) but how to recognize and encourage good ways of living among other beings.

This animism is typically respectful of Indigenous knowledges. It can be illustrated by thinking about words because different languages have words and grammatical rules that share and shape culturally important assumptions. Learning to speak English encourages the assumption that rocks, for instance, are inanimate objects. They are spoken about using the "neutral" pronoun "it," used for "inanimate objects," because they can be casually extracted and exploited without significant consequences. People are not expected to build relationships with them. In contrast, people who learn to speak Anishinaabemowin and similar Indigenous languages are encouraged to treat the world as a community in which stones are worthy of respect. Grammatically, stones (*asiniig*) are marked as "animate," and such ways of speaking (especially in stories and ceremonies) encourage people to learn to treat them decently. In short, words encapsulate and encourage particular ideas and behaviors, especially when they are repeated.

To conclude, "animism" sometimes labels a theory that some people misunderstand life, confusing what is animate or inanimate, what is human or not human. It now labels locally appropriate ways of behaving toward other beings and seeks to understand their rich implications.

About the author

Graham Harvey is professor of religious studies at the Open University in the United Kingdom. His research largely concerns the "new animism," especially in rituals and protocols through which Indigenous communities engage with the larger-than-human world. He is editor of Routledge's Vitality of Indigenous Religions series and Equinox's Religion and the Senses series.

Suggestions for further reading

In this book
See also chapters 3 (Were all religions at one time "Indigenous"?) and 45 (Do Indigenous peoples believe plants, animals, and waters have personhood?).

Elsewhere
Hallowell, A. Irving. "Ojibwa Ontology, Behavior, and World View." In *Culture in History*, edited by Stanley Diamond, 19–52. New York: Columbia University Press, 1960.

Harvey, Graham. *Handbook of Contemporary Animism*. New York: Routledge, 2013.

Tremlett, Paul, Liam Sutherland, and Graham Harvey, eds. *Edward Tylor, Religion and Culture*. London: Bloomsbury, 2017.

34

Why does it matter how we translate religious concepts in Indigenous traditions?

Josefrayn Sánchez-Perry

"We, givers of offerings, detain you!" is what a group of Aztec ritual specialists yelled as they saw an error occur at the courtyard of the temple school in the city-state of Mexico-Tenochtitlan. Having fastened himself with his main tools—a sleeveless jacket, an incense ladle, and a pouch—an "offerer of fire" stood at the entrance of the courtyard ready to perform his offering. Shortly after beginning the ceremony, however, he made a mistake. When he sat in front of the hearth to offer incense in the four cardinal directions, he rolled the offering balls the wrong way. Almost immediately, a different group, a cohort of "givers of offerings," detained him and removed him from the courtyard, demanding that he take off his regalia.

Although the difference between "offerers of fire" and "givers of offerings" may sound insignificant, it outlines an entire hierarchy of ritual labor. Aztec society invested a great deal into categories and taxonomies that positioned people into different ranks of a ritual ladder. How we translate religious concepts matters because those created for the purpose of academic comparison often flatten the idiosyncrasies of Indigenous cultures. I am mainly concerned with the use of "priest" to talk about Aztec ritual specialists, who by the sixteenth century had developed a unique way of organizing who could perform what ritual and when. In this chapter, I give a general portrayal of the Aztec organization of ritual experts, and based on this interpretation, I entertain notions of how we may interpret "priesthood" in the Aztec world.

Aztec ritual specialists trained in two settings. On the one hand, some women and men belonged to schools called the "house of unit/lineage" (*calmecac*) located in the temple precinct. Menial labor like sweeping and foraging wood was reserved for lower-status individuals, while more experienced ritual specialists led processions and ritual executions. Their lifestyle was characterized by an abstinence from alcohol and sexual activity. On the other hand, another set of women and men belonged to schools known as the "house of youth" (*telpochcalli*), which were part of an equally hierarchical system throughout neighborhood districts of the city-state. Although also required to sweep and gather wood, rather than following a life of abstinence, they trained in singing, dancing, and playing musical instruments. Further accomplished individuals collected captives during times of war but also became trainers of younger women and men. Both schools required their members to perform bloodletting from tender parts of the body.

With this brief synopsis in mind, we can entertain notions of "priesthood" in Aztec society. In his 1998 article, J. Z. Smith questioned the universality of "religion" across all cultures, noting that it was a European loanword. He was correct. There is no direct equivalent for the lexical entry in Nahuatl, the language of the Aztecs. Early efforts to find a comparable term failed when Spanish and Aztec grammarians came together to align their languages. But the absence of the term does not mean that the concept was unfamiliar. Surveying the terms "lifestyle" (*nemilztli*) and "labor" (*tequitl*) across various Nahuatl language sources from the colonial period, we can observe that Aztecs found some lifestyles and labors more important than others. Bloodletting, executions, dancing, and singing at the temple precinct, even the abstinence from sex and alcohol, had cosmological orientations that separated ritual labor from other types of labors in Aztec society.

While no word for "religion" existed, the Aztecs understood that not everyone could perform ritual activities or maintain the lifestyles that characterized a ritual specialist. Grammarians eventually settled on a Nahuatl translation of religion. The term "priest," however, proved more complicated. Aztecs had all kinds of experts, from temple specialists to members of households, from trainers to trainees, from menial laborers to exuberant specialists. Each had unique, mutually exclusive titles. What Spanish grammarians generally demonstrate is that they chose the terms "minister" (*ministro*) and "priest" (*sacerdote*) to gloss the complicated hierarchy of Aztec temple and household ritual specialists. Why does it matter how we translate religious concepts in Indigenous traditions? Aztecs thought it was important, and they made a critical note about telling their readers. "We, givers of offerings, detain you!" is a direct indication that ritual specialists in Aztec society were unique and special, and individuals had different titles based on the labors they offered. Glossing all of this linguistic diversity as "priest" conceals Aztec ritual categories. How wonderful that we have access to the records of Aztec historians who chose to express ritual diversity instead of reducing it.

About the author

Josefrayn Sánchez-Perry is an assistant professor in the Department of Theology at Loyola University of Chicago. His focus is on religions in the Americas with an interest in late postclassic and colonial Mesoamerica. His dissertation, "They Give the Sun to Drink: The Life and Labor of Aztec Ritual Specialists," is an account of Aztec ritual specialists using material culture and Nahuatl language sources. The project argues that household ritual specialists helped sustain temple religion by crafting ceramic, stonework, regalia, and food staples.

Suggestions for further reading

In this book
See also chapters 28 (What moral responsibilities do scholars and students have in studying Indigenous religions?) and 31 (Can we still use the term "shamanism"?).

Elsewhere
Bassett, Molly H. *The Fate of Earthly Things: Aztec Gods and God-Bodies.* Austin: University of Texas Press, 2015.

Cruz de la Cruz, Sabina. "Tepahtihquetl pan ce pilaltepetzin / A Village Healer." *Ethnohistory* 66(4) (2019): 647–666.

Díaz Balsera, Viviana. *Guardians of Idolatry: Gods, Demons, and Priests in Hernando Ruiz de Alarcón's Treatise on the Heathen Superstitions.* Norman: University of Oklahoma Press, 2018.

Olivier, Guilhem. *Mockeries and Metamorphoses of an Aztec God: Tezcatlipoca, "Lord of the Smoking Mirror."* Boulder: University Press of Colorado, 2003.

Tavárez, David. *The Invisible War: Indigenous Devotions, Discipline, and Dissent in Colonial Mexico.* Stanford, CA: Stanford University Press, 2011.

35

How do archaeologists study religion in the Indigenous past?

Mallory E. Matsumoto

The most important influences on any archaeological study of Indigenous religion or ritual in the past are how the archaeologist understands the concept of "religion," how religion was practiced in the historical context under study, and what kind of traces those practices may have left behind. Ultimately, archaeologists draw from a common disciplinary toolbox no matter their topic of investigation. Their methodological bread and butter are survey, excavation, laboratory study, and qualitative and quantitative analysis. Other methods that are used as relevant may include, for example, archival investigation or iconographic or linguistic analysis.

One avenue for exploring Indigenous religion archaeologically is to study associated spaces and places—after all, religion always happens somewhere. Culturally meaningful places of religion may be natural landscape features, artificial constructions, or some combination thereof; they may be fixed or mobile, and they often shift over time as the result of environmental or human activity. In some cases, archaeologists can identify religious places based on contextual knowledge. In the US Southwest, for example, foundations of a subterranean, circular structure suggest a Puebloan kiva once used for ritual and political functions; a multitiered platform with pillars and a staircase in the Andes, in turn, would be a strong candidate for an Inkan ceremonial *ushnu*.

Yet people also practice religion in abstract, measurable spaces that are not specifically defined for religion or for any activity in particular; they may make offerings over a meal at a temporary campsite or the journey itself may be part of the ritual process, as with pilgrimages. Archaeologists cannot always identify specific spaces or places associated with Indigenous religious activity. Thus, the material traces of religious practices, wherever they occur, provide key evidence for interpreting religion in the past. Relevant artifacts can vary as widely as the ways of doing religion in which they were involved. A broken clay pot, carbonized seeds from a burned offering, an ancestor's carefully positioned remains—all could represent the physical traces of religious events. Here, context is critical for interpretation. A single spearpoint excavated from an abandoned household is probably not ritually meaningful, whereas one recovered under a stone altar carved with images of sacrifice probably is.

Archaeologists can also study Indigenous religion by considering how people practiced it, especially when those practices left specific artifactual traces. Indigenous traditions varied widely in how they incorporated material culture into religion or ritual; some reserved specific ingredients for preparing ritual foods, for example, whereas others utilized the same foodstuffs for offerings and daily consumption. Because archaeological evidence is always partial and often concerns practices that are no longer used or have changed notably over time, it can be difficult for contemporary scholars to interpret. In addition, the line between religious use and production is not always clear. With some textiles, for example, the process of weaving may have been just as or more ritually meaningful than what happened to the finished product. Nonetheless, when interpreted carefully, archaeological evidence can significantly enhance our understanding of religion in the Indigenous past.

One of archaeology's inherent, enduring challenges is preservation bias: different materials decay over time at different rates, and myriad factors—from climate to natural disasters to modern urbanization to random luck—determine what survives into the present. Thus, the evidence available to archaeologists always represents a mere subset of an unknown total that once existed. One may wonder, why bother with archaeology at all? But there are many reasons why archaeology, as imperfect a tool as it is, is critical to studying Indigenous religion; I name just three here. First, archaeology is often the most direct scientific means of studying human life in the past because every life leaves behind at least some trace, however ephemeral. Second, archaeology has a robust history of focusing on practices or what people actually did in the past because they tend to leave more direct, tangible evidence than what people thought, believed, or said. And religion is, despite popular conceptions, inherently something that people do; what they believe shapes their actions, some of which may leave behind material residues. Finally, Indigenous peoples have been omitted from many accounts of religion, including documents, images, and other sources that scholars use to study history, or they are only represented from the perspective of others. With archaeology, we can mitigate this historical erasure by developing a fuller if ever incomplete understanding of how Indigenous peoples themselves practiced religion in the past.

About the author

Mallory E. Matsumoto is assistant professor in the Department of Religious Studies at the University of Texas at Austin. Her research addresses the interface between language, material culture, and religion in precolonial and colonial Maya communities of Mesoamerica. She has conducted archaeological fieldwork and archival research in Guatemala, Mexico, Hungary, Peru, and the United States.

Suggestions for further reading

In this book
See also chapters 1 (Why does the title of this book use the phrase "Indigenous religious traditions" rather than "Indigenous religions"?) and 8 (Why is "religion" a problematic category for understanding Indigenous traditions?).

Elsewhere
Bray, Tamara L., ed. *The Archaeology of Wak'as: Explorations of the Sacred in the Pre-Columbian Andes*. Boulder: University Press of Colorado, 2015.

Fowles, Severin M. *An Archaeology of Doings: Secularism and the Study of Pueblo Religion*. Albuquerque, NM: SAR, 2013.

Kyriakidis, Evangelos, ed. *The Archaeology of Ritual*. Los Angeles: Cotsen Institute of Archaeology, University of California, 2007.

Pauketat, Timothy R. *An Archaeology of the Cosmos: Rethinking Agency and Religion in Ancient America*. New York: Routledge, 2012.

36

Why reconstruct precolonial Indigenous religions in the Americas?

Yanitsa Buendía de Llaca

The conquest, colonization, and settlement of the Americas is a process in which European immigrants and their descendants actively take over land and resources from Indigenous and Native peoples to impose political, economic, and religious systems in lieu of Indigenous and Native practices. Using the present tense to describe the process of settlement and colonialism is not rhetorical but an evocation of an unfinished process that still harms and violates Indigenous peoples' rights. This process produced segregation of spaces within the different nations and racialization. In Canada and the United States, this racialization works in opposition to whiteness, but in Mexico and Latino America, it usually opposes the ideas of *mestizaje*, among other forms of racial dominance. Since colonization is an ongoing process, reconstructions of Native and Indigenous religious practices and identities are constantly challenged by historical and present impositions.

Asking if reconstruction processes are necessary may be a little dangerous because it may put the scholar into doing prescriptive research. Instead, we may want to open an invitation to always check our own assumptions, bias, and expectations of what "Indigenous" means and looks like in our imaginations versus what is being constructed by communities that are in dynamic movement and change regardless of colonization. There is a great story of an ethnographer doing fieldwork and facing her own stereotypes by encountering people that did not fit her expectations of how and what an Indigenous person was. Non-Native/Indigenous people may be inclined to ask why or why not to reconstruct precolonial religions. But within identity processes, the religious or spiritual assimilation and conversion practices are complex and in constant negotiation with what present, past, and future communities want to create for themselves.

The conversation of Indigenous and Native religions is usually tied to ideas of "purity" and "authenticity." The matter of what is "authentically" Indigenous and what counts as Indigenous religious traditions are questions that arise as Western expectation is built toward Indigenous peoples who are seen as frozen subjects of a precolonial past. However, scholars, allies, and Indigenous peoples themselves know this is far from the truth. Indigenous peoples in the Americas and around the world have continued to develop their political, social, cultural, and religious histories throughout and despite colonization.

In opposition to the process of colonization and settlement, Indigenous and Native peoples have historically adapted, resisted, and negotiated their world with the colonial world. As a consequence, Latin American Catholicism practiced in Indigenous communities has elements that belong to Indigenous world views. There are other practices that can be thought of as religious but are not categorized as religion and have survived on their own, specifically as healing forms. For example, in Mexico and the United States, *curanderismo* is a lived practice whose origins can be traced to Indigenous medicine and religion. Another example is how in Chile, the Mapuche have preserved their healing rituals despite pushback from the nation-state. Throughout the continent, Indigenous forms of healing practices are intimate; they pass from generation to generation and are practiced inside the household by a family member or designated healer in the community.

In addition to private and intimate healing practices, Indigenous religious traditions have survived in different forms. In the United States, for example, Native American nations have reclaimed different practices, objects, and human remains through the First Amendment. The nuance of religious freedom has given Native Americans the possibility to reimagine and claim their religions. This process, which is peculiar to the United States and different from the rest of the continent, has a strong history in which Native Americans have learned to use the legal system in order to negotiate and gain back the freedom that the nation-state once tried to take away in its pursuit of cultural assimilation.

In some cases where Indigenous people have "lost" their practices or languages, they have made efforts to "reconstruct" them. In this process, Indigenous people have documented themselves and reimagined what they have lost and how to bring it back. From restating a *costumbre* as religion to revitalizing traditions through dance and ceremony, different Indigenous peoples throughout the continent have regained their religious and spiritual practices. Usually, the reconstruction of religious and spiritual practices comes hand in hand with the effort made to regain "authenticity," autonomy, sovereignty, and decolonization. "Authenticity" and performativity of Indigeneity can be an intentional construction by Indigenous peoples to gain recognition by state policies but also to differentiate themselves from the different groups and movements promoting revitalization. For example, many Native Hawaiians are working on resignifying what Hawaiian identity means in opposition to Hawaiian symbols co-opted by the tourist industry. Or the struggles in Aztec dance circles to define what is more "authentic" and less close to Catholic traditions, like the type of instruments they use and the regalia they wear, are moments of performativity that target "authenticity" as being part of Native conversations.

It is not surprising, however, that these efforts are also interwoven with other aspects of social life, such as language, land, and power relations. For Indigenous peoples, both in precolonial times and currently, religion and spirituality are elements that are not considered separate from other forms of life. Going back to the examples of Native Hawaiians and the revitalization Aztec movement, we can attest that both of these cultural movements have interwoven all of these aspects. For Native Hawaiians, the revitalization of their language and culture goes hand in hand with notions of territorial governance and who owns the land. Similarly, the history of Aztec dance starts with a linguistic effort for revitalizing the *nahua* language in Mexico City, and one of the first material practices in the 1940s is the one of renaming the land to Mexico-Tenochtitlan.

Despite the fact that some communities engage with notions of "authenticity," quantifying "impure" elements (usually Christian), as outsiders to these communities, it is not only disrespectful but counterproductive to knowledge creation. As scholars, however, we can trace a history of how reconstructing Indigenous religions and spiritualities is part of a process of recovering sovereignty, pride, identity, and signifiers that strengthen communities inside the different nation-states people live in. The degrees to which the reconstruction happens may vary according to the history of colonization and the time of the conquest, and some reconstructions may look more "precolonial" than others in Western eyes. However, the common objective is for Indigenous peoples to have an experience of ownership and freedom.

About the author

Yanitsa Buendia de Llaca is an ethnographer and historian of Mexican and Latinx religions and spiritualities. Her work explores Indigenous revitalizations and Indigenous identity recognition in a transnational context.

Currently, Yanitsa teaches ethnic studies courses at California Polytechnic University, San Luis Obispo.

Suggestions for further reading

In this book
See also chapters 25 (Are Indigenous people who adapt or alter their rituals and traditions [either by choice or by historical necessity] less authentic than their ancestors?), 37 (Are Aztec dancers practicing a religion?), and 68 (What motivates Nahuas to practice their religion of *el costumbre*?).

Elsewhere
Becihalupo, Ana Mariella. *Shamans of the Foye Tree: Gender, Power, and Healing among the Chilean Mapuche.* Austin: University of Texas Press, 2007.

Friedlander, Judith. *Being Indian in Hueyapan.* New York: Palgrave Macmillan, 1975.

McMillen, Christian W. *Making Indian Law: The Hualapai Land Case and the Birth of Ethnohistory.* New Haven: Yale University Press, 2007.

Nohelani Teves, Stephanie. *Defiant Indigeneity: The Politics of Hawaiian Performance.* Chapel Hill: University of North Carolina Press, 2018.

Wenger, Tisa. *We Have a Religion: The 1920s Pueblo Indian Dance Controversy and American Religious Freedom.* Chapel Hill: University of North Carolina Press, 2009.

37
Are Aztec dancers practicing a religion?

Yanitsa Buendía de Llaca

Aztec dance originated from the Conchero movement, which was a vernacular Catholic practice carried out in small towns in the State of Mexico and neighboring states, including Querétaro, Hidalgo, and Mexico City. Every year on September 13, Concheros from Mexico and the United States congregate in the Temple of the Saint Cross (*Templo de la Santa Cruz*) in Querétaro, which has become the cradle of the celebration, to commemorate the commitment to keeping the tradition alive. The Conchero movement is a lived practice in Mexico and the United States, where dances, chants, and rituals are incorporated into Catholic worship. In a strict sense, Conchero dancers practice religion while performing their tradition (*velaciones*) alongside Catholicism.

Conchero dance has led to changes and a movement of "purification" in what we see today as Aztec dance, which seeks to be more Indigenous and less Spanish/Catholic. The difference between Conchero and Aztec dancers can be seen through material culture. Although Conchero and Aztec dancers usually share similar regalia, like wearing clothing with vibrant colors, feathered headdresses, and ankle rattles, newer groups have also marked important differences. While Conchero dancers wear colorful regalia, some Aztec dancers are trying to wear off-white clothes like the *calzón de manta* (cotton pants) used by Indigenous peoples in Central Mexico and prohibited by the government in 1887, and also the typical red belt along the waist.

Most of the people practicing Conchero and Aztec dance come from small peasant communities or families of these communities who migrated to Mexico City in search of other economic opportunities. In Mexico, Indigenous adscription is controlled by the state through cultural regulations that make people that have lost contact with their Native language and culture be considered mestizo instead of Indigenous. Thus, most of these dancers are not considered to be Indigenous in the eyes of state categories. However, they are viewed as revitalizers of pre-Hispanic Indigenous cultures. Similarly, in the United States, these dancers identified as Indigenous, but this is not accepted as such by state policies in either country.

Easier than the regalia, a way to differentiate Conchero from Aztec dancers is through the instruments they play and their proximity to Catholic belief and practice. Conchero dancers play the mandolin, a small guitar introduced by the Spanish in the conquest, and their music is mostly in Spanish with Catholic invocations to saints and virgins. Differently, Aztec dancers play the *huehuetl* and the *teponaztli*, the two main drum instruments that sometimes are accompanied by the traditional Mesoamerican flute.

Another way to see the difference between these groups is through their social organization. While Concheros gathered in *mesas*, which follow a military organization and hierarchy, where the leader of the dance circle is usually known as the "general." Aztec dancers gathered in *calpulli*, a social organization that combines ideas of family kinship and the school system in the Aztec empire. *Calpullis* are led by the figure of the *maestro* (master or teacher) and, in some cases, by their female counterpart, recognized as an *abuela* (grandmother).

While it is easy to affirm that Concheros are practicing a religion because of their affiliation with Catholicism, it is not a straightforward answer for Aztec dancers. While doing fieldwork in Mexico and the United States, I saw a wide range of vocabulary used to describe Aztec dancers' practice. Some use the term "spiritual," but for others, "spiritual" is a deeply rooted Christian term, coming from the notion of the Holy Spirit.

Instead of religion, most Aztec dancers would agree on using the word "ceremony" to describe the activities that accompanied their dances. Some of these activities are (1) following the twenty-day cycle in the Aztec calendar (*veintenas*); (2) practicing rites of passage that mark life transitions such as newborns, naming ceremonies, and deaths; and (3) the opening and closing of the dance circle every time a dance is performed. The latter is a small ritual that involves evoking the four elements of nature (water, fire, earth, wind) represented by a small altar in the center of the dancers' circle and an opening ritual that involves performing a dance, saying a prayer, or simply playing the conch (*caracol*) to the four directions (north, south, east, west).

Aztec dancers push back on Catholicism as a way of separating themselves from colonial impositions. However, when Aztec dancers use the word "ceremony" instead of "religion" to describe their own practices, we can still see a connection to the nonmaterial—when the metaphysical world is in communion with the physical/empirical world through ritual practice.

About the author

Yanitsa Buendia de Llaca is an ethnographer and historian of Mexican and Latinx religions and spiritualities. Her work explores Indigenous revitalizations and Indigenous identity recognition in a transnational context. Currently, Yanitsa teaches ethnic studies courses at California Polytechnic University, San Luis Obispo.

Suggestions for further reading

In this book
See also chapters 36 (Why reconstruct precolonial Indigenous religions in the Americas?) and 68 (What motivates Nahuas to practice their religion of *el costumbre*?).

Elsewhere
Argyriadis, Kali, Renée de la Torre, Cristina Gutiérrez Zúñiga, and Alejandra Aguilar Ros, eds. *Raíces en Movimiento: Prácticas religiosas tradicionales en contextos translocales.* Mexico: Centro de estudios mexicanos y centroamericanos, 2008. https://books.openedition.org/cemca/252?lang =en#:~:text=los%20movimientos%20religiosos.-,Ra%C3%ADces%20en %20movimiento%20analiza%20los%20procesos%20din%C3%A1micos %20de%20translocalizaci%C3%B3n%20que,contexto%20de%20los %20flujos%20globales.

Collin, Ernesto. *Indigenous Education through Dance and Ceremony.* New York: Palgrave Macmillan, 2014.

de la Peña Martinez, Francisco. "Los Hijos del Sexto Sol." In *Un estudio ethnopsicoanalítico del movimiento de la mexicanidad.* Mexico City: Instituto Nacional de Antropología e Historia, 2002.

Luna, Jennie Marie. "Danza Mexica: Indigenous Identity, Spirituality, Activism, and Performance." PhD diss., University of California, Davis, 2011.

38
What is the deal with cultural appropriation?

Gregory D. Alles

A few years ago, I heard rumors that a colleague of European background
in another department was having classes "participantly observe" shamanism. Students would drum together during class time and collectively
go on shamanic journeys. The goal was to learn about the Indigenous
experience, but to the best of my knowledge, no Indigenous person was
ever involved or consulted. As a counterpoint, I showed the film *White
Shamans and Plastic Medicine Men*, in which Native Americans critique
New Age shamans, to engage students in a discussion of both participant
observation and cultural appropriation. Afterward, one white student was
clearly upset. Her brother, she said, participated in activities like those the
film critiqued. He did so because they were meaningful to him and showed
respect for Native Americans and their traditions.

The cultural appropriation of Indigenous identities, practices, and
symbols—even bodies—is widespread. As a child, I participated in the
YMCA Indian Guide program as a putative member of the Oto tribe.
In the early 1970s, I convinced my parents to drive to Dickson Mounds
State Park in Illinois to see an exposed Indian burial site that was then on
display. In 1991, several colleagues and I organized a two-year series of
programs exploring Indigenous perspectives. One colleague, a member
of the Muscogee Creek Nation, suggested I contact a local Piscataway elder
to see whether he would conduct a sweat-lodge ceremony for us. I did so,
with more enthusiasm and naïveté than knowledge and understanding.
I received a forceful rebuke: Would I ask a Catholic priest to perform a
fake Mass?

The appropriation of Indigenous religious beliefs and practices constitutes a highly contested topic. The contestation has been particularly
acute, although not uniquely so, in locations where the New Age and
the Indigenous intersect, such as shamanism. Context matters too. The

many "Indian clubs" in Germany, which provide their members access to an imagined alternative reality, may be received variably, but in settler-colonial states like the United States and Canada, cultural appropriation inevitably assumes a place beside centuries-long policies and practices of displacement and extermination.

Several factors complicate addressing cultural appropriation in both theory and practice. One factor is that cultures and religions are artificial constructs. In reality, neither term identifies consistent, unchanging, homogeneous wholes congruous with groups of people that have strictly defined identity boundaries. Another factor is cultural flow. For the vast majority of the world's population, no aspect of culture has been untouched by outside influences, whether that be what people eat and drink, how they clothe and decorate their bodies, how they communicate with one another, how they move through space, or anything else. Yet another complication derives from the principle of religious freedom enshrined in the Universal Declaration of Human Rights. When religious practice is (improperly) subsumed under religious belief, claims of cultural appropriation seem to run afoul of the right to freedom of conscience, thought, and expression. Finally, some have attempted to negotiate cultural appropriation in terms of the laws governing copyright, patent, or trade secrets. Despite some successes, such as the United States' Native American Graves Protection and Repatriation Act (1990), legal regimes governing the use and exchange of commodities in a capitalistic market economy are often ill-suited for dealing with instances of cultural appropriation.

At heart, cultural appropriation is not about what it is legal to do, and it is not about what people have the right to do. It is about how to treat fellow human beings in the respectful manner that they deserve, especially in recognition of a continuing unequal distribution of power and privilege. Pretending to be something one is not is simply fraud, even if one manages to deceive oneself. Perpetuating misrepresentations and stereotypes of others for one's own benefit, whether economic, social, or merely psychological, is disrespectful, not a means of showing respect. Utilizing people's heritage, artifacts, and bodies, whether living or dead, in a manner that they find illicit or abusive is shameful.

These considerations do not just define ideal religious and social practice; they should also define best practices in teaching and research, including teaching and research about religions. Cultural appropriation often transposes the Indigenous to an idealized past or an inaccessible present and ignores the reality and struggles of Indigenous peoples living today. For that reason, vigilance may be especially called for in institutions like the one I work in, where no faculty member any longer self-identifies as Indigenous and where, during my teaching career, I could always count the number of Indigenous students on fewer than five fingers.

About the author

Gregory D. Alles is professor of religious studies at McDaniel College in Westminster, Maryland. A past president of the North American Association for the Study of Religion and former executive editor of *Numen*, the journal of the International Association for the History of Religions, his current research focuses on the Rathvas, an Indigenous community in Western India.

Suggestions for further reading

In this book
See also chapters 26 (Can I convert to or practice an Indigenous religious tradition if I am not an Indigenous person?) and 39 (Was the Washington R*dskins cultural appropriation?).

Elsewhere

Brown, Michael F. *Who Owns Native Culture?* Cambridge, MA: Harvard University Press, 2003.

Brunk, Conrad G., and James O. Young. *The Ethics of Cultural Appropriation*. Malden, MA: Wiley-Blackwell, 2009.

Deloria, Philip J. *Playing Indian*. New Haven: Yale University Press, 1998.

Johnson, Greg. *Sacred Claims: Repatriation and Living Tradition*. Charlottesville: University of Virginia Press, 2007.

Quijano, Aníbal. "Questioning 'Race.'" *Socialism and Democracy* 21(1) (March 2007): 45–53.

39
Was the Washington R*dskins cultural appropriation?

Matt Sheedy

"Playing Indian is a persistent tradition in American culture," writes Philip Deloria (Lakota), and dates back to at least the Boston Tea Party (1773), where the colonists who dumped tea into the Boston Harbor dressed up as Native Americans. For Deloria, "playing Indian" was a way for early American colonists to differentiate themselves from the British and soon became entangled in struggles to define national identity.

On July 3, 2020, the Washington R*dskins name was changed to the Washington Football Team. Shortly following this announcement, the Canadian Football League's Edmonton Eskimos also changed their name. In December 2020, the Cleveland Indians Major League Baseball team announced plans to change their name following the 2021 season and banned fans from wearing headdresses and face paint (a.k.a. red facing) in the team's stadium. Here we might ask the question, Was the Washington R*dskins cultural appropriation?

Like many popular terms, "cultural appropriation" describes a wide range of ideas and behaviors, from an "I'll use whatever I want" mentality to positions that define everything as appropriation. Complicating matters further, many Indigenous communities sell their own cultural products to outsiders, such as paintings, sculptures, dream catchers, beadwork, and moccasins. One important distinction here is that when such goods are made by Indigenous people, they are less likely to depict an "imaginary Indian." Despite challenges that may arise from Indigenous cultural productions, such as catering to the interests of a "white" audience or unauthorized borrowing between different Indigenous communities (e.g., a Cree artist performing Inuit throat singing), one of the effects of settler representations of Indigeneity is that it tends to condense Indigenous cultural and "spiritual" practices into a small, select set of stereotypes. In this sense, cultural appropriation is one of the most pervasive acts of erasure of Indigenous complexity.

As Michelle Raheja (Seneca) points out, "Prior to 1492 Native American community identity was often flexible. Communities and families sometimes splintered for a variety of reasons and formed new bands, nations, and confederacies." These kinds of relationships became more difficult to maintain in the nineteenth century when colonial projects in North America were mostly complete and as Indigenous people struggled to maintain cultural and spiritual practices amid forced assimilation.

A lot has been written on stereotypes about Native Americans, from the "noble savage" of Shakespeare and Rousseau to more sinister depictions of "savage Indians" as a threat to Christian civilization. Depictions of "savages" gave way to more "noble" representations in the twentieth century, since Native North Americans were no longer seen as a threat to Western expansion. While "savage" depictions still persist in popular culture, twentieth-century representations primarily served the construction of national identities. As famed Canadian painter Emily Carr wrote in 1913, "These things [in reference to totem poles and Indigenous village scenes in her paintings] should be to we Canadians what the ancient Briton's relics are to the English." Needless to say, these "relics" have been appropriated in countless ways, as seen with the Boy Scouts, who drew on images of "Indian" braves as models of strength, leadership, and masculinity. Much the same could be said for what motivates sports fans to "play Indian."

Campaigns to change the names of sports teams came about during the civil rights era, which helped spur the Red Power movement in 1968. Attempts to change the R*dskins name date back to 1972, as numerous college teams, such as Stanford and Dartmouth, decided to stop using Indigenous mascots during this time. Campaigns picked up once again in the late 1980s and early 1990s, as C. Richard King details in his book *Redskins: Insult and Brand*.

One way to interpret the current wave of name changes is through recent shifts in power following decades of activism, which has accelerated in the age of social media, from the Idle No More movement (ca. 2012) to Black Lives Matter (ca. 2013). Since this time, a revitalization of Indigenous languages and cultures has been on the rise throughout North America, while the idea of "decolonization" has entered into mainstream conversations. Why all of this is relevant for a book on Indigenous religions is simple. Since settler societies have largely defined who and what Indigenous people are, including the use of totems or trophies in the form of sports mascots, public perceptions of Indigenous culture and "spirituality" have been primarily shaped by outside interests. As a new Native American renaissance continues to unfold, more tradition-specific representations are coming to the fore as Indigenous people attempt to reclaim their own images and re-present them for a twenty-first-century audience.

About the author
Matt Sheedy holds a PhD in the study of religion and is visiting professor of North American studies at the University of Bonn, Germany. His research includes critical theories of secularism and religion and representations of atheism, Islam, Christianity, and Native American traditions in popular and political culture. His latest book is *Owning the Secular: Religious Symbols, Culture Wars, Western Fragility* (Routledge, 2021).

Suggestions for further reading
In this book
See also chapters 26 (Can I convert to or practice an Indigenous religious tradition if I am not an Indigenous person?) and 38 (What is the deal with cultural appropriation?).

Elsewhere
Deloria, Philip. *Playing Indian*. New Haven: Yale University Press, 1999.

King, C. Richard. *Redskins: Insult and Brand*. Lincoln: University of Nebraska Press, 2016.

Rajeha, Michelle. *Reservation Reelism: Redfacing Visual Sovereignty and Representations of Native Americans in Film*. Lincoln: University of Nebraska Press, 2010.

Vowel, Chelsea. "What Is Cultural Appropriation? Respecting Cultural Boundaries." In *Indigenous Writes: A Guide to First Nations, Métis, and Inuit Issues in Canada*, 80–91. Winnipeg, MB, Canada: Highwater, 2016.

40

What is decolonization, and what does it have to do with Indigenous religious traditions?

Natalie Avalos

While decolonial discourses have been present in activist circles since the nationalist movements of the middle twentieth century, they have begun to enter mainstream academia in the last few years. Decolonial thought in the United States has overlapping but distinct genealogies. One, referred to as decolonial theory, is situated among Latin American theorists, represented in the work of Anibal Quijano and Walter Mignolo, and is in conversation with postcolonial, critical, and anticolonial theorists like Frantz Fanon. The other, focused on decolonial praxis, emerged from the work of US-based women of color feminists, such as Emma Perez and Chela Sandoval, in conversation with postmodern and postcolonial thinkers like Homi Bhaba.

Like settler-colonial theory, decolonial theory makes the superstructures of colonial inequities in places like Latin America and the Caribbean visible. Decolonial theorists argue that Western imperialism operates at the level of epistemology and that modernity could be better understood as coloniality, since modern social structures were determined and continue to operate through colonial projects and their mechanisms, such as racialization. Decolonial theory challenges coloniality's hierarchies of power/knowledge by denaturalizing the white Western world's monopoly on legitimate knowledge production, who is considered an authoritative voice, and importantly for the field, the ways religious and racial discourses operated together to redefine personhood in the new world.

The latter work on decolonial praxis emerged from the intersectional discourses of women of color working in feminist and ethnic studies activist/scholar spaces. Ethnic studies is an insurgent body of scholarship forged in the late 1960s that aimed to achieve philosophical and material

liberation by enacting radical agency against imperialism, criminaliza-
tion, and enslavement that operate on the global stage. Ethnic studies
became the academic space where African American, Asian American,
Pacific, Latinx, and Native American epistemologies and histories were
researched, reclaimed, and recentered.

Native American studies emerged with ethnic studies and eventually
joined with Indigenous studies in order to mobilize toward philosophical
and material liberation, which meant explicitly advocating for Native
American and Indigenous sovereignty. Here, decolonization is explored as
both an end goal in the form of "land back"—the reallocation of Indigenous lands to Indigenous peoples—and the radical praxis that supports
this end. Native American and Indigenous studies (NAIS) challenged the
colonial legacy of knowledge production on Indigenous peoples by developing Indigenous methodologies, which take an endogenous approach
to Indigenous life, essentially deferring to Native peoples as the foremost experts of their own experience and knowledge systems. As a result,
new ethical protocols for research have been articulated, given the ways
Indigenous peoples and their epistemologies have been delegitimized,
misappropriated, and pathologized in the service of white supremacy /
racial capitalism.

A critical Indigenous studies (and decolonial) approach to understanding Indigenous religious life would incorporate critical readings from
Native scholars or those that center the voices and views of Indigenous
peoples—in essence, using work that centers Indigenous epistemologies
and asserts them as epistemologies in their own right, as opposed to
"primitive" or superstitious belief. This not only challenges the assumption
that Indigenous knowledge sits in a subservient position vis-à-vis Western
knowledges; doing so thinks beyond the normative assumptions embedded in religious studies, such as history of religion approaches, that may
seek to universalize or reimagine these complex worlds through wholly
Western categories. The work of Charles Long and Tomoko Masuzawa
and, more recently, critiques by Mallory Nye remind us that the field was
built upon colonial misreadings of the Other. These theories are mired not
only in primitivism (and Orientalism) but in a Western Christian materi-
alist framework that is generally perceived as neutral and even "objective."

Given the field's colonial history, we need to interrogate the colonialist assumptions that determine who can make truth claims about
non-Western/non-Christian religions and how as well as who has the right
to determine what constitutes legitimate scholarship. A critical step in this
direction is to recognize that there is no neutral position. As scholars, we
are always speaking from a particular place, laden with varying degrees

of power and interest. When we ignore the role of colonial/Christian theological logics still operating in the field, we marginalize and silence the work of the most vulnerable among us. Decolonizing the field means religious studies scholars can no longer make ahistorical assessments of non-Western/non-Christian scholarship and ignore their political histories, as if those political histories do not directly correlate to how knowledge is produced and power is waged.

About the author

Natalie Avalos is an assistant professor in the Ethnic Studies Department at the University of Colorado Boulder. She is currently working on her manuscript titled *The Metaphysics of Decoloniality: Transnational Indigeneities and Religious Refusal*, which explores urban Native and Tibetan refugee religious life as decolonial praxis. She is a Chicana of Apache descent, born and raised in the Bay Area.

Suggestions for further reading

In this book
See also chapters 28 (What moral responsibilities do scholars and students have in studying Indigenous religions?), 30 (Is an academic approach to Indigenous religions innately colonizing?), and 83 (What is the relationship between Indigenous religion and sovereignty?).

Elsewhere
Kovach, Margaret. *Indigenous Methodologies: Characteristics, Conversations, and Contexts.* Toronto: University of Toronto Press, 2009.

Maldonado-Torres, Nelson. "Race, Religion, and Ethics in the Modern/Colonial World." *Journal of Religious Ethics* 42(4) (2014): 691–711. https://doi.org/10.1111/jore.12078.

Mignolo, Walter. *The Darker Side of Western Modernity: Global Futures, Decolonial Options.* Durham, NC: Duke University Press, 2011.

Nye, Malory. "Decolonizing the Study of Religion." *Open Library of Humanities* 5(1) (2019): 1–45. https://doi.org/10.16995/olh.421.

Smith, Linda Tuhiwai. *Decolonizing Methodologies: Research and Indigenous Peoples.* London: Zed, 2012.

Indigenous Religious Traditions

41
What is a land-based religious tradition?

Dana Lloyd

When I ask my students what they know about Indigenous religions, they usually say something about sacred lands in response. What does it mean for land, or a specific site, to be considered sacred? What does it mean to base a whole religious tradition on the sacredness of a place? I explore these questions in this chapter, but instead of turning to the usual suspects of religious studies (e.g., Mircea Eliade) or to my own religious tradition (Judaism), for answers, I turn to Native scholars (e.g., Vine Deloria Jr.) who explain their religiosity while connecting the sacredness of the land with land dispossession.

It is important to note, first of all, that not all Indigenous traditions are the same, and therefore, different traditions relate to land differently. I am cautious not to adopt the homogenizing lens of colonialism when talking about Indigenous religious traditions as "land-based" traditions. This colonial homogenizing lens is adopted even by well-meaning people, such as US Supreme Court Justice William Brennan, who writes in a dissenting opinion that "Native Americans consider all land sacred." While Brennan points this out in order to promote the legal protection of Indigenous sacred sites, what his sweeping statement overlooks is the specificity of a relationship between a particular Indigenous people and a site that is sacred to them.

It is important to look at specific locales and specific communities so that we do not lose sight of the history and the geography of specific land-based religious traditions. To say that a religious tradition is based on land can mean different things: It could mean that a religious tradition can only be practiced in a specific location or that its continuation is dependent on the integrity of a specific place, even if the place is not easily accessible. It can mean that certain deities or ancestors reside in a specific place or that a meaningful event has taken place there (Deloria talks about "revelation"). It can mean that medicinal plants that are used by a community grow in a certain place. All these cases indicate a special relationship between a religious community and a specific place; indeed, they indicate a relationship between a people and their homeland.

Therefore, when we talk about land-based religious traditions, what we say is that a specific place is meaningful to a community as their home and their kin. Thus, for example, the Haudenosaunee Thanksgiving Address (Ohén:ton Karihwatéhkwen, or Words before All Else) gives thanks to Mother Earth: "We are all thankful to our Mother, the Earth, for she gives us all that we need for life. She supports our feet as we walk about upon her. It gives us joy that she continues to care for us as she has from the beginning of time. To our mother, we send our greetings and our thanks." To this day, these words are recited at the beginning and at the end of almost every Haudenosaunee social, political, and cultural gathering, investing these gatherings with religious meaning.

Another example is the revitalization of the Yurok Wala-we ley ga (known today as the Jump Dance), described by Yurok/Karuk leader Chris Peters as an earth-healing ceremony, which has to be conducted in a specific location in Northern California, both because of the Wo-gay (spiritual ancestors) who reside there, connecting Yurok people to this place, and because the ceremony had been traditionally conducted there until it was criminalized by the federal government following the gold rush. Peters talks about the intelligence and deep wisdom of the place, but his people's relationship to this place as their sacred homeland is also always politicized.

Standing Rock Sioux legal scholar Vine Deloria Jr. talks about Native religions as defined by Indigenous peoples' relation to place rather than to history, and Anishinaabe activist Winona LaDuke makes connections between protecting the sacred and the ecological integrity of land in Native American struggles for healing from trauma and recovering their religious traditions. And Chickasaw gender studies scholar Jodi Byrd reminds us that "for American Indians . . . the land both remembers life and its loss and serves itself as a mnemonic device that triggers the ethics of relationality with the sacred geographies that constitute indigenous peoples' histories" (2011, 118).

Thus, when we talk about land-based religious traditions, we need to remember that our (Indigenous and non-Indigenous people) relationship with the land is not only religious; it is also always political.

About the author

Dana Lloyd is assistant professor of global interdisciplinary studies at Villanova University. She holds a PhD in religion from Syracuse University and LLB and LLM degrees from Tel Aviv Law School. Her book manuscript *Arguing for This Land: Rethinking Indigenous Sacred Sites* is under contract with the University Press of Kansas.

Suggestions for further reading

In this book
See also chapters 42 (What is the relationship between Indigenous religion and land or territory?) and 51 (Was the #NoDAPL occupation at Standing Rock "spiritual" or "religious"?).

Elsewhere

Byrd, Jodi A. *The Transit of Empire: Indigenous Critiques of Colonialism*. Minneapolis: University of Minnesota Press, 2011.

Deloria, Vine, Jr. *God Is Red: A Native View of Religion*. New York: Grosset & Dunlap, 1973.

LaDuke, Winona. *Recovering the Sacred: The Power of Naming and Claiming*. Boston: South End, 2005.

Lara-Cooper, Kishan, and Walter Lara Sr., eds. *Kaʼm-tʼem: A Journey toward Healing*. Temecula, CA: Great Oak, 2019.

McLeod, Christopher, dir. *In the Light of Reverence*. Sacred Land Film Project, 2001.

42

What is the relationship between Indigenous religion and land or territory?

Chris Jocks

If we know only one thing about Native people that isn't a Hollywood cliché, it may be that their cultures and societies are land based. And it's true; relationship to land or territory is an essential dimension of anything Indigenous—for example, art, politics, or health. So what about religion? Most human beings at some point in their lives have felt a sense of awe, a sense of a beyond-human presence, in nature. Especially when they were children. So we may imagine that Native cultures cultivate those experiences more intensely and make them more prominent in peoples' lives, compared with settler societies. This is a start, but to go any deeper, we really have to stop and deconstruct the question.

The challenge is that this question is a typical English sentence built on a string of ponderous nouns. The most ponderous of all is "religion," for reasons discussed in other chapters. But "land" and "territory" are equally unsuitable. All they can do is mark out spatial boundaries—necessary in legal and political arenas but unable to carry us deeper. "Relationship" could be the key to unlocking this riddle if it too weren't boxed up as a noun, because what this question really needs to explore is whether human beings accept and return relationships with other beings on the ground they share. *What are some characteristics of the ways Indigenous people get along with their relatives at home?* Across multiple Indigenous traditions, we can identify three important characteristics: kinship, responsibility, and respect.

Kinship is a fundamental principle of most Indigenous cultural practices. It certainly is so in the Kanien'kehá:ka (Mohawk) world I was born into, as well as other Indigenous worlds I have been privileged to learn from. Kinship is understood as the primary experience of all beings and is rooted in places. Land or territories are not just sectors of physical space;

they are the seedbeds of relationships. Knowledge, medicine, subsistence, and care are taught to humans by older entities—plants and animals and others—and elder relatives with whom our ancestors gathered in places and made agreements. In many such life systems, the earth is our first mother, the source of all our relationships. Even when a people is displaced, as so many have been under colonization, as they recover, they ask permission and introduce themselves into the relationships of their new homes.

This emphasis on kinship leads to social systems built around responsibility rather than privilege or domination. It is our responsibility to maintain good relationships with all the beings with whom we share place. Naturally, this responsibility includes proper care and protection of territory, especially those distinctive places where the generosity of revered and beloved beings has been and continues to be received. Kinship is not a status; it's a responsibility. In Kanien'kéha, the Mohawk language, most kinship terms are verbs; kinship is proven in action.

The most natural response to such a system of responsibility—kinship, knowledge, and mutual care—is one of gratitude and respect. Ceremonial expression cultivates and deepens this response. Awareness of place serves to remind Indigenous people of specific events and exchanges in that history of care, kinship, and struggle. Traveling through traditional territory is itself a ceremony that builds knowledge and respect.

Nations with military might and aggressive hunger for other peoples' territories and resources have wreaked havoc and disruption on these Indigenous ways of life, as we all know. Relations between human beings and their places of origin, including their other-than-human kin, have been disrupted or severed. Communication is lost when Indigenous languages are starved. Revered, sacred places have been degraded and destroyed. Indigenous people have been forcibly removed from the seedbeds of their ways of life. It is no surprise when social, ecological, and spiritual dysfunction proliferates. Violence begets violence. In this context, Indigenous people displaced from their homelands may not always have an opportunity to learn these ways, but often they still seek to build Indigeneity through new forms of expression, culturally informed but responsive to fractured modern and postmodern experiences. Relationship with land or territory is nurtured through memory, aspiration, and political action in places of displacement. Think of this the next time you hear "Land Back!"

About the author

Chris Jocks, Kahnawà:ke Mohawk, is senior lecturer in Applied Indigenous Studies at Northern Arizona University. He earned his PhD in

Religious Studies under the direction of Inés Talamantez at the University of California, Santa Barbara, in 1994. His work includes publications on the conceptual incongruity between Indigenous and settler state societies and nations, as manifest in law, religion, and social practices. He is also engaged with local Indigenous community advocacy in northern Arizona.

Suggestions for further reading

In this book
See also chapters 43 (What does it mean for an Indigenous religion to be "place based"?) and 48 (Are Indigenous peoples inherently environmentalists?).

Elsewhere
Crawford O'Brien, Suzanne, with Inés Talamantez. *Religion and Culture in Native America*. Lanham, MD: Rowman & Littlefield, 2021.

Irwin, Lee, ed. *Native American Spirituality: A Critical Reader*. Lincoln: University of Nebraska Press, 2000.

Kimmerer, Robin Wall. *Braiding Sweetgrass: Indigenous Wisdom, Scientific Knowledge, and the Teachings of Plants*. Minneapolis, MN: Milkweed Editions, 2013.

43
What does it mean for an Indigenous religion to be "place based"?

Abel R. Gomez

Land or place is important in nearly all religions. Indigenous and non-Indigenous scholars, however, have often described Indigenous religions, cosmologies, and practices as particularly "land based" or "place based." Distinct groups typically adopt the term "Indigenous" as a political, cultural, and/or national identity because they identify as the original people of a given place. In an increasingly globalized world, "Indigenous" also refers to comparable relationships that such distinct peoples sustain with their specific homelands.

Standing Rock Sioux scholar Vine Deloria Jr. once wrote, "American Indians hold their land—places—as having the highest possible meaning, and all their statements are made with this reference point in mind." This chapter will examine Indigenous relations to land in terms of creation accounts, ancestral ceremonial grounds, and emerging transnational spaces.

While the ways that land features within Indigenous religious practices vary, Indigenous peoples' relations to particular places are often foregrounded in creation stories. One example of this is a creation narrative from the Kanaka Maoli or Native peoples of Hawai'i. Their creation story recounts that in the beginning, Wākea, the Sky Father, and Papahānaumoku, the Earth Mother, birthed the Hawaiian Islands. The sacred mountain called Mauna a Wākea, or Mauna Kea for short, is the firstborn of this union. Because Hawaiian creation narratives recount the Hawaiian people emerging from the land, the land is viewed as *kūpuna*, or ancestor, suggesting a direct genealogical relationship to this place. Such relationships are also connected to *mālama 'āina*, care of land, a Kanaka Maoli ethic of responsibility to the land. While every people has their own specific creation account, many Indigenous peoples share a pattern of ancestral relationships to particular areas of land since the beginning of time.

Indigenous peoples also speak of particular places as sites of power or revelation. Places like Onondaga Lake for the Haudenosaunee (Iroquois) Confederacy, Ĥe Sápa (the Black Hills) for the Oceti Sakowin (Sioux), and Dookʼoʼoosłííd (the San Francisco Peaks) for the Diné (Navajo), Hopi, Zuni, and others have long been associated with sacred power. Cultural teachings based on generations of relationship to these places suggest that such sites are locations of powerful spiritual forces. Through culturally specific practices, Indigenous peoples engage in ceremonial exchanges with the forces within specific places for a number of reasons, ultimately to fulfill covenants that their people have made with sacred beings for the perpetuation of life.

The depth of relationship that Indigenous peoples maintain to land as sites of creation or ancestral ceremonial grounds offers a very different sense of place from those held by immigrant or settler peoples living in the United States. Indeed, Indigenous peoples often speak of being not simply from a place but *of* a place. They trace relationships to ancestral lands in terms of countless generations of ceremonial exchange with place. This generates a profound sense of belonging to ancestral lands. Because of this, Indigenous religious practices are often not portable in the same ways that other religions are. Each group of people and each land have their own distinct religious practices, sacred narratives, and cultural traditions that relate specifically to that area of land.

Like other elements of Indigenous religions, these sacred places are not always accessible to individuals outside of a given tribal nation. Many Indigenous peoples prefer not to disclose the locations of ceremonial sites or burial grounds to protect such places from New Age appropriation or grave robbing. Unfortunately, the ongoing impacts of colonialism across the world often mean that Indigenous peoples are forced to disclose culturally sensitive information about their places when they are threatened by deforestation, mineral extraction, or pollution.

The sense of belonging to the land that Indigenous peoples have does not mean they are "stuck" in the past or in place. Indigenous peoples also create new places for religious practice. Intertribal communities of urban Indians in places like San Francisco or Minneapolis often participate in religious practices in Native community centers or powwows. Such spaces are increasingly important for various diasporic Indigenous peoples. Indigenous peoples also practice various forms of ceremony in sites of transnational solidarity with Indigenous peoples from around the world, in places like the United Nations, or at high-profile sacred sites protection movements, like Standing Rock, South Dakota. In the wake of the global pandemic of the coronavirus, some Indigenous peoples have also participated in ceremonies through cyberspace.

The connections that Indigenous peoples sustain with place are both ancestral and emerging. These relationships point to Indigenous peoples' deep roots to their homeland as recounted in sacred narratives and cultural traditions as well as to their dynamic relations to new places today.

About the author

Abel R. Gomez is an assistant professor of Native American and Indigenous spiritual traditions in the Religion Department at Texas Christian University. He holds a PhD from the Religion Department at Syracuse University. His research focus is on sacred sites, decolonization, and Indigenous survival among the Ohlone peoples of the San Francisco–Monterey region.

Suggestions for further reading

In this book
See also chapters 2 (What makes a religion an "Indigenous religion"?), 41 (What is a land-based religious tradition?), and 42 (What is the relationship between Indigenous religion and land or territory?).

Elsewhere
Basso, Keith. *Wisdom Sits in Places: Landscape and Language among the Western Apache*. Albuquerque: University of New Mexico Press, 1996.

Deloria, Vine, Jr. *God Is Red: A Native View of Religion*. Golden, CO: Fulcrum, 2003.

Goeman, Mishuana. *Mark My Words: Native Women Mapping Our Nations*. Minneapolis: University of Minnesota Press, 2013.

Kelley, Dennis F. *Tradition, Performance, and Religion in Native America: Ancestral Ways, Modern Selves*. New York: Routledge, 2014.

44

If Native American religious traditions are place based, how do "urban Indians" practice their religion?

Dennis Kelley

The complexity of Indigenous traditions begins with the very nature of the term "Indigenous," due to the fact that it doesn't really mean anything unless there is such a thing as "not-Indigenous." In other words, the very discussion of Indigenous cultures and issues is inexorably linked to colonialism.

Indigenous traditions seek to maintain ancestral connections to particular places, the natural cycles of those places, and the ongoing relationship with those connections. I refer to this process as "embeddedness." Embeddedness incorporates the natural cycles of particular places in the formation of traditions, identities, and values. There are three interconnected concepts associated with embeddedness: place, power, and protocol. Briefly, "place" refers to a deep connection to the natural cycles of those particular places that form the Indigenous culture's world view. Power relates to the broad concept of "sacred" in that Indigenous traditions recognize the immanent nature of the creative energy in the universe and the need for a proper relationship to it. This leads to the protocols—practices and behaviors—for living life in a good way essential for the maintenance of these relationships.

Embeddedness can be seen in contrast to the colonizing powers that enter into the lands of others and alter that system of reciprocity and respect. Colonial systems see the land and its resources as "inanimate," and that land is a possession and seen primarily as a storehouse for resources. The story of the world after the arrival of Europeans in the Western Hemisphere as well as the desire for land in the African subcontinent and South Asia is one of the displacement and death of countless tribal peoples.

While many different tribal peoples around the world have been removed to lands other than their ancestral places and many have been relocated to urbanized areas or, indeed, have had their ancestral places urbanized underneath them, the desire to maintain Indigenous traditional identities remains strong. The question of how these communities accomplish this has answers as varied as the many communities experiencing this trauma around the world. But two major themes can help—tribal peoples who remain in or very near their ancestral places while living primarily in urban centers and those that have been far removed from their homelands to urban centers elsewhere.

In the first instance, people can relate to some of their traditional places and their natural cycles (seasonal changes, precipitation cycles, flora and fauna, etc.) on a regular basis but are often prevented from engaging with these places. The maintenance of Indigeneity for these communities is often a matter of gaining political and social power in the colonial system and forcing a change in the economic and sociopolitical barriers erected to keep Indigenous people from having access to places and from performing the proper ceremonies. A good example of this is the efforts of First Nations tribal communities in Canada, where long-fought battles in both political and legal arenas have resulted in many concessions made for First Nation access to places and the decision-making processes associated with Canadian economic development.

The second category is more complex given the many parts of the picture. Indigenous communities that have been removed from their homelands to urban centers at a distance have to necessarily make allowances for both different types of landscapes and a variety of tribal identities in forming Indigenous collectives. For example, in the United States, removal policies often resulted in American Indian people of several different tribal traditions relocating to the same urban areas and maintaining connections to Indigeneity by forming pan-tribal communities. In these contexts, traditional expressions of place, power, and protocol could re-form around common themes shared by all and that are able to be realized given the urbanized environs. One example is in Los Angeles, California, where Native people from both the Los Angeles–area tribes and those that came to California from elsewhere have made efforts to come together with a common goal to maintain the connections to Indigenous values and to teach children to honor their Indigenous heritage.

Place, then, being more than a spot on a map from which Indigenous people can be removed, lives in the ways Indigenous communities interact with the world regardless of where they are—though of course refraining from forcing these communities off their lands is very much the preferable option. However, Indigeneity is a world view established in specific contexts that always guides the values, behavior, and relationships of Indigenous people regardless of their dwelling places. Power and the reciprocal relationships to the other-than-human world can be a guiding factor in any context such that protocol becomes the key way communities can maintain ancestral connections to Indigenous identities, whether that means constructing ceremonial practices that accommodate multiple tribal identities or incorporating protest, political action, and community organizing into urban Indigenous sacred practices.

About the author

Dennis Kelley is an associate professor of religious studies at the University of Missouri, Columbia. His research area is the intersection between religious, ethnic, and national identities, specifically in how they are negotiated and maintained through embodied practice in contemporary American Indian communities.

Suggestions for further reading

In this book
See also chapters 41 (What is a land-based religious tradition?) and 43 (What does it mean for an Indigenous religion to be "place based"?).

Elsewhere
Bird-Naytowhow, Kelley, Andrew R. Hatala, Tamara Pearl, Andrew Judge, and Erynne Sjoblom. "Ceremonies of Relationship: Engaging Urban Indigenous Youth in Community-Based Research." *International Journal of Qualitative Methods* 16 (2017): 1–14.

Dennis Kelley. *Tradition, Performance, and Religion in Native America: Ancestral Ways, Modern Selves.* New York: Routledge, 2015.

Kulis, Stephen S., and Monica Tsethlikai. "Urban American Indian Youth Spirituality and Religion: A Latent Class Analysis." *Journal for the Scientific Study of Religion* 55 (2016): 677–697.

45

Do Indigenous peoples believe plants, animals, and waters have personhood?

Meaghan Weatherdon

What does it mean when Indigenous peoples declare trees, deer, birds, or beaver as their relatives? Why are Indigenous activists across the globe petitioning the courts to have rivers designated as legal persons under the law? What kind of ethical responsibilities and moral imperatives arise when more-than-human beings are thought to possess personhood? Indigenous world views and knowledge systems offer ways of relating to the world that challenge modern society's and Western thinking's anthropocentric focus. Many Indigenous cultures possess teachings, stories, and cultural practices that convey an understanding that other beings are persons and may even be regarded as more-than-human in that they are understood to possess abilities and knowledges that in many ways exceed human capabilities.

It has been difficult for Western academics to grapple with Indigenous ways of being and relating. As Graham Harvey illustrates in his discussion of "animism" in this volume, sometimes early scholars of religion accused Indigenous peoples of anthropomorphizing their natural surroundings, believing they lacked the science and reason to explain natural events. Departing from these earlier imperialist appraisals of Indigenous religiosity, anthropologist A. Irving Hallowell (1892–1974), working with the Beren River Ojibwe, expanded scholarly understandings of Indigenous notions of personhood. By centering on Ojibwe world views in his analysis, Hallowell discerned that within an Ojibwe ontology, holding personhood does not necessitate a being to be human or even humanlike. Within an Ojibwe ontology, personhood is an expansive category of meaning that is constituted and cultivated through a being's interactions and relations with other beings.

Indigenous thinkers, storytellers, and activists insist that an orientation toward other beings as persons in fact incites a deeper understanding of humanity's interdependencies with and moral obligations toward other life-forms. The famous Cherokee storyteller Thomas King, for example, has written a version of the Haudenosaunee Creation Story of Skywoman in order to explicate a Haudenosaunee world view in which humans are understood not as separate from or above nature but rather as existing within an interconnected web of relations. In his telling of Skywoman, King describes how the world came into being when a young woman fell from the sky world to a place where there was nothing but water. King explains how all the animals of the water world collaborated to bring Skywoman to safety. The water birds caught her falling and brought her to land on top of a Turtle's back. Then one by one, each animal took its turn trying to swim to the bottom of the waters and retrieve mud for Skywoman so that she could live comfortably on the Turtle's back. Finally, it is Otter who returns to the surface successfully with mud in hand. Skywoman then uses this mud to create the Earth, or Turtle Island. While analyzing the significance of the Skywoman story, King underscores how within Skywoman's version of the world, creation is a collaborative endeavor. He suggests the story of Skywoman imparts an understanding that human beings exist in a reciprocal rather than hierarchical relationship with other aspects of creation.

During an era characterized by ecological uncertainty in which humanity is facing global climate change, drastic declines in biodiversity, and multiple water crises, Indigenous activists insist modern society has much to learn from Indigenous ways of relating to the world around them. Shinnecock scholar and water activist Kelsey Leonard, for example, advocates for granting the legal status of personhood to bodies of water. She asks, If corporations are granted legal personhood in courts of law within the United States, why can not the same protections be guaranteed for water? According to Leonard, humans need to move from viewing water as primarily a resource toward viewing water as a source of life and living relation. Viewing water as a living relation will transform how society makes decisions surrounding water management and encourage people to protect water with the same level of care and concern they afford their family members. These ideas are gaining traction around the world. In New Zealand, for example, the Maori peoples successfully petitioned the New Zealand Parliament to declare their ancestral river, Whanganui, as a legal person on March 20, 2017. These environmental initiatives demonstrate how Indigenous conceptions of personhood are influencing current legal and political landscapes and encouraging societies to cultivate an understanding of plants, animals, and waters that no longer focuses solely on their instrumental value but instead aims to centralize the intrinsic value of the nonhuman world.

About the author

Meaghan Weatherdon is an assistant professor in the Department of Theology and Religious Studies at the University of San Diego. She specializes in the study of Indigenous religions and spiritualities on Turtle Island with a particular focus on intersections between spirituality, youth self-determination, and land-based activism.

Suggestions for further reading

In this book
See also chapters 33 (What is animism?) and 69 (What are ancestor spirits, and what role do they play in Hawaiian religious life?).

Elsewhere
Hallowell, Alfred Irving. *Ojibwa Ontology, Behaviour, and Worldview*. New York: Columbia University Press, 1960.

Harvey, Graham. *Animism, Respecting the Living World*. Cambridge: Wakefield, 2005.

King, Thomas. *The Truth about Stories: A Native Narrative*. Minneapolis: University of Minnesota Press, 2008.

Leonard, Kelsey. "Why Lakes and Rivers Should Have the Same Rights as Humans." Filmed December 5, 2019, in Palm Springs, CA. TEDWomen video, 13:13. https://www.ted.com/talks/kelsey_leonard_why_lakes _and_rivers_should_have_the_same_rights_as_humans.

46

What does it mean when Indigenous peoples say animals are sacred?

Kelsey Dayle John

Saying that animals are sacred is a simple statement that holds a complex critique about human-centered value systems. When Indigenous folks say animals are sacred, they mean that animals matter and that they shouldn't matter less than humans. To explain this, it is important to also understand the current moment where the phrase "Black Lives Matter" has become the rallying cry against anti-Blackness and white supremacy. Black Lives Matter, as many activists and leaders of the movement have explained, doesn't mean that all lives don't matter or that Black lives matter more than other lives; instead, it centers on Black lives by critiquing the systems infiltrated with the idea that Black lives do not matter or that they somehow matter less than white lives. It's a statement that gets at the root of white supremacy.

Critical animal studies scholars connect modern-day racism to the proliferation of original forms of speciesism. Speciesism is the act of valuing one species over another, like people might consider a horse to be more valuable than a mouse based on its utilitarian output. Ultimately, the species highest in this imaginary hierarchy is the human. With humans as the superior species, humans create structures that oppress lower species because of their position on an imaginary value scale (think about how human networks treat mice as test subjects while certain horse breeds might sell for hundreds of thousands of dollars). Billy Ray Belcourt explains that white supremacy, capitalism, settler colonialism, and speciesism are all related and mutually reinforce one another, creating a hierarchy where the "less than human" are exploited.

Many Indigenous persons resist the idea that humans are somehow superior to animals or that there exists a hierarchy of human/animal at all. This is an idea reflected in many Indigenous religious traditions and practices. Indigenous persons and their stories describe their knowledge systems, ceremonies, and lives to be interconnected with lands, animals, and humans. Many Indigenous persons will advocate that there is no difference between humans and animals and that both are *persons*. They explain that the qualification for personhood is not being of the human species but that being a creature in the world signifies personhood. Returning to white supremacy, Black and Indigenous folks have historically been compared to animals as a way to designate their status as "less than human." But where did the less-than-human hierarchy begin? Maneesha Deckha connects the racialization of Black and Brown humans as it is perpetuated with the existing idea that animals were less than humans, which leads white Europeans to compare people of color to animals to enforce their superiority and ultimately systems of hierarchy and exploitation (think about the transatlantic slave trade and the forced removal of Indigenous persons).

So when Indigenous folks say animals are sacred, they are resisting the Western hierarchy of speciesism that places humans in a position of superiority over animals, especially when this superiority results in practices that harm or oppress animals and humans. Furthermore, Indigenous folks are speaking about the interconnectedness of their religious traditions, where every person (regardless of species) has a purpose, a place, and agency. They are also providing a deep critique of human-centered and racial hierarchies that persist through colonial world views.

About the author

Kelsey Dayle John (Diné) is an assistant professor with a joint appointment in gender and women's studies and American Indian studies. She holds a PhD in Cultural Foundations of Education from Syracuse University. Her work is centered on animal relationalities, particularly horse/human relationships, as ways of knowing, healing, and decolonizing education. Alongside her work in Indigenous animal studies, Kelsey's research interests also include Indigenous feminisms, decolonizing methodologies, and tribal colleges and universities.

Suggestions for further reading

In this book
See also chapters 42 (What is the relationship between Indigenous religion and land or territory?) and 45 (Do Indigenous peoples believe plants, animals, and waters have personhood?).

Elsewhere

Belcourt, B. R. "Animal Bodies, Colonial Subjects: (Re)locating Animality in Decolonial Thought." *Societies* 5(1) (2015): 1–11.

Deckha, M. "Postcolonial." In *Critical Terms for Animal Studies*, edited by L. Gruen, 280–293. Chicago: University of Chicago Press, 2015.

Fielder, Brigitte. "Why Animal Studies Must Be Antiracist: A Conversation with Benedicte Boisseron." *Edge Effects*, March 26, 2020. https://edgeeffects .net/afro-dog-benedicte-boisseron/#:~:text=Why%20Animal%20Studies %20Must%20Be%20Antiracist:%20A%20Conversation%20with %20B%C3%A9n%C3%A9dicte%20Boisseron&text=Scholarly%20and %20activist%20discussions%20of,kinds%20of%20oppression%E2%80 %94including%20racism.

John, K. D. "Animal Colonialism—Illustrating Intersections between Animal Studies and Settler Colonial Studies through Diné Horsemanship." *Humanimalia: A Journal of Human/Animal Interface Studies* 19(2) (2019): 42–68. https://www.depauw.edu/humanimalia/issue%2020/john.html.

47

What role does pilgrimage play in Indigenous religious life?

Paul L. Gareau and Jeanine LeBlanc

Pilgrimage is a global phenomenon. It traverses place and time and sociopolitical and ethnocultural contexts. But when engaging the question "What role does pilgrimage play in Indigenous religious life?," *pilgrimage* is usually defined in Western and Christian values and terms. By that definition, pilgrimage is an act of religious devotion involving singular or collective experiences of journeying outside of one's everyday life toward a "sacred" site that is contextualized and managed by a complex religious institution. Often, Indigenous pilgrimage is perceived or misinterpreted as an act of assimilation. And you wouldn't be wrong to think this when considering the complex history of religion and settler colonialism with regards to the Doctrine of Discovery, the concept of terra nullius (i.e., empty lands), Manifest Destiny, and Christian missionary evangelicalism. But this is a deterministic view that focuses only on settler colonialism as an ideological process that bulldozes Indigenous ways of being and knowing the world. The problem is a matter of perception, interpretation, and world view.

Indigenous experiences and perspectives need to be centered in this discussion on pilgrimage by focusing on *religion and the sacred as relations*. Indigenous relations are political, informed by kinship structures of language and governance that help generate and maintain reciprocal connections between collective nations and other peoples (human and more-than-humans). Vine Deloria Jr. is a foundational thinker in helping define the "sacred" in Indigenous terms of relations. He pushes back against a Western understanding of the sacred being a binary between this material world and a transcendental spiritual world. A key insight from Deloria is that Indigenous peoples coconstitute connections with and in relation to humans and more-than-humans. Sacred places become sedimented by generations of visitors and ceremonies, and these sediments are understood by generations of storytelling. These storied places are like gravity wells that draw peoples together along seasonal paths and across traditional territories. Movement is the lifeblood of Indigenous engagement with these traditional forms and relational formations. Movement helps define the contours of Indigenous nations and helps reconnect and affirm relations with other peoples, humans and more-than-humans. Therefore, storied places and traditional territories are a matter of good relations that need to be continually maintained.

Speaking from our different communities, the Mi'kmaq nation engages in this complex relationality with regards to Catholic pilgrimage across Mi'kma'ki, the traditional territory in what we now call the Maritimes in Eastern Canada. Pilgrimage has always been a time for visiting with relations. We boat across the Bras D'or Lake to Mniku (Chapel Island), a long-standing storied and sacred place for the Mi'kmaq nation where ancestors are buried and live, to honor our relation and grandmother St. Anne at Se'tta'newimk / St. Anne's Mission. The Métis are a postcontact Indigenous nation situated in the Métis homeland, which is the Parkland and Prairie regions of what we now call Western Canada and the Northern US. We also engage in pilgrimage to sacred and storied places across the Métis homeland, like Manito Sakahigan / Lac Ste. Anne, north of Edmonton, Alberta. We are excited to reconnect with the land; with the waters; with family and friends; with ancestors, Ste. Anne, and God; and with all other relations, human and more-than-human.

Relations are central to everything we do on pilgrimage. It informs Indigenous nationhood, meaning our internal symbols and values that shape the contours of our collective identities. Relations also inform Indigenous peoplehood as an external force outside of our nations, orienting us to make and maintain kinship connections with other collectivities, both human and more-than-human. Pilgrimage facilitates these political dynamics through visiting, which renews and restores nationhood and peoplehood connections, and exercises reciprocity and responsibility with multiple relatives. Pilgrimage, therefore, is more than an individual action of redemption, healing, and religious devotion. It is an opportunity for visiting and relating that helps resist the settler-colonial project that continually seeks to delegitimize and marginalize Indigenous peoples. In the end, Indigenous pilgrimage represents self-determination that resists colonialism by affirming the sovereignty of good relations.

About the authors

Paul L. Gareau is Métis and an associate professor in the Faculty of Native Studies at the University of Alberta. His research and teaching center on theory and methodology around religion and relationality, gender, Indigenous epistemologies, land and place, and sovereignty/peoplehood.

Jeanine LeBlanc is Mi'kmaw and a doctoral candidate at the Faculty of Native Studies at the University of Alberta in Edmonton, Alberta, Canada. Her research explores Mi'kmaw women's lived experiences of religion, Indigenous women's engagement with religion, and Indigenous feminisms.

Suggestions for further reading

In this book
See also chapters 42 (What is the relationship between Indigenous religion and land or territory?) and 51 (Was the #NoDAPL occupation at Standing Rock "spiritual" or "religious"?).

Elsewhere
Andersen, Chris. "Peoplehood and the Nation Form: Core Concepts for a Critical Métis Studies." In *A People and a Nation: New Directions in Contemporary Métis Studies*, edited by Jennifer Adese and Chris Andersen, 18–39. Vancouver: University of British Columbia Press, 2021.

Gaudet, Janice Cindy. "Keeoukaywin: The Visiting Way—Fostering an Indigenous Research Methodology." *Aboriginal Policy Studies* 7(2) (2019): 47–64. https://doi.org/10.5663/aps.v7i2.29336.

Lelièvre, Michelle. *Unsettling Mobility: Mediating Mi'kmaw Sovereignty in Post-contact Nova Scotia*. Tucson: University of Arizona Press, 2017.

Moreton-Robinson, Aileen. "Relationality: A Key Presupposition of an Indigenous Social Research Paradigm." In *Sources and Methods in Indigenous Studies*, edited by Chris Andersen and Jean M. O'Brien, 69–77. New York: Routledge, 2016.

Schermerhorn, Seth. *Walking to Magdalena: Personhood and Place in Tohono O'odham Songs, Sticks, and Stories*. Lincoln: University of Nebraska Press, 2019.

48
Are Indigenous peoples inherently environmentalists?

Dennis Kelley

When I begin my American Indian Religious Traditions course, I ask the students to briefly recount what they have learned about Native Americans in their educational careers to date. One of the most common themes is that Indigenous people have an inherent connection to nature and that Indigenous people uniquely relate to the natural world in some way. However, that connection may not specifically conform to "environmentalism," a term that arose in the nineteenth century in reference to protecting natural resources in the rapidly industrializing world.

While the *concept* of preserving natural environments goes back at least to the sixth century BCE among Jains in South Asia, "environmentalist" is most often used to refer to a set of principles and practices oriented toward protecting and preserving landscapes seen as inherently separate from human communities. Environmentalists in the nineteenth century, especially people like Aldo Leopold and John Muir, emphasized a moral imperative to protect some natural spaces from the polluting effects of modern industry. While Indigeneity shares these basic concerns, and certainly contemporary Indigenous people can identify as "environmentalists," Indigenous approaches to the natural world differ in key ways.

I often think of Indigenous cultures as "embedded" in opposition to what Anthony Giddens calls the "disembedded" nature of modernity. Giddens points out that modern societies became removed from the contexts of medieval village life and instead produced urbanized spaces disconnected from traditions and the natural cycles of particular places. In contrast, Indigenous communities developed and maintain their religious identities and socioeconomic systems in relationships with *particular* places, like landscapes and their natural cycles. Indigenous communities are *of* places rather than merely *in* them.

This produces deeply realized connections to the natural world that see humans not as separate from nature in the first place but rather in a reciprocal relationship with it, a fundamentally sacred set of responsibilities often modeled after one's bond to family. Just like a family nurtures and cares for children, provides contexts for understanding one's role in the world, and teaches the relevant skills to navigate that world, the earth does that for humans. In fact, it is accurate to say that much of what constitutes Indigenous "religions" are systematized practices and ideas that nurture and perpetuate the proper relationships inherent in this connected, embedded reality. These relationship maintenance systems are often referred to in Native communities as "doing things in a good way," meaning that there are proper ways to maintain these interconnected relationships between the people, the ancestors, and the other-than-human world.

One example that might illuminate this idea comes from the California Indian tribes on the Klamath River. Salmon are a key resource but are also sentient beings with their own societies. The Klamath, Hupa, Yurok, Karuk, and Shasta have developed practices to enact the sacred responsibilities they have toward the salmon. For example, when the first salmon begin the journey upriver from the ocean to spawn, ceremonies are held away from the river, as it is improper to let the first salmon see the people. Then when the fishing begins, there are limits inherent in the fishing techniques and practices that ensure only what the people need is taken. Failure to behave properly toward the salmon—and indeed, in general—would be to risk the salmon refusing to allow themselves to be taken to feed the people. These protocols, then, both maintain the health of the salmon population by ensuring that enough salmon make the journey to perpetuate the species and establish other social protocols that preserve a sense of communitarianism and promote good communal relations.

Certainly it can be said that these practices among the Klamath River tribes are "environmentalist" in nature, since they preserve the integrity of an important natural resource, but these ideas go much deeper in that the salmon are helping maintain proper human relationships, teaching the people about self-sacrifice, and allowing for opportunities to engage in positive interpersonal relations. Proper protocols are a way of life in an environment with many such communities of other-than-humans, with the people responsible for the diplomatic interactions with populations of equally deserving beings rather than a superior species taking responsibility to protect an idealized nature that exists in isolation from humans.

The idea that Indigenous peoples are "inherently" environmentalists obscures the deeply embedded nature of the relationships these communities have to *particular* landscapes and the natural cycles of those places.

As an elder once told me, "White people often talk about protecting *the* environment, but we are here to protect *our* environment."

About the author

Dennis Kelley is an associate professor of religious studies at the University of Missouri, Columbia. His research area is the intersection between religious, ethnic, and national identities, specifically in how they are negotiated and maintained through embodied practice in contemporary American Indian communities.

Suggestions for further reading

In this book
See also chapters 42 (What is the relationship between Indigenous religion and land or territory?) and 50 (How does resource extraction impact Native American religious practices?).

Elsewhere
Krech, Shepard, III. "Reflections on Conservation, Sustainability, and Environmentalism in Indigenous North America." *American Anthropologist* 107 (2005): 78–86.

Nadasdy, Paul. "Transcending the Debate over the Ecologically Noble Indian: Indigenous Peoples and Environmentalism." *Ethnohistory* 52(2) (2005): 291–331.

Vincent, Eve, and Timothy Neale. *Unstable Relations: Indigenous People and Environmentalism in Contemporary Australia.* Perth: University of Western Australia Press, 2016.

49

What is the Idle No More movement, and what's a round dance?

Matt Sheedy

The Idle No More (INM) movement began with a Tweet in late October 2012 as part of a teach-in by four women in Saskatoon, Saskatchewan, against Bill C-45. This bill would have enabled the Canadian government to roll back treaty rights on First Nations reserves, among other proposed legislation. INM caught on in Canada and later internationally after Chief Theresa Spence of Attawapiskat First Nation (Treaty 9, present-day Ontario) staged a hunger strike in a teepee on Victoria Island beneath the gothic towers of Canada's parliament on December 11, 2012. As media attention to Chief Spence's hunger strike grew, videos of round dances in shopping malls, in front of government buildings, and in the streets began to appear on YouTube, as those participating took up the mantle of #IdleNoMore.

Round dances are commonly attributed to Plains Cree traditions (possibly received from the Assiniboine) and have been linked to healing ceremonies, honoring ancestors, and forms of prayer and gift giving. They also typically include a drum circle, as participants hold hands and move in a circle around it. Depending on the event, this can be done in full regalia, as is common during ceremony, or less formally, especially during protests and acts of civil disobedience.

Unlike previous uprisings that gained national attention in Canada, such as the Oka Crisis in 1990, which included a seventy-eight-day armed standoff between the Mohawk community of Kanesatake (just outside of Montreal) and the Canadian military, INM saw relatively few confrontations with the authorities. Part of the reason for this was that Bill C-45 impacted *all* First Nations people and not just an isolated community, along with many non-Indigenous citizens who opposed the deregulatory policies of the Conservative Party of Canada. Additionally, by centering on round dances as the central performative act of INM, non-Indigenous allies could participate more easily, which helped shift the familiar "we must return to law and order" narrative of previous conflicts (like the Oka Crisis) toward one of cooperation. For Anishinaabe scholar and activist Niigaan Sinclair, the round dance is a symbol of being in relation to one another, as the constant movement and holding of hands require that people work together. For Sinclair and others, the round dance became a metaphor for reconciliation and for honoring treaty relationships between First Nations and the Canadian state.

Since the round dance did not initially symbolize reconciliation, it cannot be said to have a static or singular meaning; rather, its meaning has been reimagined in relation to contemporary concerns. This does not mean that traditional interpretations don't still hold sway for certain communities, like the Plains Cree; instead, it simply means that the round dance has taken on new meanings, which includes, following INM, being a recognizable symbol of pan-Indigenous ritual or "spirituality." Adding to the pan-Indigenous appeal of the round dance is the fact that many First Nations communities also incorporate drumming into their ceremonial practices, which commonly symbolizes the heartbeat of "Mother Earth" and of the people. The fact that round dances were effective in drawing attention to Indigenous issues via social media also suggests that non-Indigenous people are more likely to identify it with Indigenous religion or spirituality *today*.

During the height of INM in the winter of 2012–2013, Mi'kmaq scholar and activist Pamela Palmater appeared in numerous media interviews where she stated, "First Nations, with our constitutionally protected Aboriginal treaty rights, are Canadians' last best hope to protect the lands, waters, plants, and animals from complete destruction—which doesn't just benefit our children, but the children of all Canadians." By linking Indigenous treaty rights to environmental concerns that impact *all* Canadians, Palmater simultaneously performed two functions. First, she demystified the long-standing trope that Indigenous people are "natural ecologists" that (typically white) settlers selectively draw on for their own interests. Instead of mystifying Indigenous spirituality, her appeal to treaty rights linked Indigenous people with political power. Second and relatedly, Palmater reversed the stereotype that Indigenous people are in need of aid from settler society. This sentiment was commonly reflected by referring to Indigenous people as "land defenders/protectors" and, relatedly, with the slogan "defend/protect the sacred." This became popular during the standoff at Elsipogtog First Nation (October 2013) and later during the massive protest against the Dakota Access Pipeline at Standing Rock Reservation (2016–2017).

However Indigenous nations and individuals may interpret round dances or "the sacred," these newer iterations have contributed to the resignification of Indigenous spirituality for both Native North Americans and settlers alike.

About the author

Matt Sheedy holds a PhD in the study of religion and is visiting professor of North American studies at the University of Bonn, Germany. His research includes critical theories of secularism and religion and representations of atheism, Islam, Christianity, and Native American traditions in popular and political culture. His latest book is *Owning the Secular: Religious Symbols, Culture Wars, Western Fragility* (Routledge, 2021).

Suggestions for further reading

In this book
See also chapters 51 (Was the #NoDAPL occupation at Standing Rock "spiritual" or "religious"?) and 71 (What is the Ghost Dance?).

Elsewhere
Coulthard, Glen Sean. "Conclusion: Lessons from Idle No More; The Future of Indigenous Activism." In *Red Skin, White Masks: Rejecting the Colonial Politics of Recognition*, 151–179. Minneapolis: University of Minnesota Press, 2014.

Kino-nda-niimi Collective. *The Winter We Danced: Voices from the Past, the Future, and the Idle No More Movement*. Winnipeg, MB, Canada: Arbeiter Ring, 2014.

McNally, Michael D. *Defend the Sacred: Native American Religious Freedom beyond the First Amendment*. Princeton, NJ: Princeton University Press, 2020.

Palmater, Pamela. "Feathers versus Guns: The Throne Speech and Canada's War with the Mi'kmaw Nation at Elsipogtog." *Rabble*, October 18, 2013. http://rabble.ca/blogs/bloggers/pamela-palmater/2013/10/feathers-versus -guns-throne-speech-and-canadas-war-mikmaw-nat.

50

How does resource extraction impact Native American religious practices?

Richard J. Callahan Jr.

Most readers of this book take aspects of their lifestyles, such as electricity, cell phones, heat and air conditioning, and motorized transportation, for granted. Most of us are implicated in the global extractive economy that is required to make these things possible. And in many cases, natural resource extraction has direct impacts on the religious practices and well-being of Native American and other Indigenous populations.

While the quantity and extent of extractive enterprises are as high now as they have ever been, the quest for particular natural resources has long shaped the interactions between Indigenous and non-Indigenous peoples. From hunting whales for oil and baleen across the world's oceans; to drilling for oil in the fields of Oklahoma, Alberta, Alaska, and elsewhere; to mining coal, uranium, plutonium, silver, and copper; to fracking natural gas and extracting lithium—in so many cases, natural resources required for the way of life that dominates global capitalism lie in the lands or the waters of Native peoples.

For land-based religions and cultures, the violence and destruction of resource extraction are inherently disruptive. It may destroy sacred land, it may threaten health and well-being, or it may prevent human communities from maintaining proper relations with other-than-human beings. I will briefly discuss three examples that illustrate these points.

Chi'chil Biłdagoteel, or Oak Flat, in Arizona is sacred land to the Western Apache. It is the residence of Ga'an, spirit beings, and the site of ceremonies. It is also the location of one of the largest deposits of copper ore in the world. The US government has passed legislation that would transfer Oak Flat to global mining companies to extract the copper. A group of Western Apache activists has opposed this transfer and framed their legal and moral arguments as a case of First Amendment religious freedom rights. If Chi'chil Biłdagoteel is turned into a copper mine, San Carlos leader Wendsler Nosie explains, it will destroy his community's ability to practice their religion.

Oil pipelines, promoted as a safe and efficient method to transport oil from the point of extraction to processing or distribution sites, have become hotly contested sites of Native opposition. In the case of the Dakota Access Pipeline (DAPL), Lakota and Dakota members of the Standing Rock reservation objected to the pipeline's path under the Missouri River, the source not only of the reservation's drinking water but of life itself. Arguing that "water is life," water protectors from Standing Rock and Indigenous and non-Indigenous communities from across the Americas and the world came together to share ceremony, prayer, and struggle against exploitative extractive capitalism. In so doing, they produced new forms and meanings of spiritual activism, drawing attention to the ways that pipelines and resource extraction disrupt sacred land, ancient burial sites, and the well-being of life itself (human and other-than-human) throughout the world.

Writing about an oil spill in Alberta, Canada, Metís scholar Zoe Todd has called attention to an important ontological dimension of fossil fuels that has a direct relationship to what might be termed religious or spiritual impacts of resource extraction. Noting that so-called fossil fuels were once, millions of years ago, living animals, Todd emphasizes that they are a kind of kin to humans. Treating these remains as an energy source—extracting them from their resting places and transforming them into fuel—weaponizes "these fossil-kin, these long-dead beings, and transforms them into threats to our very existence as humans." What does it mean to think about the responsibilities of relationship and the obligations of reciprocity between human and nonhuman beings when we recognize fossil fuels as kin, "as agential more-than-human beings in their own right," and when we take account of the dependence of modern life on the destruction of fossil fuels as energy?

For scholars of religion, Indigenous perspectives on natural resource extraction illuminate ontological and epistemological dimensions of relationality and interdependence between human and other-than-human beings in ways that powerfully problematize the Eurocentric foundations of the discipline.

About the author

Richard J. Callahan Jr. is an assistant professor in religious studies at Gonzaga University. He is the author of *Work and Faith in the Kentucky Coal Fields: Subject to Dust*; editor of *New Territories, New Perspectives: The Religious Impact of the Louisiana Purchase*; and coeditor of *The Bloomsbury Reader in the Study of Religion and Popular Culture*. His work is particularly interested in the intersections and coconstitutions of religion, labor, and natural resource extraction.

Suggestions for further reading

In this book
See also chapters 51 (Was the #NoDAPL occupation at Standing Rock "spiritual" or "religious"?) and 48 (Are Indigenous peoples inherently environmentalists?).

Elsewhere
Erdrich, Louise. "Not Just Another Pipeline." *New York Times*, December 28, 2020. https://www.nytimes.com/2020/12/28/opinion/minnesota-line-3 -enbridge-pipeline.html.

Estes, Nick, and Jaskiran Dhillon, eds. *Standing with Standing Rock: Voices from the #NoDAPL Movement*. Minneapolis: University of Minnesota Press, 2019.

Frankel, Todd C., and Peter Whoriskey. "Tossed Aside in the 'White Gold' Rush: Indigenous People Are Left Poor as Tech World Takes Lithium from under Their Feet." *Washington Post*, December 19, 2016. https://www .washingtonpost.com/graphics/business/batteries/tossed-aside-in-the -lithium-rush/.

Native News Online Staff. "Apache Stronghold Files Lawsuit in Federal Court to Stop Oak Flat Transfer." *Native News Online*, January 13, 2021. https://nativenewsonline.net/sovereignty/apache-stronghold-files-lawsuit -in-federal-court-to-stop-oak-flat-transfer.

Todd, Zoe. "Fish, Kin and Hope: Tending to Water Violations in Amiskwaciwâskahikan and Treaty Six Territory." *Afterall: A Journal of Art, Context and Inquiry* 43(1) (2017): 102–107.

51

Was the #NoDAPL occupation at Standing Rock "spiritual" or "religious"?

Richard J. Callahan Jr.

When thousands of people gathered on the Standing Rock Reservation to oppose the development of the Dakota Access Pipeline between the spring of 2016 and early 2017, many news outlets reported the event as an environmental or political protest. Some outlets, however, framed it a little bit differently. "The 'Spiritual Battle' over the Dakota Access Pipeline," read a headline for a story by Emily McFarlane Miller from the *Religion News Service* in September 2016. In November, Dr. Rosalyn LaPier, a professor of environmental studies and member of the Blackfeet Tribe, published a piece in the online journal the *Conversation* titled "Why Understanding Native American Religion Is Important for Resolving the Dakota Access Pipeline Crisis." According to the authors of these articles, and the Lakota and other Indigenous people quoted in them, the occupation may have had environmental and political urgency, but it was also spiritual or religious. How was it spiritual or religious? There are several factors to consider in answering that question.

First, opposition to the pipeline was grounded in concern that any leaks would pollute the Missouri River with oil. The river is the primary source of drinking water for the Standing Rock Reservation. But more than that, as the slogan that came to represent the struggle reflects, for Lakota people (and many others), *"Mní wičhóni,"* or "water is life." This phrase represents the idea that there is no life without water. Water is, literally, required for life. And it has a life of its own. It is, therefore, for Lakota people, sacred. The people live in relation with water, as they do with the land and the human and other-than-human beings that inhabit the land. One might say that "religion" or "spirituality" (concepts derived from European Christian origins) mean, in part, for Lakota people, maintaining proper relations. Ceremony enacts the reciprocity of these relations. So protecting the water was a spiritual activity.

Second, beyond water, pipeline construction threatened sacred land, which also included burial sites. Opposition to the project included the strong sense not only that graves were being destroyed and land itself being brutally torn apart but that this disregard for Native sovereignty and ontology was a continuation of a long legacy of colonial erasure and devastation. To fight back was spiritually important not only in terms of protecting and preserving relations to land and other-than-human beings in this place but also in terms of resisting the erasure of a way of being, asserting life and existence in the face of destruction.

Third, the language of spirituality and sacrality was evident throughout the event. Participants insisted that they were "water protectors," not "protesters." Individuals and groups performed ceremonial activities regularly in the encampments. When speaking to the press, some individuals explained their opposition to the pipeline in language that explicitly described their actions in terms of spirituality and religious value. As religion scholars Greg Johnson and Siv Ellen Kraft note, by November, the language of "prayer" and "ceremony" was ubiquitous: reminders to "be in ceremony," "act in ceremony," "wear ceremony" were commonly heard in the camps and in public statements. The water protectors claimed to be acting "in prayer" and "prayerfully." This language was disseminated, too, in popular music videos by acts such as Nahko Bear, Prolific the Rapper, and Taboo, framing the occupation for a wider audience as a religious event. Johnson and Kraft explore how this language of ceremony, spirituality, and prayer also acted to bridge the local and the global, as Indigenous peoples from across the Americas, and even across the world, joined the occupation and enacted a global Indigenous identity that asserted a shared perspective on both opposition to colonial disenfranchisement and the sacredness of water and earth.

Fourth, as the religious significance of the #NoDAPL movement extended beyond Standing Rock and the Lakota people to global Indigenous communities, it resonated with non-Indigenous religious communities as well. Christian, Muslim, Jewish, and other religious groups visited Standing Rock to pray, march, and resist in solidarity, also defending the assertion that "water is life." Each of these communities likely had different reasons for the religious and spiritual significance of their actions and the occupation, but together, the overwhelming result was a sense of the sacredness of water and an opposition to pipeline construction in this place.

A closing thought: While many Indigenous people considered the opposition to the Dakota Access Pipeline (and other similar projects) to have sacred, spiritual, and religious significance, non-Natives should be careful not to carelessly attribute spirituality to Indigenous peoples without knowledge about why something might be considered spiritual within a particular tribal context. Too often, non-Indigenous people have attributed spiritual authenticity or power to Indigenous peoples in a romantic manner that has little to do with Indigenous cultures. And it is important to acknowledge that Native communities, like any community, are diverse and that everybody may not share the same interpretation of events. It is best to listen to a variety of voices and perspectives to determine how *they* understand what they are doing.

About the author

Richard J. Callahan Jr. is an assistant professor in religious studies at Gonzaga University. He is the author of *Work and Faith in the Kentucky Coal Fields: Subject to Dust*; editor of *New Territories, New Perspectives: The Religious Impact of the Louisiana Purchase*; and coeditor of *The Bloomsbury Reader in the Study of Religion and Popular Culture*. His work is particularly interested in the intersections and coconstitutions of religion, labor, and natural resource extraction.

Suggestions for further reading

In this book
See also chapters 53 (Why is the public expression of Indigenous religion political?) and 42 (What is the relationship between Indigenous religion and land or territory?).

Elsewhere
Elbein, Saul. "The Youth Group That Launched a Movement at Standing Rock." *New York Times*, January 31, 2017. https://www.nytimes.com/2017/01/31/magazine/the-youth-group-that-launched-a-movement-at-standing-rock.html.

Estes, Nick. *Our History Is the Future: Standing Rock versus the Dakota Access Pipeline, and the Long Tradition of Indigenous Resistance*. New York: Verso, 2019.

Johnson, Greg, and Siv Ellen Kraft. "Standing Rock Religion(s): Ceremonies, Social Media, and Music Videos." *Numen* 65 (2018): 499–530.

LaPier, Rosalyn. "Why Understanding Native American Religion Is Important for Resolving the Dakota Access Pipeline Crisis." *Conversation,*

November 2, 2016. https://theconversation.com/why-understanding-native
-american-religion-is-important-for-resolving-the-dakota-access-pipeline
-crisis-68032.

McFarlan Miller, Emily. "The 'Spiritual Battle' over the Dakota Access
Pipeline." Religion News Service, September 16, 2016. https://religionnews
.com/2016/09/16/the-splainer-the-spiritual-battle-over-the-dakota
-access-pipeline/.

52

Do Hawaiian religious practices have any political significance?

Marie Alohalani Brown

Politics, in its most basic sense, refers to the ways that we engage with one another in small and large communities to organize ourselves. A critical element of politics is power relations: the degree to which an individual or group has the power to influence or control others. If we consider Hawaiian religious practices through the lens of power relations, their nuanced political significance is evident.

From a Hawaiian religious-cultural-political perspective, power relations include relationships between humans and the more-than-human entities termed "akua" that compose the island world. Such entities embody elements (e.g., earth, water, air, fire) and natural phenomena: meteorological-atmospheric (e.g., rain, thunder, lightning, wind, rainbows, clouds), geological (e.g., volcanic activity, earthquake, mountain, rocks), hydrologic-oceanographic (e.g., rivers, oceans, waves, currents, tides, tsunamis), and flora and fauna. In short, akua are nature deities, and as such, their power far eclipses that of humans. Humans cannot control natural phenomena such as storms, earthquakes, lava flows, and tsunamis—they can only survive them. Prayer and ritual are ways to navigate akua-human power relations.

Mana underpins Hawaiian religious traditions. Significantly, the Hawaiian word for that which in English is termed "religion" is "Hoʻomana"—Hoʻo + mana. "Hoʻo" means to cause something to happen. Thus, the Hawaiian understanding of "religion" is to cause, create, or increase mana. Mana is essentially a power that has a "divine" (other than or beyond the human) origin. That said, "power" fails to fully capture the nuances of this complex concept. For example, mana can also be understood as an entity in its own right, an essence, an energy, an ability, a capacity to effect positive or negative outcomes; it is intangible, yet its manifestations are tangible. Mana can be spiritual, intellectual, or physical; is intrinsic but can be increased or diminished; grants authority; and determines status. Everything in the natural world is imbued with mana.

Through prayers and rituals, Ho'omana practitioners can increase the mana of an akua and their own, petition an akua to intervene, and/ or evoke and direct mana to achieve an intended result. Historically, these desired outcomes include protection, inspiration, guidance, knowledge, and healing. They also include causing harm to another, gaining favor with akua, attaining healthy crops, being successful at fishing, winning a battle, obtaining political power or lessening another's political power, overcoming another's mana, and stopping or redirecting a lava flow.

In Hawaiian history, religion and politics have always been tightly intertwined. Ho'omana, like other religions, is a dynamic system that has evolved over time. At one point, so long ago that its origins are the topic of myths, a new religious system founded on older beliefs but established new practices emerged—the 'Ai Kapu. For countless generations, the *'Ai Kapu* was the core of Hawaiian political-social organization and regulated nearly every aspect of Hawaiian life. This religious-cultural-political-social system was based on the idea of food and food consumption ('ai) as sacred (kapu) and therefore in need of regulation. 'Ai is sacred because most, if not all, of the flora and fauna our ancestors ate are forms of akua—a belief that pre- dates the 'Ai Kapu. Although the 'Ai Kapu was officially officially abolished in 1819, Ho'omana practitioners continue to honor certain elements of that system, including the belief that certain flora and fauna are akua forms.

The political significance of Hawaiian religious practices continues today in other ways. Despite efforts to Christianize Hawaiians and shame them for practicing their traditional religion, Ho'omana is experiencing a revival. As more practitioners incorporate Ho'omana practices to protect the sacred, these practitioner-activists increase the visibility of Ho'omana. Notably, from July 2019 to March 2020, to protect Mauna Kea (a sacred mountain) from further desecration by preventing the construction of the Thirty Meter Telescope (TMT), anywhere from twenty to a hundred kia'i (protectors) participated in 'aha (ceremony) three times a day for eight months. The intent of the chants and hula (here, a form of kinetic prayer) performed in these 'aha was to manifest mana to protect Mauna Kea. Because thousands of visitors witnessed or participated in these 'aha, actions that were filmed and made available to the public, there is a growing global awareness about Ho'omana as a living religion. Hawaiians have fought and continue to fight for their right to practice their religious traditions. Efforts to protect the sacred include preventing the desecration of ancestral remains in burial grounds, preserving water sources, and protecting flora and fauna in danger of extinction. These efforts are not only religious-cultural stands but pushback against a political system that devalues Hawaiian religious traditions and what Hawaiians hold sacred.

About the author

Marie Alohalani Brown, a Kanaka ʻŌiwi (Hawaiian), is an associate professor in the Department of Religion at the University of Hawaiʻi–Mānoa and a specialist in Hawaiian religion. Her research is primarily carried out in nineteenth- and twentieth-century Hawaiian-language materials. Her works include *Facing the Spears of Change: The Life and Legacy of John Papa ʻĪʻī*, which won the biennial Palapala Poʻokela Award for the best book on Hawaiian language, culture, and history (2016, 2017); *The Penguin Book of Mermaids* (2019), for which she is coeditor along with Cristina Bacchilega; and *Ka Poʻe Moʻo Akua: Hawaiian Reptilian Deities* (University of Hawaiʻi Press, 2022).

Suggestions for further reading

In this book
See also chapters 69 (What are ancestor spirits, and what role do they play in Hawaiian religious life?) and 33 (What is animism?).

Elsewhere
Brown, Marie Alohalani. "Mauna Kea: Hoʻomana Hawaiʻi and Protecting the Sacred." In "Indigenous Knowledge, Spiritualities, and Science," edited by Robin M. Wright. Special issue, *Journal for the Study of Religion, Nature, and Culture* 10(2) (August 2016): 155–169.

Brown, Marie Alohalani. "Mourning the Land: Kanikau in Noho Hewa: The Wrongful Occupation of Hawaiʻi." *American Indian Quarterly* 38(3) (Summer 2014): 347–395.

Handy, E. S. Craighill, and Mary Kawena Pukui. *The Polynesian Family System in Ka-ʻu, Hawaiʻi*. Honolulu: Tuttle, 2011.

Hoʻomanawanui, Kuʻualoha. *Voices of Fire: Reweaving the Literary Lei of Pele and Hiʻiaka*. Minneapolis: University of Minnesota Press, 2014.

53

Why is the public expression of Indigenous religion political?

Stacie Swain

There are several key terms at play in this question. Of course, there is the notion of "Indigenous religion," the unifying subject of this book. But what are "public expressions" of an Indigenous religion, and what do we mean by "political"?

When you think of a public expression of an Indigenous religion, you might think of local elders blessing events or colorful dances, drumming, and regalia. Alternatively, you might think of more controversial flash-point events from the news cycle, such as when Indigenous peoples erect camps in the path of oil and gas projects, blockade bridges and roads, or occupy parks and other sites. These latter activities often contain elements that appear to be religious or spiritual: they are ceremonial in nature, sacred fires are kept burning, prayers and songs are common, and slogans like "Water Is Life" and "Defend the Sacred" adorn clothing and banners. Here, it can appear as though Indigenous peoples are publicly expressing their religion or making religious claims in order to politicize a particular item, issue, or place.

This interpretation suggests one way in which public expressions of Indigenous religion can be understood as political: like other religions, Indigenous religion properly belongs to the private sphere; however, like other religions, it can sometimes enter the public sphere and be made political through the actions of its adherents. Upon entry into the public sphere, Indigenous religious claims can serve as a way to contest dominant norms, economic processes, or political regimes and thus be understood as a form of resistance.

Do Indigenous peoples' actions and claims, however, always constitute a *reaction* to the colonial state or society? Or are Indigenous peoples *continuing* activities from within their own political traditions and adapting them to modern contexts, despite the ongoing occupation of their lands?

The answer to this question depends on whether we understand the colonial state form to be the sole locus of politics or whether we recognize that Indigenous peoples have their own political systems that have survived attempted genocide, displacement, and assimilation.

Indigenous peoples compose diverse nations that range in size and form. Prior to and since the onset of colonization, these nations have governed themselves according to their own principles, values, and relationships to territory. Indigenous peoples also have laws and procedures for how they relate to one another and build alliances between nations. These alliances may include diplomatic relationships with individuals and groups that post-Enlightenment ways of knowing do not typically understand as social beings or political communities—the earth itself, animals, water creatures, plants, mountains, and other parts of the environment. While these relationships and the procedures that maintain them differ from nation to nation, they can be understood as political responsibilities that have developed through long-term observation and interactions with the environment. Knowledge of these responsibilities and how to uphold them are passed down through names, songs, stories, landmarks, and ceremonies; failing to uphold these collectively held responsibilities to care for the land and other-than-human beings can have material, not solely spiritual, impacts upon both place and people.

Both imperialism and colonialism have shaped a modern notion of politics that does not account for this interpretation of Indigenous politics. Once imperial states established access to Indigenous lands, they governed from distant cities or undertook colonization by occupying territory and establishing local institutions, which were modeled on their own political systems. Within the so-called New World, an understanding of politics based on these systems took shape and became solidified over time. The idea of the public sphere also originates within the imperial and colonial notion of politics. The modern state system arose from a context of Christian sectarian conflict, with the result that religion was split from political institutions and relegated to the private sphere. Now state institutions govern the public sphere on behalf of their citizens, who make up the public and whose religions are meant to be interiorized belief systems modeled upon Protestantism and subordinated to the state—not collectively held political responsibilities that refuse to be domesticated. Contemporary liberal democratic regimes rest upon distinctions between religion/politics and public/private in addition to the conviction that the state form is the only type of political system that exists or is possible.

What appears to be "public expressions of Indigenous religion" can lead us to question the distinction between religion and politics. If we take imperialism and colonialism into account, they can also lead us to question the state's monopoly on how these concepts themselves are defined and normalized. If such expressions are understood as dimensions of Indigenous nationhood, they invite us to consider different possibilities for what politics—as well as political constructs like citizenship and the public sphere—can look like.

About the author

Stacie Swain is a Ukrainian-British doctoral student in the Department of Political Science and the Indigenous Nationhood Program at the University of Victoria in ləkʷəŋən territories (Victoria, BC). Her research considers Indigenous ceremony and the categories of religion and politics, particularly in relation to settler colonialism, Indigenous legal orders, and the governance of public space.

Suggestions for further reading

In this book
See also chapters 55 (Is Indigenous law religious?) and 49 (What is the Idle No More movement, and what's a round dance?).

Elsewhere
Cadena, Marisol de la. "Indigenous Cosmopolitics in the Andes: Conceptual Reflections beyond 'Politics.'" *Cultural Anthropology* 25(2) (2010): 334–370. https://doi.org/10.1111/j.1548-1360.2010.01061.x.

Magnusson, Warren. "Decentering the State, or Looking for Politics." In *Organizing Dissent: Contemporary Social Movements in Theory and Practice: Studies in the Politics of Counter-hegemony*, edited by William K. Carroll, 69–80. Toronto: Garamond, 1992.

Martin, Craig. *Masking Hegemony: A Genealogy of Liberalism, Religion, and the Private Sphere*. Religion in Culture. London: Equinox, 2010.

Nelson, Melissa K. "Wrestling with Fire: Indigenous Women's Resistance and Resurgence." *American Indian Culture and Research Journal* 43(3) (2019): 69–84.

Simpson, Leanne. "Looking after Gdoo-Naaganinaa: Precolonial Nishnaabeg Diplomatic and Treaty Relationships." *Wicazo Sa Review* 23(2) (2008): 29–42. https://doi.org/10.1353/wic.0.0001.

54
Why were Native American religious traditions outlawed?

Jennifer Graber

While Euro-Americans had long suppressed Native religious traditions through intimidation and violence, US officials criminalized them with the 1883 Code of Indian Offenses. Prohibited acts included marriage customs, ceremonial dances, healing practices, and mourning rites. Violations were adjudicated in newly established courts on reservations. Punishments ranged from fines to imprisonment. Lasting until 1934, the code may surprise present-day readers, as it obviously violates the First Amendment guarantee of free religious exercise. Officials circumvented constitutional protections in two ways. First, they conceived of the government's relationship with Native people as a guardian to a ward. They likened the code to wise parents guiding wayward children. Second, officials did not regard Native rituals as religion. Instead, they saw them as "heathenish" cultural obstacles to Native people's assimilation. Further, challenges to the code on First Amendment grounds would likely have been unsuccessful. In an 1879 case about Latter-day Saint plural marriage, the Supreme Court had ruled that Congress could not mandate religious *belief*, but it could outlaw religious *practices* deemed unlawful.

The code coincided with two other efforts to undermine Native cultures. The first, land allotment, broke up communally held reservation lands by assigning individual plots to Native men and making the "surplus" available to non-Native people. Allotment resulted in extensive land loss and weakened tribal political structures. Second, officials established off-reservation boarding schools that separated Native children from their families. In this way, the code operated as part of a larger campaign to dismantle Native ways of life.

While courts were not required to keep records, other sources suggest how the code was implemented. For instance, reservation officials often struggled to find Native men willing to serve the courts. Some never managed to form them at all. Records also show that courts did not adjudicate "offenses" uniformly. They inordinately punished Native forms of long-term partnership in an effort to enforce Victorian marriage norms. On the other hand, courts rarely prosecuted ceremonial dance participants, at least in the early years. Some Native nations still held Sun Dances attended by thousands, making the prosecution of individual practitioners nearly impossible. That doesn't mean large-scale rituals evaded suppression. Rather, reservation agents typically employed soldiers to suppress dances. We have a few records of mourners appearing before the courts, despite the ongoing practice of giveaways and property destruction. At least one Lakota man was imprisoned for working as a "medicine man," but we have no evidence of other such cases. Clearly, courts varied across Indian country. Even so, the code functioned as part of a broader program of cultural suppression that had devastating effects.

Native people responded to the code in a number of ways. Sometimes they practiced in secret, such as mourning customs observed under the cover of night. They adapted other traditions by associating them with Christian rites and symbols, allowing them to "hide in plain sight." In some cases, such as the Kiowas "putting away" their Sun Dance, they discontinued criminalized practices. Native people also challenged the code. Umatillas argued that punishments for offenses such as adultery were illegal, as non-Native citizens faced no similar sanctions. They also disputed the courts' legitimacy, as they were not created by Congress, which has exclusive authority to establish them.

Native people also invoked the First Amendment and the category of religion. For instance, Pueblos responded to dance restrictions by asserting their religious nature. They succeeded in securing protection for ceremonial dancing. Practitioners of ritual peyote ingestion challenged punishments connected to the code's sanction for intoxication. They claimed peyote functioned as a "sacrament" and established the Native American Church (NAC) to protect their ritual practice.

Efforts by Native people and their allies eventually led to the code's demise. Some advocates came from the Society of American Indians, a Native rights group founded in 1915. One member, Charles Eastman (Dakota Sioux), sought to educate the public about Native ritual life. "We also have a religion which was given to our forefathers," he wrote in a popular book. It "has been handed down to us, their children." In 1923, non-Native reformers founded the American Indian Defense Association (AIDA) in response to dance restrictions. AIDA members then collaborated with Native leaders to study reservation conditions. Their findings, including the 1928 Meriam Report, criticized federal officials for undermining Native cultures. These efforts prompted new perspectives on Native ritual practices. As a result, federal officials published a 1934 circular on "Indian Religious Freedom and Indian Culture," which not only ended the code and courts but also forbade "interference with Indian religious life or ceremonial expression."

About the author

Jennifer Graber is Shive, Lindsay, and Gray Professor in the History of Christianity and associate director of the Native American and Indigenous Studies Program at the University of Texas in Austin. Her first book, *The Furnace of Affliction: Prisons and Religion in Antebellum America*, explores the intersection of church and state during the founding of the nation's first prisons. Her latest book, *The Gods of Indian Country: Religion and the Struggle for the American West*, considers religious transformations among Kiowa Indians and Anglo Americans during their conflict over Indian territory, or what is now known as Oklahoma.

Suggestions for further reading

In this book
See also chapters 40 (What is decolonization, and what does it have to do with Indigenous religious traditions?) and 58 (Is peyote a medicine or a drug?).

Elsewhere
Deloria, Vine, Jr., and Clifford M. Lytle. *American Indians, American Justice*. Austin: University of Texas Press, 1983.

McNally, Michael D. *Defend the Sacred: Native American Religious Freedom beyond the First Amendment*. Princeton, NJ: Princeton University Press, 2020.

Wenger, Tisa. "Indian Dances and the Politics of Religious Freedom, 1870–1930." *Journal of the American Academy of Religion* 79(4) (December 1, 2011): 850–878.

Wilkins, David E. *American Indian Sovereignty and the U.S. Supreme Court: The Masking of Justice*. Austin: University of Texas Press, 1997.

55

Is Indigenous law religious?

Dana Lloyd

When we talk about Indigenous peoples, law, and religion, we may refer to any of the following: federal Indian law, tribal law, or international law. We may think about documents such as treaties between the US government and a specific tribal nation or the UN Declaration on the Rights of Indigenous Peoples. Some of these include references to religious traditions or practices, but Indigenous scholars and legal practitioners clarify that for many of their communities, there is no distinction between law, creation stories, and ceremony.

Does this make Indigenous law religious? If so, is it religious in the same way as Jewish *Halacha* or Islamic *Sharia*? And what is its status as law? Should the state recognize Indigenous legal systems as legitimate competitors of the state's official (secular) legal system? These questions have different answers in different contexts. In the United States, where I live and work, the federal government recognizes some Indigenous/tribal legal systems as valid, depending on tribal organization and on the state in which the tribal nation resides. In states such as California, tribes have jurisdiction over their people in legal cases related to adoption, for example. In these cases, tribal courts' ruling can be based on religious values, and the state or federal government will not intervene. Other Indigenous nations do not recognize the federal government's authority over their people; for example, the Haudenosaunee have their own passports, and they govern their communities according to the Great Law of Peace, which is their oral constitution, seen by some religious studies scholars as a religious system.

OK, so are these legal systems religious? To answer this question, we need to unfold the relationship between religion, cosmology, tradition, and culture. Religious studies scholars have understood religion broadly to include beliefs, practices, and material culture. All of these things construct our identities as both individuals and groups (national, ethnic, racial, religious). And so practicing Indigenous law that is based on so-called religious values is tightly related to identity and to survival. If

Indigenous groups do not adhere to their traditional values, in law and in other spheres of life, they are in danger of losing their distinct identities. At the same time, it is important to acknowledge that introducing traditional values into tribal legal systems is complicated because the state wants these legal systems to resemble Anglo-American legal systems as much as possible, and it conditions recognition and funding on such structural resemblance. It is also important to note that incorporating traditional values into tribal law would never lead to full restoration of precontact societies—it would, however, create new forms of tribal lives and help in healing tribal communities from centuries of trauma.

Indigenous law is rich. It includes stories and dreams, and it asks to shape relationships among human beings and between humans and the nonhuman environment. This means that Indigenous law is based on creation stories; it governs relationships with sacred lands and waters as well as with the Creator; and it includes not only what we see in American courtroom TV drama (two lawyers interrogating witnesses in front of a judge wearing a robe and twelve jurors) but also things that are oftentimes classified as ritual, such as burning tobacco.

Therefore, for Indigenous peoples, law and religion are not two separate things. This might mean that the category of "religion" or "religious" does not fit to describe Indigenous communities at all. However, Indigenous law is labeled "religious" by settlers. They do this in order to distinguish Indigenous ("religious") law from the (secular) law settlers themselves practice. As a result, Indigenous law is also portrayed as a "primitive" form of law, and this portrayal has served to promote oppressive, even genocidal policies against Native nations in the United States and elsewhere. On the other hand, because of the free exercise of religion that the US Bill of Rights guarantees, portraying Indigenous law as religious practice potentially allows Indigenous communities to exercise jurisdiction over their people and territory in the name of religious freedom.

And so, the answer to the question posed in the title of this chapter— "Is Indigenous law religious?"—changes based on circumstances and on whom you ask.

About the author

Dana Lloyd is assistant professor of global interdisciplinary studies at Villanova University. She holds a PhD in religion from Syracuse University and LLB and LLM degrees from Tel Aviv Law School. Her book manuscript *Arguing for This Land: Rethinking Indigenous Sacred Sites* is under contract with the University Press of Kansas.

Suggestions for further reading

In this book

See also chapters 8 (Why is "religion" a problematic category for understanding Indigenous traditions?) and 51 (Was the #NoDAPL occupation at Standing Rock "spiritual" or "religious"?).

Elsewhere

Borrows, John. *Law's Indigenous Ethics*. Toronto: University of Toronto Press, 2019.

Echo-Hawk, Walter R. *In the Courts of the Conqueror: The Ten Worst Indian Law Cases Ever Decided*. Golden, CO: Fulcrum, 2010.

Makepeace, Anne, dir. *Tribal Justice*. Lakeville, CT: Makepeace Productions, 2017.

Richland, Justin B. *Arguing with Tradition: The Language of Law in Hopi Tribal Court*. Chicago: University of Chicago Press, 2004.

56
Do Indigenous people have churches?

Pamela E. Klassen and Roxanne L. Korpan

Indigenous people on Turtle Island are leaders and members of Christian churches across a wide range of denominations; Indigenous Christians have worshipped, preached, and prophesied for more than four centuries. Some of the most powerful Indigenous advocates and public intellectuals have been Christian clergy or theologians—from Kahkewaquonaby (Peter Jones), the nineteenth-century Ojibwe chief and Methodist minister, to Vine Deloria Jr., the twentieth-century Lakota philosopher and lawyer. At the same time, many Indigenous people are sharply critical of Christianity as an ideological support for colonialism and white supremacy. Two prominent examples are the Catholic Doctrine of Discovery, which has long provided sanction for colonizers to claim Indigenous territory, and Christian-run residential schools, which were a church-state project of genocidal assimilation that often violently separated Indigenous children from their families, land, language, and spirituality.

Christian missionaries were in the vanguard of Spanish, French, and British colonizers, arriving alongside—or often before—fur traders, soldiers, and colonial officials. At almost every turn, quite literally, colonizers depended on Indigenous people to help them survive and find their way in geographical, cultural, and linguistic terrain that was unfamiliar to them. White missionaries relied on Indigenous people to allow them to pass through or remain on their territory, to translate and interpret for them, and eventually to contribute to the construction and sustenance of churches through raising money, taking on roles as clergy and in women's societies, and filling the pews and singing in the choir. Despite this dependence, churches drew racist distinctions between the "white work" and the "Indian work" of their missions.

Many Indigenous Christians understood joining churches not necessarily as a "conversion" to new beliefs but as a way to access spiritual, material, and political resources of settler society. At a time when white settlers and capitalist resource extraction were destroying Indigenous hunting and fishing grounds and colonial governments were forcing Indigenous people to reserves or reservations, churches provided access to learning English literacy and legal representation. Indigenous Christians, for example, often used biblical arguments to write petitions to colonial authorities to reclaim and defend their land.

Despite the assimilationist history and legacy of Christianity, many Indigenous communities are still home to many churches across a variety of denominations. The churches found in Indigenous nations today can be loosely grouped into three categories: fully Indigenous-run churches, such as the Native American Church; historic Christian churches that have acknowledged, up to a point, their role in colonialism and attempted genocide and increasingly support a Christianity shaped by Indigenous spiritual practices; and mission churches that continue to see themselves as having a mission from God to convert Indigenous people from traditional ways, which they view as "heathen." Indigenous people are part of all of these churches, often as clergy and lay leaders. Since at least the early twentieth century, many churches have worked with a policy of "indigenization," which sought to build up Indigenous Christian leadership and reshape Christianity through adapting, instead of expunging, specific Indigenous rituals and spiritual practices. For example, the Immaculate Conception Church on M'Chigeeng First Nation (Manitoulin Island) was built in 1972 as a round building with a conical roof resembling a tipi and includes paintings of the stations of the cross by Anishinaabe artist Leland Bell and inspired by the Ojibwe Three Fires Midewiwin society and artists of the Woodland School.

Today, the denominational divisions among varieties of Christianity can lead to intense conflict within specific Indigenous nations, both among Christians and with those who are not Christian. While some Indigenous Christians still want to "cast out" Indigenous spiritual practices and organizations as supposedly heathen, other Indigenous people have understood Christianity as a resource for supporting Indigenous sovereignty and well-being. Elders and clergy in many communities provide leadership rooted in a combination of Christian theology and sacrament and Indigenous knowledge and practice. For example, Indigenous Anglicans have redrawn the maps of their church to acknowledge Indigenous jurisdiction; the Right Reverend Lydia Mamakwa became the first bishop of the Indigenous Spiritual Ministry of Mishamikoweesh, a fully Indigenous diocese. The unceasing demand for the pope to apologize for the role of the Roman Catholic Church in the Canadian residential school system shows that Indigenous people continue to hold churches accountable for their role in the violence and dispossession of settler colonialism. At the same time, many Indigenous people still participate in churches as congregants and critics, preachers and prophets.

About the authors

Pamela E. Klassen is a professor in the Department for the Study of Religion at the University of Toronto. She is the author of *The Story of Radio Mind: A Missionary's Journey on Indigenous Land* (University of Chicago Press, 2018) and the cocreator of Kiinawin Kawindomowin Story Nations (www.storynations.utoronto.ca). She is a settler scholar whose research focuses on religion, public memory, and Indigenous-settler relations, with specific attention to treaties and questions of land and jurisdiction.

Roxanne L. Korpan is a settler scholar and doctoral candidate in the Department for the Study of Religion at the University of Toronto whose research focuses on intersections of Christianity, colonialism, media, and Indigenous sovereignty in nineteenth-century Canada. Her dissertation analyzes the Anishinaabemowin bible translations of Kahkewaquonaby (Peter Jones), a Methodist minister and chief of the Mississaugas of the Credit. She is the author of the article "Scriptural Relations: Colonial Formations of Anishinaabemowin Bibles in Nineteenth-Century Canada," *Material Religion* 17(2) (2021): 147–176.

Suggestions for further reading

In this book
See also chapters 57 (What is the Native American Church?) and 63 (Why is distinguishing a Native American world view from a eurochristian one important?).

Elsewhere
Bradford, Tolly, and Chelsea Horton, eds. *Mixed Blessings: Indigenous Encounters with Christianity in Canada.* Vancouver: University of British Columbia Press, 2016.

Graber, Jennifer. *The Gods of Indian Country: Religion and the Struggle for the American West.* Oxford: Oxford University Press, 2018.

Hare, Jan, and Jean Barman. *Good Intentions Gone Awry: Emma Crosby and the Methodist Mission on the Northwest Coast.* Vancouver: University of British Columbia Press, 2006.

Robertson, Leslie, with the Kwaguł Gixsam Clan. *Standing Up with Ga'axsta'las: Jane Constance Cook and the Politics of Memory, Church, and Custom.* Vancouver: University of British Columbia Press, 2012.

Wheeler, Winona. "The Journals and Voices of a Church of England Catechist: Askenotoow (Charles Pratt), 1851–1884." In *Reading beyond Words: Contexts for Native History* (2nd edition), edited by Jennifer H. Brown and Elizabeth Vibert, 237–261. Peterborough, ON: Broadview, 2003.

57
What is the Native American Church?

Lisa Poirier

The Native American Church is a religious organization that was first officially incorporated in Oklahoma in 1918. The church's charter documents were drafted in response to the US federal government's opposition to the spread of the medicinal and religious use of the buttons of the peyote cactus (*Lophophora williamsii*) by Native peoples who had been forcibly relocated to Oklahoma. Seeking protection for their ceremonial use of this sacred plant, they formed the Native American Church.

Long before the official establishment of the Native American Church, Indigenous peoples of North America had used the buttons of the peyote cactus in the performance of their traditional rituals. In the 1500s, a Spanish missionary described it as being used by Aztecs to achieve visions. The Wixáritari (also known as Huichol) of Central Mexico still make an annual pilgrimage to Wirikuta, the sacred place in San Luis Potosi where the peyote cactus grows, to harvest buttons. These buttons are ingested during the performance of rituals that keep the Wixáritari in relationship with their sacred powers.

The habitat of the peyote cactus extends north of San Luis Potosi, all the way to the Rio Grande region of Texas, and is most concentrated in the Chihuahuan Desert between the United States and Mexico. The Lipan Apache of this area knew the sacred power of the peyote. After almost two hundred years of resistance to Spanish, Mexican, and US settler-colonial incursion, the US government forcibly removed the Apache to Oklahoma Territory, alongside the Kiowa and Comanche. These involuntary relocations were traumatic for every Native group. Removal meant alienation from the sustaining relationships they had cultivated with the flora and fauna of their traditional lands and with the sacred powers with whom they shared those lands. Moreover, missionaries and government agents in

Oklahoma Territory were pressuring Native people to convert to Christianity but were met with resistance to joining white churches.

The Apache shared the knowledge of the power of the peyote cactus with their new neighbors in southeastern Oklahoma, and the peyote's power to bring visions and to heal made it quite popular, both as a way to reconnect with sacred power and as a medicine to heal spiritual and physical, individual and collective trauma.

Quanah Parker, a Comanche chief famous for his strategic leadership during these stressful times, became one of peyote's most vocal proponents. He gave testimony about its transformative healing power and was instrumental in its spread. Another important advocate for the religious use of peyote was James Mooney, an American anthropologist. Just as the US Congress was moving to outlaw peyote, Mooney encouraged the Native peoples of Oklahoma to create an official church to protect their peyote-related religious practices from government persecution.

In 1918, at a meeting in El Reno, Oklahoma, the Native American Church was legally incorporated. At this meeting, leaders from many Native nations gave testimony about the positive effects of peyote. Their stories focused on the healing power of the peyote, which helped sick people recover from their illnesses, including alcoholism. Thus, the creation of a Christian church protected peyote religion from governmental forces bent on its suppression.

Since its inception, the Native American Church has been supratribal; many Native nations have chapters. In worship meetings, water drums and gourd rattles accompany healing songs sung in turn by church members. Learning traditional songs and eventually sharing one's own song is a part of participation in the central ritual of the church. The singing, the drumming, and the ingestion of the sacred peyote connect practitioners with sacred power. The peyote brings visions, and while these visions are personal to each individual, participation in the church requires responsibility to the community.

After preparatory fasting, all-night worship meetings are led by the Roadman of that church. Roadmen are highly respected in their communities and are experienced with the sacred power of peyote. At the beginning of a meeting, the Roadman will invoke the Four Directions. He may also blow an eagle-bone whistle, making the call of the Water Bird, which is thought of as a messenger carrying the prayers of the worshippers. There are special roles for women as well. The Water Woman of each church, usually a close relative of the Roadman, brings water at midnight and again in the morning to refresh the people. Her prayer gives counsel to the church members and signals the end of the ceremony. In the morning, a group of women joins the Water Woman in bringing the three sacred foods (corn, meat, and berries) to help everyone break their fast.

From its inception, the Native American Church has had strong Christian influences, and most practitioners identify as Christians. Its distinctiveness from other Christian churches is peyote, which church members identify as the special sacrament that God created for the exclusive use of Native people. Today, the Native American Church of North America has chapters in over seventy Indigenous nations in the United States and Canada. It is the largest Native American religious group, with over a quarter million members.

About the author

Lisa Poirier is an associate professor in the Department of Religious Studies at DePaul University in Chicago. She lives and works on the traditional lands of the Council of the Three Fires—the Ojibwe, Odawa, and Potawatomi Nations. At DePaul, she teaches classes about Native American religions, theory and method in the study of religion, new religious movements, and gender and sexuality in religion.

Suggestions for further reading

In this book
See also chapters 25 (Are Indigenous people who adapt or alter their rituals and traditions [either by choice or by historical necessity] less authentic than their ancestors?) and 56 (Do Indigenous people have churches?).

Elsewhere
Bouayad, Aurelien. "The Cactus and the Anthropologist: The Evolution of Cultural Expertise on the Entheogenic Use of Peyote in the United States." *Laws* 8(2) (2019): 1–22. https://doi.org/10.3390/laws8020012.

Maroukis, Thomas Constantine. *The Peyote Road: Religious Freedom and the Native American Church.* Norman: University of Oklahoma Press, 2012.

Smith, Huston, and Reuben Snake, eds. *One Nation under God: The Triumph of the Native American Church.* Santa Fe, NM: Clear Light, 1996.

Swan, Daniel C. *Peyote Religious Art: Symbols of Faith and Belief.* Jackson: University Press of Mississippi, 1999.

58

Is peyote a medicine or a drug?

Jennifer Graber

Sixteenth-century Nahuatl speakers in Mesoamerica used the word *peyotl* to describe several medicinal plants, including a small cactus they harvested, dried, and ingested to treat illness, find lost items, and seek visions. Since then, Indigenous peoples throughout North America have used this cactus for physical healing and consumed it in ritual settings. Their oral traditions tell of powerful beings who gifted them with peyote in times of need. Their peyote rites operate within wider ritual systems that work to ensure their people's health and flourishing.

Euro-American missionaries to Native peoples often misidentified peyote, confusing it with an unrelated plant called mescal. They objected to ritual peyote use, or "mescal beans," considering it an obstacle to Christianization and "civilization." They spearheaded efforts to punish and later criminalize it. In the early twentieth-century United States, Native practitioners responded by seeking First Amendment protection for the religious "sacrament" of peyote ingestion. They organized a body called the Native American Church (NAC) and secured accommodations for the practice in many states.

While NAC members claim a variety of perspectives, most view peyote as both a plant medicine and a nonhuman person. They typically address the cactus as "Father Peyote." In contrast, Western scientists have focused on peyote's psychoactive alkaloids, particularly mescaline. Early investigators described the "kaleidoscopic play of colors" brought on by peyote-induced "hallucinations." At midcentury, artists such as Aldous Huxley advocated mescaline-fueled enlightenment, even as they associated peyote's origins with Mexican Indians' "primitive religion." In the 1970s, US officials commenced a "war on drugs," designating peyote a Schedule 1 controlled substance along with heroin and LSD. Peyote consumption continues to be criminalized to various degrees across North America.

Clearly, what we call the peyote cactus has great significance. Because concern about illegal drugs looms large, Native peoples' relation to peyote as both healing plant and revered nonhuman person is often understood in those terms. But considering peyote's place within Indigenous religious systems allows for a dramatically different understanding. For instance, Native people engage in peyote rites in group settings under the direction of experienced leaders. Gatherings involve a variety of ritual acts, such as singing, praying, drumming, burning cedar, petitioning, and partaking in food and drink. Practitioners have developed an extensive material culture for the ritual itself, including sensors and rattles, as well as elaborate symbolism seen in Kiowa silverwork and depictions of visions in Huichol yarn paintings. Some Indigenous groups make pilgrimage to peyote gardens, trekking over three hundred miles to harvest the cactus. Still others have combined peyote rites with Christian forms, including altars that feature the cactus beside a Bible or a Mexican chapel named El Santo de Jesús Peyotes. As one scholar of the Lakota has observed, the physiological effects of ingesting peyote are only one aspect of a "total religious setting."

Over time, state authorities have recognized ritual peyote ingestion as something other than drug use. After a 1990 Supreme Court decision left practitioners vulnerable to prosecution, the US Congress acted in 1994 to ensure the protection of peyote's ceremonial ingestion. Canada, also, allows exemptions from drug laws for some Indigenous peoples.

This legal wrangling, even when Native peyotists are accommodated, raises questions about religion and race. Like many free exercise accommodations, the law stipulates that peyote ingestion stem from "sincere" religious belief. But as scholars have asked, how does one demonstrate or prove sincerity? Accommodations also raise questions about the nature of Native "religion." For instance, the previously mentioned 1994 amendment protects peyote rites as part of "traditional Indian religion." But who decides what is traditional? For example, when peyote practitioners founded the Native American Church of Navajoland, some elders objected. They viewed peyote rites, which had been established in the last half century, to fall outside Navajo "traditions" that dated back centuries, if not millennia. Another issue is state laws that allow peyote exemptions only for those who can prove they have at least 25 percent Native blood. Some practitioners, especially those married to non-Natives, have challenged these laws, arguing that religious freedom protections should not hinge on race or ethnicity.

So is peyote a medicine or a drug? First and foremost, peyote is a plant. Depending on the observer's position, it might also be a vehicle for hallucinatory experience, a medicine for the ailing body, an addictive drug, an object of religious devotion, or a powerful nonhuman person who heals and guides practitioners. And for some, it might be more than one of those things.

About the author

Jennifer Graber is Shive, Lindsay, and Gray Professor in the History of Christianity and associate director of the Native American and Indigenous Studies Program at the University of Texas in Austin. Her first book, *The Furnace of Affliction: Prisons and Religion in Antebellum America*, explores the intersection of church and state during the founding of the nation's first prisons. Her latest book, *The Gods of Indian Country: Religion and the Struggle for the American West*, considers religious transformations among Kiowa Indians and Anglo Americans during their conflict over Indian territory, or what is now known as Oklahoma.

Suggestions for further reading

In this book
See also chapters 57 (What is the Native American Church?) and 61 (What role does healing play in Native American and Indigenous religious traditions?).

Elsewhere
Dawson, Alexander S. *The Peyote Effect: From the Inquisition to the War on Drugs*. Berkeley: University of California Press, 2018.

Maroukis, Thomas Constantine. *The Peyote Road: Religious Freedom and the Native American Church*. Norman: University of Oklahoma Press, 2010.

Schaefer, Stacy B. *Amada's Blessings from the Peyote Gardens of South Texas*. Albuquerque: University of New Mexico Press, 2015.

Schaefer, Stacy B. *People of the Peyote: Huichol Indian History, Religion, and Survival*. Albuquerque: University of New Mexico Press, 1996.

Tone-Pah-Hote, Jenny. "Circulating Silver: Peyote Jewelry and the Making of Region." In *Crafting an Indigenous Nation: Kiowa Expressive Culture in the Progressive Era*, 32–57. Chapel Hill: University of North Carolina Press, 2019.

59

What are Native American foodways, and how are they religious?

Andrea McComb Sanchez

One commonality among the incredible diversity of Native communities is that "religion" is not a separate and discrete aspect of life; instead, interactions with the sacred are interwoven with all parts of life. Important expressions of this interconnectedness are found in foodways, which include farming, hunting, gathering, fishing, and the preparation and eating of food.

A conceptual framework that connects place, narratives, community, ceremony, responsibility, and proper relationships can help us understand how foodways are part of religious traditions. We can begin with place, which includes the land, water, and the ecosystems within both. Each tribe or nation has a particular place that is home, and Native American religious traditions are thought to originate within and/or emerge from those particular places and are part of a people's continuing connection to their ancestral home. As part of the ecosystem of place, the plant and animal beings live *with* humans and also give themselves as food; humans, therefore, are responsible for treating plants, animals, and the land they share fairly.

Knowledge about plants and animals and their relationships with humans, such as past interactions, how to hunt or fish in respectful ways, and how to properly grow and gather can be found within narratives or stories. These narratives are oral and are tied to specific places on the landscape. Many narratives are about or are a part of ceremonies.

These narratives are also connected and unique to each community. Native American religious traditions are local, not universal; they are from and are for each specific community. Community is not restricted to humans. Included within the community are ancestors and other spiritual beings and plant and animal beings, some of which are referred to directly as "relatives." Many of the plants and animals that are considered relatives have been integral to a community's survival—for example, salmon for the Coast Salish and bison for the Lakota. The saguaro cactus is considered a relative of the Tohono O'odham, and its fruit is needed for the ceremony that calls down the clouds and brings the rain that is necessary for farming.

Ceremony is another component of this framework and includes ritual actions and spiritual complexes, but it can also be used to discuss particular ways of being and acting more broadly. Ceremonies are connected to the land in a variety of ways, from ritual materials and implements that are harvested in specific places to the inclusion of plant and animal beings in ritual action and intention. One of the most important ceremonies for the Coast Salish, for example, is the First Salmon Ceremony, which welcomes and honors their relative the salmon. All aspects of foodways—hunting, harvesting, planting, preparation, and the serving and eating of food—can be accompanied by ceremonial activities such as dancing, praying, and singing. Many ceremonies have the preparation and consumption of food at their center. Traditions hold that the community is responsible for maintaining proper relationships with the land, plant and animal beings, ancestors, and spiritual beings, and ceremony is an integral way that this is enacted. People are also responsible for living correctly, which includes holding and participating in ceremonies that lead to the well-being of all things. People get the food they need to survive, and the beings that provide that food thrive. It is meant to be a relationship of balance and reciprocity.

Indigenous food sovereignty movements are the contemporary rec-lamation and revitalization of Native foodways, which were disrupted by colonialism through the loss of land, the intentional attempted destruction of traditions, and the introduction of commodity foods. People involved in Indigenous foods movements assert that traditional foodways help bring back the sacred into communities through the telling of the narratives connected to foodways and through people's participation in ceremonies that are necessary to hunt, fish, gather, and plant correctly and respon-sibly. Those who participate argue that being involved in any aspect of foodways, from the acquisition of the beings that become food to the preparation and the eating of food, connects people directly with their ancestors. Native foods are also understood as medicine, good for the body, mind, and spirit. Engaging in traditional foodways is viewed as central to restoring and maintaining correct relationships with the earth, water, and animal and plant relatives and is considered an important aspect of decolonization. Thus, participating in Native foodways also revitalizes the religious traditions specific to those foodways.

About the author

Andrea McComb Sanchez is an assistant professor of religious studies at the University of Arizona. Her work addresses Native American religious traditions, religion and the environment, religion and colonialism in North America, and religion in the American southwest.

Suggestions for further reading

In this book
See also chapters 42 (What is the relationship between Indigenous religion and land or territory?) and 55 (Is Indigenous law religious?).

Elsewhere
Crawford O'Brien, Suzanne. "Salmon as Sacrament: First Salmon Ceremonies in the Pacific Northwest." In *Religion, Food, and Eating in North America*, edited by Benjamin E. Zeller, Marie W. Dallam, Reid L. Neilson, and Nora L. Rubel, 114–133. New York: Columbia University Press, 2014.

LaPier, Rosalyn. "How Native American Food Is Tied to Important Sacred Stories." *Conversation*, June 15, 2018.

Mihesuah, Devon A., and Elizabeth Hoover, eds. *Indigenous Food Sovereignty in the United States: Restoring Cultural Knowledge, Protecting Environments, and Regaining Health*. Norman: University of Oklahoma Press, 2019.

Pesantubbee, Michelene, and Michael Zogry, eds. *Native Foodways: Indigenous North American Religious Traditions and Foods*. New York: SUNY, 2021.

60
What is a sweat lodge?

Suzanne Owen

The sweat lodge is a domed structure made with a frame of pliable saplings covered with canvas, blankets, or other materials to make it dark inside, likened to being in a womb. Several dozen stones are heated in a fire not far from the lodge. Often there is a small mound outside to act as an altar.

The sweat lodge also refers to the ceremony that takes place within the lodge. The ceremony usually has four rounds correlating to the four directions, elements (air, fire, water, earth), and stages of life (childhood, youth, maturity, elderhood). There are songs and prayers throughout the ceremony, which can last several hours. The leader pours water onto the heated stones inside the dome to create steam while an attendant remains outside to open the flap in between the rounds and to bring in the stones.

Sweat lodge ceremonies are widely practiced among Plains Indian groups and have been incorporated into other Indigenous cultures in the Americas, sometimes controversially, especially where this might have displaced local Indigenous traditions. Other cultures may have, or have had, similar practices—such as the northern European sauna tradition—but these differ greatly in their ritual elements and customs or protocols.

In Lakota, the name for the ceremony is *inipi* or *inikagapi* ("for making life/breath") and is used either for purification and prayer prior to (and sometimes after) other ceremonies or on its own for healing and prayer. In the case of the latter, the ceremony has been provided as a treatment for Native Americans in recovery from addiction. Key to its use is the view that healing takes place within community, and when the Lakota and many others enter a lodge, they say "all my relations" in acknowledgment of this, inclusive of nonhuman relations with animals, plants, and so on.

Two questions that may be asked about the sweat lodge ceremony are (1) whether it is dangerous and (2) in which circumstances it is considered a misappropriation. The two are related in that a case of misappropriation in Sedona, Arizona, in 2009 led to the deaths of three participants (two during the ceremony and one nine days later) and hospitalizations of many others. Sweat lodges have long been a feature of back-to-nature or Native American–style retreats and workshops, in some instances led by Native Americans. In the Sedona case, the leader was not Native American and had no connection to any Native American community. Participants were charged up to $10,000 and had been fasting since the day before, apparently without water. It seemed there were too many participants inside the dome, and even when several of them began to complain of their discomfort, they were discouraged from leaving the lodge.

For Native Americans, several elements of this tragedy mark it as a misappropriation, starting with the leader having little or no training. Usually, the leader would be expected to have had long years of training under the guidance of a teacher connected to a Native American community. Another feature of misappropriation in the Sedona case is that participants had paid to attend. They might argue that they had paid for the retreat rather than the sweat lodge per se, but having paid, they would expect to be able to attend. In a Native American community, the ceremony would not be for sale, though a donation may be offered afterward. Participation is by invitation or permission of the sweat lodge keeper (the one who "pours the sweat").

Participants would usually prepare by abstaining from drugs and alcohol for at least four days prior to the ceremony, not only out of respect for the community, but for the health of the individual. Women would not participate in a mixed sweat if they were menstruating, which is already regarded as a time of cleansing and renewal of their power. Some women go to a "moon lodge" during this time. In mixed sweats, participants wear light clothing. It can get quite hot during a ceremony. There are breaks in between the rounds where the flap is opened, letting in fresh air, but if a participant experiences any discomfort, they might be advised to lie on the ground where the air is cooler, or they may leave at any time. The Lakota, as do many others (in their own language), say "All my relations" to alert the attendant, who opens the flap.

When studying a ceremony such as the sweat lodge, it is worth observing these discourses around leading, participating, sharing, and appropriating but also the power relations involved, including that of the scholar. Trust is developed over time in a community with the sweat lodge keeper and other participants. During the ceremony, participants often reveal personal struggles and insights. In general, what is spoken in the lodge stays in the lodge.

About the author

Suzanne Owen is a reader in religious studies at Leeds Trinity University researching Indigeneity in Newfoundland and contemporary British

Druidry. Her monograph, *The Appropriation of Native American Spirituality*, was published by Continuum (now Bloomsbury) in 2008.

Suggestions for further reading

In this book
See also chapters 38 (What is the deal with cultural appropriation?) and 66 (What is a nagual/nahual/nawal?).

Elsewhere
Bucko, Raymond. *The Lakota Ritual of the Sweat Lodge*. Lincoln: University of Nebraska Press, 1998.

Irwin, Lee, ed. *Native American Spirituality: A Critical Reader*. Lincoln: University of Nebraska Press, 2000.

Irwin, Lee. "Walking the Line: Pipe and Sweat Ceremonies in Prison." *Nova Religio: The Journal of Alternative and Emergent Religions* 9(3) (2006): 39–60.

Waegemakers Schiff, Jeannette, and Kerrie Moore. "The Impact of the Sweat Lodge Ceremony on Dimensions of Well-Being." *American Indian and Alaska Native Mental Health Research: The Journal of the National Center* 13 (2006): 48–69.

61

What role does healing play in Native American and Indigenous religious traditions?

Or, What's religious about health and healing in Indigenous religious traditions?

Suzanne Crawford O'Brien

To understand the relationship between Indigenous religious traditions and healing, we first need to ask what we mean by *healing*. This is important because there is a big difference between curing and healing, between disease and illness. Disease has to do with a discrete ailment, the diagnosis one might receive from a doctor. Illness is about how that disease is experienced. Curing is about removing a disease, but healing means restoring the whole person to balance. There may be cures for certain discrete diseases, but the side effects and broader impacts on one's life and sense of self must be healed. *Healing* may happen when a cure is not possible, even in the midst of chronic or terminal disease. How illnesses are experienced and what it means to be healthy are culturally specific and so will vary by community.

At the same time, some broad themes can be found among Indigenous communities. The first of these is the notion that colonialism is at the root of illness. Statistically, the greatest threats to Native North Americans' health and well-being are diabetes, heart disease, obesity, alcohol and drug addiction, suicide, and violence—all of which can be attributed to the history of colonialism. Addressing these threats to Indigenous health and well-being requires decolonizing: restoring peoples' relationships with their land, with traditional foods and ways of living; restoring healthy self-identities rooted in community; and engaging in ceremonial activism to protect Indigenous resources, land, and water. Decolonizing is difficult, but Indigenous religious traditions provide the tools for doing this work.

A second theme is the notion that a healthy self is not an isolated individual but one that exists within a web of healthy relationships: with one's human community, with one's ancestors, and with the natural world. These relationships have been placed under heavy strain—and sometimes broken—by the impacts of colonialism. Restoring relationships thus entails recovering traditional ways of being in community: reclaiming healthy relationships between couples, among extended families, and with one's ancestors. It means restoring a relationship with one's Indigenous homeland.

A third common theme is the understanding that restoring relationships is *spiritual* work and that Indigenous religious traditions and philosophies provide the needed tools for this work. For instance, Indigenous nations and families maintain their own stories with instructions for how to live in right relationship with each other. In partnership with the land itself, these stories serve as sacred texts, teaching healthy ways of living and being. Indigenous ceremonies also provide tools for restoring relationships with one's ancestors and with the spirits of the natural world. There are rites and ceremonies to restore relationships with one's human community, such as ceremonies of peacemaking and adoption. There are complex ceremonies that call individuals' spirits back or reconnect them to the forces that animate their landscape to remind them of both who they are meant to be and what they are called to do with their lives. The very act of preparing and conducting such complex ceremonies can heal relationships: the sheer amount of work required to conduct large gatherings simply requires collaboration. Participating in ceremonies heals relationships, as the symbols, stories, and ritual actions communicate core values, ethics, and teachings about the right way to live in the world. Smaller, more intimate rituals and ceremonies—such as the sweat lodge or a Native American Church peyote ceremony—are also vital spaces for healing relationships because they provide spaces for openness, vulnerability, and speaking from one's heart.

A fourth common theme is that Indigenous healing ceremonies are holistic, addressing the physical, mental, spiritual, and emotional aspects of illness. While often conducted in partnership with biomedical care, there is a common understanding that while standard medical care addresses only the physical complaint, Indigenous traditions address the underlying spiritual cause of illness, restoring harmony and balance. Consider, for instance, the common practice of herbal medicine found among Indigenous communities around the world. Such practices are not just about the chemical properties of plants but also about building a spiritual relationship with the plant itself, supporting mental strength through working with the plants, and emotional resiliency through engaging with the land.

Healing is inextricably tied to Indigenous religious life because at heart, it is about healing the soul wounds of colonialism. Healing happens in many different ways: in protests that become ceremonies, through working with plants, through walking with a story that gives guidance and encouragement, or through receiving a healing ceremony that restores hope, meaning, and purpose.

About the author

Suzanne Crawford O'Brien is professor of religion and culture and chair of the Native American and Indigenous Studies Program at Pacific Lutheran University. She is the author of *Coming Full Circle: Spirituality and Wellness among Native Communities in the Pacific Northwest* (University of Nebraska, 2014) and is coauthor with Inés Talamantez of *Religion and Culture in Native America* (Rowman & Littlefield, 2020).

Suggestions for further reading

In this book
See also chapters 58 (Is peyote a medicine or a drug?) and 47 (What role does pilgrimage play in Indigenous religious life?).

Elsewhere
Calabrese, Joseph. *A Different Medicine: Postcolonial Healing in the Native American Church*. Oxford: Oxford University Press, 2013.

Crawford O'Brien, Suzanne, ed. *Religion and Healing in Native America: Pathways for Renewal*. Westport, CT: Praeger, 2008.

Duran, Eduardo. *Healing the Soul Wound: Trauma-Informed Counseling for Indigenous Communities*. New York: Teachers College Press, 2019.

Jacob, Michelle. *Yakama Rising: Indigenous Cultural Revitalization, Activism, and Healing*. Tucson: University of Arizona Press, 2014.

Million, Dian. *Therapeutic Nations: Healing in an Age of Indigenous Human Rights*. Tucson: University of Arizona Press, 2013.

62

Is Voudou dangerous?

Emily Suzanne Clark

This is a question I frequently field. Popular culture has long depicted Voudou or Voodoo as a danger. In Disney's 2009 film *The Princess and the Frog*, viewers witness Voudou as both villain and potential friend. It is not uncommon for mainstream American culture to regard diasporic African religions as exotic or dangerous. There is also a clear reason for this depiction: white supremacy. But before answering the main question, I would like to pose a question in response: Is Voudou dangerous to whom? To whom or what does Voudou allegedly pose a danger? Why are some religions seen as dangerous and others not?

Voudou or Voodoo is a religion of the African diaspora that developed in New Orleans. "Voudou," a francophone spelling, was common in the nineteenth century before the popular Americanized spelling "Voodoo" dominated the scene. However it is spelled, Voudou is a powerful tradition. Far too complicated to unpack in a short chapter, Voudou is an often misunderstood religion of the African diaspora. It is a tradition at times difficult to define because of how it has changed over the years and due to outsiders seeing it as dangerous. Practitioners of Voudou, sometimes called Voudousants or Voudouists, engage with spiritual powers in and beyond their world. Those can be powerful spirits (gods, goddesses, ancestors) and sources of power in the everyday world, such as graveyard dirt, certain roots, candles, and various foods and beverages. Interactions with this field of religious powers can enable helping or harming one's immediate environment. New Orleans newspapers are full of stories about Voudouists affirming the "truth" of Voudou, defending their practice, and sometimes expressing fear of fellow practitioners. And this makes sense; all religions have the power to strengthen community bonds or turn people against one another. Any religion can provide safety and pose a threat, all at the same time.

Outsiders viewed Voudou as dangerous because it was a clear result of syncretism. If you believed that traditional Christianity was the only moral or good religion, then a tradition that combined elements of various African religions, French and Spanish Catholicism, and newly developed practices and ideas would certainly upset your simple binary of good and evil. That syncretism troubled what powerful white citizens saw as the natural order of things. First, it incorporated Christianity but also removed the tradition from its alleged pure religious origins and intermixed it with traditions seen as evil. Those supposed evil traditions were African. White Europeans and Euro-Americans viewed Africa as a place without history, without culture, without religion, and without morality. For them, this helped justify slavery and colonialism. To mix the supposed "true" religion with evil ones could only create a dangerous tradition in their eyes.

The religions viewed by the powerful as alternative were categorized as dangerous. Those alternative religions refused to fit the presumed "normal" mode of religion. Voudou offered authority to women and seemed to attract the marginalized and minoritized. The tradition also troubled dominant assumptions about religion because it did not have the formality of Christianity. Without the institutional elements of Christianity, like a sacred text, authority figures with seminary training, and steepled edifices, Voudou appeared to have an underground element, which kept it beyond the reach of white authorities. Where outsiders might criticize the tradition for a seeming lack of stability, insiders to the tradition would see the value of adaptability. Adaptability could mean power for practitioners, and for outsiders, it reinforced how Voudou was beyond their control.

Religions that resist white supremacy are often categorized as dangerous. Despite being labeled as dangerous and even rendered illegal at times in Louisiana history, Voudou persisted. White supremacy and traditional Christianity could not destroy it. While now a tourist attraction, there were multiple points in Louisiana history when Voudou was illegal. During the territory's past as a French colony, Catholicism was the only legal religion. In the late eighteenth century, Voudou was put on trial for the first of multiple times when a group of enslaved African men was charged with poisoning a slaver, his dogs, and his overseer. During the nineteenth century, the police barged into homes when they suspected Voudou activity. The city classified meetings of Voudou practitioners as unlawful assemblies due to a mixture of alleged superstitious magic, presumptions of illicit sexual activities, and social interactions across the color line. Voudou possessed spiritual power that white Christianity could not. It offered power beyond the grasp of white citizens that they could not control. This made it powerful and, to outsiders, dangerous.

About the author

Emily Suzanne Clark is associate professor of religious studies at Gonzaga University, where she teaches undergraduate courses in American religions. She is the author of *A Luminous Brotherhood: Afro-Creole Spiritualism in Nineteenth-Century New Orleans* (University of North Carolina Press, 2016) and coeditor of *Race and New Religious Movements: A Documentary Reader* (Bloomsbury, 2019). She has also published on New Orleans Voudou, Jesuit missions in the Pacific Northwest, and the Moorish Science Temple.

Suggestions for further reading

In this book
See also chapters 19 (Is Voudou an American religion or an Indigenous religion?) and 16 (What makes Vodou an Indigenous tradition?).

Elsewhere
Clark, Emily Suzanne. "Nineteenth-Century New Orleans Voudou: An American Religion." *American Religion* 2(1) (2020): 131–155.

Gordon, Michelle Y. "'Midnight Scenes and Orgies': Public Narratives of Voodoo in New Orleans and Nineteenth-Century Discourses of White Supremacy." *American Quarterly* 64(4) (2012): 767–786.

Morrow Long, Carolyn. "Perceptions of New Orleans Voodoo: Sin, Fraud, Entertainment, and Religion." *Nova Religio: The Journal of Alternative and Emergent Religions* 6(1) (2002): 86–104.

Roberts, Kodi. *Voodoo and Power: The Politics of Religion in New Orleans, 1881–1940*. Baton Rouge: Louisiana State University, 2015.

63

Why is distinguishing a Native American world view from a eurochristian one important?

George "Tink" E. Tinker

By my fifth year on the Iliff faculty, I had experienced persistent interactions with my faculty colleagues and with Iliff staff that reminded me that my position at the school was indeed a colonial compromise. They really did expect me to mirror the structures of their own discourse. I was to teach about Indians but to teach about Indians using the modalities that had been crafted by a century of eurochristian academics in anthropology and history, using their categories of analysis, their own theories, and their own jargon-laden language. They seemed oblivious to the possibility that Indian folk might want to talk about the Indian world using our own modes of discourse, our own theories and methods. So I did have to make the compromise of studying and learning much of their sophisticated discourses—out of self-defense and in order to fight for a decolonizing project that they never quite understood.

By the time I finished writing my book *Missionary Conquest* in 1993, however, it finally became ever clearer to me that my attempt to hold the gospel and Indian traditional culture in constructive tension was doomed to failure. Rather, I realized that *any* degree of conformity or assimilation to the christian gospel necessitated the deconstruction and ultimate extinguishing of a Native world view, so Chief Justice Marshall's legal language in *Johnson v. M'Intosh* about the ascendancy of a "superior [eurochristian] genius" necessitated a dramatic shift in world view for Native folk—from Native to eurochristian. I came to understand that these are in actuality two very different world views, eurochristian and Indian, that stand in dramatic conflict with one another. All we can expect from the more liberal colonizer missionary is to add a bit of familiarity and comfort for the colonized subject to entice us into the web of the eurochristian world view, to wrest us away from our egalitarian world of communityist harmony and balance and reduce us to the captivity of hierarchy and power structures with promises of individual salvation in heaven. Adding familiarity and comfort is precisely what the (eurochristian/White) jesuits do in South Dakota, for instance, when they place a Lakota-style pipe on the altar next to their sacrament of holy communion. They even have learned to use Lakota words and phrases, except they have reinterpreted them with their own christian meaning, so that at one point, they renamed their confessional room in the church at Red Cloud mission the *hanblecea* room, totally erasing the traditional meaning of that ceremony and investing it with a new colonialist christian meaning.

Colonialism and its eurochristian world view stand as the center of that rupture that has and continues to fragment, shatter, and divide the Indigenous communities and their cultures in this hemisphere. Yet the original foundation of that Indigenous world view and our cultures are still held firm by enough folk that we need not entirely despair. Through the first two decades of this eurochristian twenty-first-century, for instance, urban Indians in Denver where I live are still able to gather in order to *wada* (talk) with our relatives in the *wanagi* (spirit) world in ceremony. That has been a moment and a place each week where Indian folk from various Nations were able to speak to their ancestral *wanagi* relatives, to reclaim languages that have been historically silenced by colonization.

In our struggle to decolonize ourselves, language was always key. It is deeply embedded in how we think as well as in how we think and talk about the consequences of colonial compromise for Indigenous peoples. The words that we use reveal the embedded assumptions that mark the difference between an Indigenous world view and a eurochristian world view. Forcing the conversion of Indian folk to eurochristianity (i.e., to christianity) was explicitly intended to shift the culture and world view of Natives to encourage assimilation to the eurochristian social whole, to erase Indians entirely—and just as readily, to put Indian land and natural resources at the disposal of eurochristian invaders.

Of course, the real surprise is that American Indians still have substantial chunks and pieces of the surface structure of the old world view and cultures and pieces of our lands. We are still here. We still dance, and powwows are ubiquitous, of course.

About the author

Tink Tinker, a citizen of the Osage Nation (wazhazhe), is the Clifford Baldridge Emeritus Professor of American Indian Cultures and Religious Traditions at Iliff School of Theology. During his thirty-three-year professorate at Iliff, Dr. Tinker brought a distinctly American Indian perspective to a predominantly White, eurochristian school, as he continues to do in lectures across the continent. His publications include *American Indian Liberation: A Theology of Sovereignty* (Orbis, 2008); *Spirit and Resistance: American Indian Liberation and Political Theology* (Fortress, 2004); and nearly a hundred journal articles and chapters for edited volumes.

Suggestions for further reading

In this book
See also chapters 26 (Can I convert to or practice an Indigenous religious tradition if I am not an Indigenous person?) and 65 (What do Indigenous religious traditions in the Americas have in common?).

Elsewhere
Tinker, George E. "The Irrelevance of Euro-Christian Dichotomies for Indigenous Peoples: Beyond Non-violence to a Vision of Cosmic Balance." In *Peacemaking and the Challenge of Violence in World Religions*, edited by Irfan A. Omar and Joshua Burns, 206–229. Malden, MA: Wiley-Blackwell, 2015.

Tinker, George E. "Jesus, the Gospel, and Genocide." In *The Colonial Compromise: The Threat of the Gospel to the Indigenous Worldview*, edited by Miguel de la Torre, 133–160. Lanham, MD: Lexington Books / Fortress Academic, 2020.

Tinker, George E. *Missionary Conquest: The Gospel and Native American Cultural Genocide*. Minneapolis, MN: Fortress, 1993.

Tinker, George E. "Religious Studies: The Final Colonization of American Indians, Part 1." Religious Theory, e-supplement to *Journal of Cultural and Religious Theory*, June 1, 2020. http://jcrt.org/religioustheory/2020/06/01/religious-studies-the-final-colonization-of-american-indians-part-1-tink-tinker-wazhazhe-udsethe/.

Tinker, George E. "Religious Studies: The Final Colonization of American Indians, Part 2." Religious Theory, e-supplement to *Journal of Cultural and Religious Theory*, June 9, 2020. http://jcrt.org/religioustheory/2020/06/09/religious-studies-the-final-colonization-of-american-indians-part-1-tink-tinker-wazhazhe-udsethe-2/.

Tinker, George E. "Why I Don't Believe in a Creator." In *Buffalo Shout, Salmon Cry: Conversations on Creation, Land Justice, and Life Together*, edited by Steve Heinrichs, 167–179. Waterloo, ON: Herald, 2013.

64

Do Indigenous peoples have "gods"?

Patrisia Gonzales

In asking this question, one must also ask, What and how are "gods" in the minds of those asking, and who are the "gods" among Indigenous peoples?

What exactly do the gods stand in for? Powers? Energies? Sacred agents and spiritual agencies? The "gods," as a concept, may reflect the non-Indigenous attempt to describe in one word the deep Indigenous analysis of how life functions, which has evolved over millennia. It is difficult to not contrast the existence of the "gods" with the embedded Judeo-Christian "God" as the oppositional concept of what is true and correct. Such projections led conquerors and colonizers to burn people at the stake because the European invaders believed Indigenous peoples either had no religion or had a religion that was heathen and contrary to church theology. Indigenous concepts of the powers of the universe and the deep cosmologies, Indigenous knowledge systems, and sciences of Indigenous peoples were reduced to related binaries of gods in opposition to the devil, demons, and witchery. Prior to colonization, Christian concepts of the devil and the Christian evil were nonexistent in Indigenous languages of the Americas and were introduced by European colonizers as they persecuted Indigenous peoples for their beliefs. The idea of whether Indigenous peoples worshipped gods—and whether they had souls—formed the justification for European colonization. Vine Deloria Jr. notes in *God Is Red* that Judeo-Christian religions offer a universalized concept of religion in contrast to the place-based spiritual teachings of Indigenous peoples. Deloria's book *The World We Used to Live In* refers to a "basic unity" of a "spiritual universe" that is expressed distinctively among Indigenous peoples.

Notions of gods, godlings, undergods, and so on—which are embedded in Judeo-Christian teachings—have been used to describe how Indigenous peoples understand the natural world, the spiritual world, and the order of the universe. This spiritual and cosmological order is alive with an expansive field of possibilities that is expressed through powers, presences, and nonhuman personhood, such as the Holy People of the Diné, who are protective, sacred beings. The spirit of the water is recognized by many Indigenous peoples as a living being, and there are ceremonial leaders and elders recognized for their ability to pray water into existence during scarcity. Numerous Native nations recognize animals, such as the buffalo, as a nation with rights and powers that may impact the human world at multiple levels. Powers to heal; to protect; to draw knowledge, insight, and wisdom; and to create movement or harness an accumulation of actions are other examples of unseen spiritual power and energies. These become manifest in ceremonies, healing, and the leadership of Indigenous peoples. For instance, several chiefs who signed treaties with the United States rose to leadership because of their command of spiritual power. Some non-Native scientists, such as F. David Peat in his book *Blackfoot Physics*, have sought to inform their frameworks with Indigenous knowledge systems and the possibilities of the universe that falls outside accepted Western sciences.

However, the larger answer to this question lies within Indigenous languages and cultures themselves, in which a nuanced understanding of the sacred is based on deep philosophies of Indigenous peoples and their distinct relationship with the cosmos and their territories. Water-based Indigenous cultures whose teachings evolved from extensive relations with their waterways carry specialized knowledge that is distinct from Indigenous peoples who emerged from arid lands, where a sacred and physical relationship with water is crucial but enacted within a distinct context. Once the filters of the Western mind are removed, a variety of expressions are evident of the powers of life, of the impulse of the universe, of that which creates and forms and organizes.

Some Indigenous peoples may use "gods," "dioses," or "deities," but how they deploy the term may be different from how someone outside their culture conceives of it. Deloria notes that the idea of one Creator is not necessarily a uniform idea among Indigenous peoples. Today, an Indigenous understanding of unified power is present in the English language as Creator or Great Spirit. The Indigenous concept of the Great Mystery, held by some Indigenous nations, is used to convey that not all things in the profundity of the spiritual world may be understood or articulated but must be respectfully acknowledged and honored as a deep experience of life. Indigenous languages may convey layered words and meanings, where there are multiple forces and expressions of a great power or various creators.

About the author

Dr. Patrisia Gonzales is the author of *Red Medicine: Traditional Indigenous Rites of Birthing and Healing* (University of Arizona Press, 2015) and *Traditional Indian Medicine* (Kendall Hunt, 2017). The granddaughter of Kickapoo/Comanche and Macehual peoples, she descends from three generations of bonesetters, herbalists, midwives, and traditional doctors. She teaches courses on Indigenous medicine at the University of Arizona. She is a mother maker, baby catcher, and herbalist and has collaborated with Macehual knowledge keepers in Mexico since 1990.

Suggestions for further reading

In this book
See also chapters 45 (Do Indigenous peoples believe plants, animals, and waters have personhood?), 66 (What is a nagual/nahual/nawal?), and 69 (What are ancestor spirits, and what role do they play in Hawaiian religious life?).

Elsewhere
Deloria, Vine, Jr. *God Is Red: A Native View of Religion*. Golden, CO: Fulcrum, 2003.

Deloria, Vine, Jr. *The World We Used to Live In: Remembering the Powers of the Medicine Men*. Golden, CO: Fulcrum, 2006.

Peat, F. David. *Blackfoot Physics: A Journey into the Native American Universe*. Boston: Weiser, 2005.

65

What do Indigenous religious traditions in the Americas have in common?

Inés Hernández-Ávila

The English language fails to describe, explain, or contemplate "religion" in relation to Indigenous peoples in the Americas. The (mis)representation of Indigenous peoples by scholars who presume the ascendency of the West and use the intricacies of the English language (or other "major world languages," such as Spanish, French, German, and others) to describe and analyze Indigenous "religious traditions" (often without having taken the time to study the languages of the peoples they are writing about) is sadly common.

In the now globally recognized field of Native American and Indigenous studies, it is becoming increasingly clear that we must (re)turn to Indigenous languages in order to deeply and more fully consider the belief systems they encode. These belief systems can guide scholars to more profound understandings of what "religion" means to and for Indigenous peoples in the Americas. We must also remember that there is no one Native American or Indigenous culture but rather hundreds upon hundreds of Indigenous cultures throughout North, Central, and South America, each with a distinct language and a unique way of interpreting their lives, their worlds, and their beings.

This writer assumes that readers have more than a sense of the fraught historical relationship Native American and Indigenous peoples have had with the respective nation-states in which they find themselves and the commonalities of those lived experiences over the centuries: dispossession, genocide, ethnocide, forced assimilation, and intense missionization, to name some. This is the backdrop for what we are witnessing as an immense movement of Indigenous cultural, linguistic, and spiritual revitalization in the Americas. For precision, we must go to the Indigenous language of each people to seek the "religious" conceptualizations that reside in the language.

In English, "spirituality" and "religion," in effect, are generic terms for what Indigenous peoples would call their ways of knowing (epistemologies) and ways of being (ontologies). When we explore and contemplate these ways of knowing and being, some concepts emerge as having currency—indeed, centrality—in relation to Indigenous peoples and their belief systems. For instance, the idea of a "good life" in relation to all that lives is key to understanding these "religious traditions." The "good life" is not one of individualistic, capitalistic accumulation; it is not one that places the human being above all other beings; it is not one where the individual seeks power over other beings; it is not one that considers the earth as exploitable and human beings expendable.

The "good life" is a life with dignity in which the human being is raised to understand his/her/their sacred place in the world and his/her/their responsibility to contribute to the sustenance of family, community, culture, land, water, kinships with humans, and all the more-than-human beings that live on this earth. The "good life" is one that recognizes that each unique Indigenous people has their own Creation story that must be respected. Indigenous peoples do not impose their Creation stories on each other, although their historical proximity to one another or the fact that their languages are very closely related may enable mutual concepts.

Another element that emerges often is the attention to the heart in Indigenous cultures. How do we grow as Indigenous human beings? How do we learn, from even before birth, how to be, how to relate, how to mature with wisdom, how to take our place as caretakers of the earth and all the more-than-human beings? We are taught to be guided by our hearts. We are taught to listen with our hearts, to see with our hearts, to speak from our hearts, to create from our hearts, and to strive to contribute to a collective heart that ideally teaches us about consensus, governance, sacred obligations, and the well-being of all of life. These teachings take place informally in the home—how to be a good person, how to treat others, how to always show respect, and how to care for others, for the earth, for the more-than-human beings. They also take place in sacred spaces beyond the home, in ceremony, in song, with dance, in acts of (re)creation that renew, replenish, and heal the community.

Indigenous religious traditions in the Americas have in common a radical (rooted) relationality that speaks to the longevity of Indigenous peoples in this hemisphere; their sacred awareness of themselves as original peoples, as First Nations, and as Native Nations; and their accountability to ensuring that life is sustained in the most healthy way possible on this planet.

About the author

Inés Hernandez-Avila (Niimiipuu/Nez Perce, enrolled on the Colville Reservation, and Tejana) is professor of Native American studies at the University of California, Davis. She is a scholar, poet, visual artist, and cultural worker. Her research/teaching areas include contemporary Native American / Indigenous literature (United States and Mexico) and Indigenous religious traditions.

Suggestions for further reading

In this book
See also chapters 2 (What makes a religion an "Indigenous religion"?) and 8 (Why is "religion" a problematic category for understanding Indigenous traditions?).

Elsewhere
Echo-Hawk, Walter. *In the Light of Justice: The Rise of Human Rights in Native America and the U.N. Declaration on the Rights of Indigenous Peoples.* Golden, CO: Fulcrum, 2013.

Fitzwater, Dylan. *Autonomy Is in Our Hearts: Zapatista Autonomous Government through the Lens of the Tsotsil Language.* Oakland, CA: PM, 2019.

Gross, Lawrence. *Anishinaabe Ways of Knowing and Being.* Oxfordshire, UK: Routledge, 2016.

Heath Justice, Daniel. *Why Indigenous Literatures Matter.* Waterloo, ON: Wilfred Laurier University Press, 2018.

66

What is a nagual/nahual/nawal?

Mallory E. Matsumoto

One of the most complex and enigmatic phenomena associated with Indigenous religion in Mesoamerica is the nagual. Sometimes written as "nahual" or "nawal," the term is derived from Nahuatl *nahual*, or "transform, convert, disguise, trick," but has been applied to related traditions beyond Central Mexico. Across the region, naguals are generally conceptualized as nonhuman or other-than-human entities, often with an animal form, that inhabit the liminal space between the human world and the realm of gods and ancestors. Depending on the tradition, however, nahuals may be ascribed different functions, powers, or attributes. The broad distribution of nagualism and its manifold variations in Mesoamerica today reflect its ancient origins and innumerable modifications over more than one and a half millennia.

One common view situates the nagual as a "companion spirit" belonging to an individual, intimately linked to but existing outside of her or him. A person usually acquires a nagual at birth but often does not discover its guise until an encounter with the corresponding animal later in life—for instance, while walking alone in the forest or during a dream. In some traditions, only some (usually important) persons have a nagual, whereas in others, they may belong to people at all levels of society. The role that naguals play in human lives varies widely among Mesoamerican communities, and it has surely changed significantly over time. For some, naguals are more neutral companions, spiritually tied to individuals without actively shaping the course of their lives short of the nagual's own accident, injury, or death. In other traditions, however, they may be attributed positive or negative influence and wield the power to shape the course of a war, deter or inflict natural disaster, or guide benevolent rains to agricultural fields.

If a nagual is kidnapped, wounded, or killed, the person to whom it belongs becomes gravely ill and usually dies if not treated by a local healer, whose curing practices include work to restore the nagual. Although some incidents are unfortunate accidents—a man falls ill after his nagual, who takes the form of a deer, is hit by a truck, for example—in others, someone may target another's nagual to inflict harm on him or her. Thus, it is important to know one's nagual and to guard it, both by avoiding behaviors that could jeopardize its well-being and by protecting it from others. Similarly, care must be taken when encountering an unknown animal because it could be someone else's nagual. Consequently, Indigenous healers, sometimes referred to as priests, shamans, or sorcerers, can wield great power by guiding naguals to do good or do harm and by taking the appropriate steps to restore a nagual under duress.

The temporal and cultural depth of nagualism is best attested by Classic Maya hieroglyphic records from as early as the fifth century CE. There, naguals are called *wahy* or *wahyis*, a Classic Mayan term that means "sleep" or "dream" and references naguals' associations with nighttime and the untethered world of dreams. In Classic Maya imagery, naguals appear as animals such as turkeys, peccaries, toads, or jaguars or as hybrid beings that combine features from animals, gods, and humans. They are often shown dancing or participating in sacrifices or other, more ambiguous events. Repeating cohorts of naguals across images indicates that some were associated with specific ritual practices or mythological narratives. Interestingly, Classic Maya naguals are almost never mentioned or illustrated on large stone monuments or architecture; instead, these beings are largely confined to painted ceramic vases and other portable media that could be easily handled by or moved between individuals.

Much scholarly fascination with nagualism is driven by the great diversity of manifestations over time but also among and even within cultural groups. Yet it also reflects the fact that even through this diversity, naguals and nagualism offer an entry point for understanding Indigenous Mesoamerican concepts of self and soul. Generally, nagualism is not limited to nor even situated within what most Western scholars would understand as "religion." The bond between nagual and person is not forged by or contingent on specific religious practices; it is as much a part of human daily existence as are the practices that maintain it. Today, respecting and engaging with one's nagual is important, even necessary to individuals who practice or self-affiliate with a range of religious traditions. Nagualism intimately intertwines Mesoamerican peoples, their communities, the human world, and the other-than-human realm, making it crucial to interpreting past and present Indigenous culture and society.

About the author

Mallory E. Matsumoto is assistant professor in the Department of Religious Studies at the University of Texas at Austin. Her research addresses the interface between language, material culture, and religion in precolonial and colonial Maya communities of Mesoamerica. She has conducted archaeological fieldwork and archival research in Guatemala, Mexico, Hungary, Peru, and the United States.

Suggestions for further reading

In this book

See also chapters 64 (Do Indigenous peoples have "gods"?) and 69 (What are ancestor spirits, and what role do they play in Hawaiian religious life?).

Elsewhere

Houston, Stephen D., and David Stuart. "The Way Glyph: Evidence for 'Co-essences' among the Classic Maya." *Research Reports on Ancient Maya Writing* 30 (1989): 1–16.

Martínez González, Roberto. *El nahualismo*. Mexico City: Nacional Autónoma de México, 2011.

Pitarch Ramón, Pedro. *The Jaguar and the Priest: An Ethnography of Tzeltal Souls*. Austin: University of Texas Press, 2010.

Velásquez García, Erik. "New Ideas about the *Wahyis* Spirits Painted on Maya Vessels: Sorcery, Maladies, and Dream Feasts in Prehispanic Art." *PARI Journal* 20(4) (2020): 15–28.

67

What are sacred bundles, and why are they important in Indigenous cultures in the Americas?

Molly H. Bassett

In the mid-sixteenth century, Fray Gerónimo de Mendieta, author of the *Historia eclesiástica indiana*, noted that Andrés de Olmos had called *tlaquimilolli*, "sacred bundles," the *"principal ídolo"* of the Mexica (Aztec). Olmos's terminology—"principal idol"—betrays his own iconoclastic views of Mesoamerican effigies. However, we need not take his word on the importance of bundles in the Americas. Evidence of their centrality in ordinary and ceremonial life abounds. Throughout the Americas, everyday bundles and sacred bundles played—and, in some cultures, continue to play—significant roles in commerce, society, and ceremony.

Among Nahuatl speakers like the Mexica, everyday bundles functioned as both an easy way to carry goods and a quantifier. Quantifiers associate a particular amount of something with a certain term (e.g., a "ream" of paper contains five hundred sheets). Mexica merchants knew that a single *quimilli*, "bundle," contained twenty soft items, like blankets or shirts. The Codex Mendoza includes colorful depictions of bundles of *mantas* (blankets) and other goods extracted by the Mexica from polities across Mesoamerica. Illustrations in the Florentine Codex show long-distance merchants hefting pack frames loaded with bundles of goods along paths across hilly terrain. *Quimilli* simplified the work of merchants by ensuring a certain quantity of goods in an easily transportable package.

The weight of bundles was borne by merchants and also by rulers. Maya rulers spoke of their responsibilities of governance as a burdensome bundle that they took up and then passed on to their successors. Descriptions of Mexica rulers' accession rites make the Maya metaphor more concrete. During the transition from noble to ruler, a candidate was "bundled" in special ritual attire, including a cape decorated with bones and a veil, for a period of four days. After the period of seclusion, he emerged as *tlahtoani*, the "speaker" or ruler.

Wrapping and bundles were important in Mesoamerican medicine and healing too. The Florentine Codex describes people wrapping snake-bites and binding broken bones. The bite of a venomous snake could lead to the loss of a limb, but this trauma could be averted by sucking the venom from the wound and then binding it with maguey fibers. The bandaged area was then held over hot coals and rubbed with good tobacco. For centuries, bonesetters throughout Mesoamerica have wrapped broken bones or inflamed extremities to ease pain and encourage healing. Contemporary self-taught bonesetters in Guatemala use their hands or ritual objects to ascertain the type and extent of a dislocation, fracture, or break. After manually realigning the joint or bone, they bind it using removable materials rather than casts. Removable bindings allow the bonesetters to regularly assess healing.

Both Mesoamericans and the Inka enshrouded the dead in bundles. The Mexica bound bodies in preparation for cremation, in the case of commoners, or funerary rites, in the case of rulers. Maya iconography and archaeological records confirm that rulers were bundled in textiles tied with ropes before burial. In the Andes, the arid climate contributed to the excellent preservation of funerary bundles wrapped in multiple layers of elaborate and colorful textiles. Inside each bundle, a corpse sat in a flexed position surrounded by consumables, luxury items, and personal effects. The textiles that wrapped bundles in the Paracas Necropolis are famous for their intricate patterns embroidered in alpaca wool on a cotton textile base.

Sacred bundles are the most precious kind of bundle. María Nieves Zedeño explains that among Native Americans of the North American Great Plains, bundles originated in dreams or visions that showed a person how to construct and handle the bundle. Medicine bundles help curers diagnose and cure illnesses, while ceremonial bundles are personal bundles that connect the holder to cosmologically significant events or ideas. Called tlaquimilolli in Nahuatl, sacred bundles were one form gods took among the Mexica. Tlaquimilolli contained objects associated with a particular deity that were bound by animal pelts and textiles. Together, the objects and layered wrappings ritually recollected a given *teotl*, "god." Gods spoke to their devotees from inside the sacred bundle. On the peregrination to found the Mexica capital Tenochtitlan, the patron god Huitzilopochtli, "Hummingbird Left-Hand Side," frequently communicated with priests from the sacred bundle. The Codex Boturini depicts a priest carrying

Huitzilopochtli's bundle like a backpack, and the god's anthropomorphic form emerges from it wearing a hummingbird headdress. From ordinary bundles used in marketplace exchanges to the sacred bundles that communicate with healers and priests, bundles have shaped Native American cultures.

About the author

Molly H. Bassett is an associate professor and chair in the Department of Religious Studies at Georgia State University. She published *The Fate of Earthly Things* with the University of Texas Press in 2015. Her current book project explores bundles as theory and method in the study of Mesoamerican religions. A fourth-generation Appalachian, she lives in Atlanta, Georgia, with her spouse, kids, and animal companions.

Suggestions for further reading

In this book
See also chapters 66 (What is a nagual/nahual/nawal?) and 68 (What motivates Nahuas to practice their religion of *el costumbre*?).

Elsewhere
Bassett, Molly H. *The Fate of Earthly Things: Aztec Gods and God-Bodies.* Austin: University of Texas Press, 2015.

Guernsey, J., and F. K. Reilly III. *Sacred Bundles, Ritual Acts of Wrapping and Binding in Mesoamerica.* Barnardsville, NC: Boundary End Archaeological Research Center, 2006.

Houston, Stephen, David Stuart, and Karl Taube. *The Memory of Bones: Body, Being, and Experience among the Classic Maya.* Austin: University of Texas Press, 2006.

Scherer, Andrew K. *Mortuary Landscapes of the Classic Maya: Rituals of Body and Soul.* Austin: University of Texas Press, 2015.

Zedeño, María Nieves. "Bundled Worlds: The Roles and Interactions of Complex Objects from the North American Plains." *Journal of Archaeological Method and Theory* 15 (2008): 362–378.

68

What motivates Nahuas to practice their religion of *el costumbre*?

Abelardo de la Cruz

I am a *macehualli* (Native person) who was born and grew up in a Nahua community in the northern part of the state of Veracruz, Mexico. From the time I was a child, my parents shared with me the practice of *el costumbre* (meaning "the customs" or "traditions"). I witnessed our customs performed in rituals such as *yancuic xihuitl* (held at the New Year) and *ahuaquiztlan* (asking for water in times of heat and drought in April and May) and during *elotitlan* (in the time of the young corn in September). Together with my parents, I participated in community rituals in the *xochicalli* ("flower house") or *casa de costumbre* a shrine for holding el costumbre rituals. The rituals are held in honor of deities associated with nature to make supplications or petitions to *chicomexochitl* (Seven Flower, the maize), *atl* (the water), *tlixihuantzin* (the fire), *ehecatl* (the wind), and *tlalli* (the earth).

El costumbre is a system of beliefs that the inhabitants of the municipality of Chicontepec consider their local religion. The followers of el costumbre share beliefs, practices, and the value of living together in the religion inherited from their grandparents while also accepting some influence from Catholicism. The religious ceremonies of el costumbre are practiced only in the xochicalli, never in the Catholic chapel. The majority of the believers respect and tolerate Catholicism, but they also bless the maize. They make the sign of the cross and use holy water from Catholic practice on el costumbre ritual altars.

The towns in the municipality of Chicontepec experienced increased contact with Catholicism in the 1980s through catechizations overseen by the Chicontepec parish. Afterward, Nahuas received instruction in Catholic sacraments, and they started baptizing, taking the rites of first communion and confirmation, and marrying in the Catholic Church.

From time to time, they also participated in community masses. For that reason, el costumbre has to be understood as continuing to validate Nahua beliefs and culture mixed with elements of Catholicism. In the Nahuatl language, religious beliefs are called *tlaneltoquilli*. In current religious thought, people who carry out tlaneltoquilli ceremonies equate the practices with el costumbre. Nahuas appear to be Christians because of their tolerance of Catholicism, but in reality, the people follow their own religion.

The Chicontepec region is hilly, covered in patches of tropical forest. It often rains in the mountain ranges throughout the year, but sometimes too much rain falls, especially in the summer. The year-round climate is generally warm and humid, but in the absence of rain, it can be extremely hot, especially during the springtime, a period known as *ahuaquiztlan*. Nahuas call their geographic environment *tonentlan* (meaning something like "our place we travel frequently and are familiar with"). In the absence of rain, the region's wells, streams, and water held in dams often dry up.

The extreme heat destroys almost everything, including the cultivated maize and the vegetation that provides sustenance for people and animals. The farm animals can easily die from dehydration. Because of the immense need people have for water, Nahuas make a ritual request for rain, known as *atlatlacualtiliztli*, before the Nahua gods. For four days and three nights, the *huehuehtlacatl* ("wise man"), together with the *tlaneltocanih* ("believers"), leads petitions for rain in the xochicalli. The petitions are accompanied by sacred music, dances, bird sacrifices, and offerings of food and beverages, and they end with a pilgrimage to a communal sacred mountain to make the final offerings and sacrifices.

In such times of drought and extreme heat under a broiling sun, Nahuas ask the deities to send rain in order that they may survive. But when the rains arrive, they are sometimes accompanied by heavy, destructive ehecatl and become dangerous hurricanes that threaten to destroy the *altepetl* ("community") and the cultivated crops. The people always request rain in moderation because they do not want to receive an overabundance. Out of the necessity to live and to reduce suffering, Nahuas request sufficient rain from the gods with the greatest respect and thereby strengthen and express their religious commitment.

About the author

Abelardo de la Cruz is from Chicontepec, Veracruz, Mexico. He has a PhD in anthropology from the University at Albany (SUNY). He collaborates at the Instituto de Docencia e Investigación Etnológica de Zacatecas and serves as Nahuatl instructor at the University of Utah.

Suggestions for further reading

In this book
See also chapters 36 (Why reconstruct precolonial Indigenous religions in the Americas?), 67 (What are sacred bundles, and why are they important in Indigenous cultures in the Americas?), and 76 (Did colonial missions destroy Indigenous religions?).

Elsewhere
Bassett, Molly H. *The Fate of Earthly Things: Aztec Gods and God-Bodies.* Austin: University of Texas Press, 2015.

Sandstrom, Alan R. *Corn Is Our Blood: Culture and Ethnic Identity in a Contemporary Aztec Indian Village* (1st edition). The Civilization of the American Indian Series. Norman: University of Oklahoma Press, 1991.

Tavárez, David Eduardo. *Words and Worlds Turned Around: Indigenous Christianities in Colonial Latin America.* Boulder: University Press of Colorado, 2017.

69

What are ancestor spirits, and what role do they play in Hawaiian religious life?

Marie Alohalani Brown

The foundation of traditional Hawaiian culture is the belief that everything in the island world—land, sea, sky, and everything therein, including akua (deities) and humans—is interconnected and genealogically related. As creation chants attest, Hawaiians are kin to the nonhuman, albeit the kinship degree can be remote or near. Thus, the use of "ancestor" as a descriptor is not limited to human relatives. For example, should an akua have a child with a human, the human child's progeny would be the akua's direct descendants. For this lineage, the akua would be an 'aumakua ('aumākua, plural)—'au (group) + makua (parent, parental relatives, and progenitor)—a family god. 'Aumākua play an important role in Hawaiian cultural-religious traditions as ancestral guardians who protect and comfort their descendants, impart knowledge, offer guidance, bestow spiritual or physical strength, escort their progeny upon their death to the spirit world, and intervene on behalf of descendants to ensure that their prayers to other akua are received.

Many akua have human forms, but when people think of ancestral guardians, they most often envision 'aumākua with nonhuman forms, such as a shark, owl, eel, or moʻo (lizard; a Hawaiian reptilian water deity). Perhaps this is because another way that a family obtained an 'aumakua was when a deceased relative underwent a ceremony called kākūʻai. The kākūʻai transformed the deceased into a nonhuman form, often an animal, which would then go on to exist in that akua form to protect the family. An 'aumakua might also be born into the family in a nonhuman form. Children born in nonhuman forms are considered akua. Because of the supposed resemblance of miscarried fetuses to fish or lizards, they were dedicated to a shark or moʻo akua.

218 INDIGENOUS RELIGIOUS TRADITIONS IN FIVE MINUTES

Although ancestor spirits known as ʻaumākua are beneficial deities, should descendants offend them, they can mete out punishment in the form of misfortune, illness, death, or a refusal to escort the offender into the spirit world. Without an escort, the offender would then forever wander the areas it frequented when it was alive. A most grievous infraction is to eat or otherwise harm the kino lau (many forms or bodies) of one's ʻaumakua because these forms are sacred to it. By way of example, a family who has an ʻaumakua with a shark form cannot eat or otherwise harm sharks in general because the ʻaumakua and nonakua sharks have that form in common. Here, it is important to note that a shark ʻaumakua is a specific shark—not sharks collectively. As another example, if a family counts a moʻo among its ʻaumākua, they must not harm the ordinary (non-akua) lizards because lizards as a collective are sacred to these reptilian water deities.

ʻAumākua include the collective ancestors and near relatives who preceded their kin in death and then became spirits. Significantly, spirits are a type of akua, a concept often translated into English as "god" or "deity," words that have a marked Christian inflection. Yet Hawaiian and Christian understandings of what constitutes a "deity" differ substantially. Notably, things that fall under the category of akua include the usual powerful entities gendered as gods and goddesses but also spirits, ghosts, and even corpses. Whether we call these ancestor spirits "ʻaumākua" or "kūpuna" (grandparents, ancestors), the fact remains that many Hawaiians continue to acknowledge their existence. The belief in ʻaumākua is one that even some Hawaiians who had embraced Christianity in the nineteenth century refused to leave behind. Indeed, a Hawaiian lay church leader was criticized in 1888 for setting apart time in his Christian services to pray and make offerings to ʻaumakua.

Although death results in the separation of the deceased from the living, who must then dwell in different planes of existence, ancestor spirits and their descendants are nevertheless still united by familial ties of love. Hawaiians continue to call upon them, and in turn, these spirit relatives may make their presence known in the course of the day or evening or visit them in dreams. A twenty-line traditional prayer to ʻaumākua, Nā ʻAumākua (Ancestors), attests to their importance in Hawaiian religious and political life. Hawaiians have also evoked their ʻaumākua in times of need as a collective by chanting this prayer. Kiaʻi chanted Nā ʻAumākua four times a day in the daily ceremonies held at Mauna Kea for eight months (July 2019–March 2020) to ask their ancestors to help them protect this sacred mountain.

About the author

Marie Alohalani Brown, a Kanaka ʻŌiwi (Hawaiian), is an associate professor in the Department of Religion at the University of Hawaiʻi–Mānoa and a specialist in Hawaiian religion. Her research is primarily carried out in nineteenth- and twentieth-century Hawaiian-language materials. Her works include *Facing the Spears of Change: The Life and Legacy of John Papa ʻĪʻī*, which won the biennial Palapala Poʻokela Award for the best book on Hawaiian language, culture, and history (2016, 2017); *The Penguin Book of Mermaids* (2019), for which she is coeditor along with Cristina Bacchilega; and *Ka Poʻe Moʻo Akua: Hawaiian Reptilian Deities* (University of Hawaiʻi Press, 2022).

Suggestions for further reading

In this book
See also chapters 64 (Do Indigenous peoples have "gods"?) and 66 (What is a nagual/nahual/nawal?).

Elsewhere
Handy, E. S. Craighill, and Mary Kawena Pukui. *The Polynesian Family System in Ka-ʻu, Hawaiʻi*. Honolulu: Tuttle, 2011.

Pukui, Mary Kawena, E. W. Haertig, and Catherine Lee. *Nānā I Ke Kumu (Look to the Source)* (volume 1). Honolulu: Hui Hānai, 1972.

Pukui, Mary Kawena, E. W. Haertig, and Catherine Lee. *Nānā I Ke Kumu (Look to the Source)* (volume 2). Honolulu: Hui Hānai, 1979.

70

Do all Indigenous peoples in North America practice the same ceremonies as one another?

Meaghan Weatherdon

Ceremony is an integral aspect of life within many Indigenous cultures. People meet in ceremony for a variety of reasons, including to acknowledge a person's passage throughout the life stages, to seek healing and new knowledge, to mark momentous occasions or seasonal cycles, and to offer gratitude to the lands, spirits, and ancestors. As Michi Saagiig Nishnaabeg scholar Leanne Betasamosake Simpson suggests, ceremonies are a way of continually generating meaning. In this sense, ceremonies can be understood as embodied theories that empower individuals and communities of people to make sense of the world around them and their place in it. As generative practices, ceremonies also allow people to envision and enact their futures.

The answer to the question proposed above as to whether or not all Indigenous peoples in North America practice the same ceremonies as one another is no. Indigenous peoples' ceremonies are as diverse as Indigenous cultures. These ceremonies vary widely across geographic locales and communities. They also change and innovate as they are passed down across the generations. Yet any answer to the question above must also contend with the ways in which Indigenous peoples from different cultural backgrounds often do share and/or practice the same or similar versions of ceremony. Indigenous communities engage in cultural borrowing, ceremonial exchange, and religious reinvention to gain new insights, establish networks of affinity, and foster solidarity, especially in times of uncertainty.

Ceremonies give form and expression to Indigenous peoples' historic and ongoing relationships with their lands, enabling them to cultivate a sense of place and community. For this reason, they tend to vary widely across cultures and regions. For example, the coming-of-age ceremonies practiced by the Cree peoples living in the subarctic of northeastern Canada look and operate differently from the coming-of-age ceremonies that belong to the Hoopa Valley peoples who live on the other side of the hemisphere in Northwestern California. In Iiyiyiu Aschii, the Cree have recently revitalized the First Snowshoe Walk Ceremony, or Pimuhtihâusunâniû. The First Snowshoe Walk Ceremony is held during the wintertime when children as young as five years old are ready to take their first steps in their snowshoes and join their families during long and difficult winter journeys. This ceremony imparts vital knowledge for survival and celebrates a young person's deepening connections to land, growing autonomy, and heightening sense of responsibility to their community. In Northwestern California, the Hoopa Valley tribe has been reviving the Flower Dance, or Ch'ilwa:l, a women's coming-of-age ceremony, which is held in celebration of a young woman when she starts menstruating. Like the First Snowshoe Walk Ceremony, the Flower Dance is a public ceremony that brings the community together. It involves many practices, such as running, singing, dancing, and bathing, lasting anywhere from three to ten days. Throughout this time, the young woman is offered teachings that help her prepare for her future life as a woman. Each ceremony, though distinct in intention and form, works to cultivate personhood and embed the initiate in supportive networks of belonging.

There are other ceremonies that span vast geographies and are practiced widely by many different Indigenous communities. In this volume, Tiffany Hale describes how the Ghost Dance of the late nineteenth century, which began in Walker River Valley, Nevada, with the prophet Wovoka, spread west across the Great Plains. Hale explains how as the Ghost Dance was taken up by various communities, practitioners retained common elements at the same time that they adapted the ceremony to new cultural contexts. During a time in which Native Americans were suffering greatly from the violence and ecological disaster of Westward colonial expansion, the Ghost Dance provided a sense of hope and togetherness to those who danced.

Indigenous communities engage in processes of intertribal sharing and cultural borrowing, in which ceremonies are gifted from one community to another according to collectively recognized protocols. For example, when working with Miawpukek Mi'kmaq of Conne River in Newfoundland, Canada, anthropologist of Indigenous religions Suzanne Owen discovered the community had inherited elements of Lakota spirituality, such as powwow dancing and the sweat lodge ceremony. Contrary to the assumption that the introduction of new ceremonial forms would replace Mi'kmaq spirituality, Owen found that the introduction of Lakota spirituality in Mi'kma'ki stimulated a revival of Mi'kmaq cultural pride and motivated a return to Mi'kmaq ceremony as well. Taken together, these brief examples illustrate how ceremonial reciprocity generates creativity, empowers Indigenous peoples to adapt to shifting contexts, and affords opportunities for decolonization.

About the author

Meaghan Weatherdon is an assistant professor in the Department of Theology and Religious Studies at the University of San Diego. She specializes in the study of Indigenous religions and spiritualities on Turtle Island with a particular focus on intersections between spirituality, youth self-determination, and land-based activism.

Suggestions for further reading

In this book
See also chapters 49 (What is the Idle No More movement, and what's a round dance?), 53 (Why is the public expression of Indigenous religion political?), and 71 (What is the Ghost Dance?).

Elsewhere
Baldy, Cutcha Risling. *We Are Dancing for You: Native Feminisms and the Revitalization of Women's Coming of Age Ceremonies.* Seattle: University of Washington Press, 2018.

Crawford O'Brien, Suzanne, with Inés Talamantez. *Religion and Culture in Native America.* Lanham, MD: Rowman & Littlefield, 2021.

Iseke, Judy. "Spirituality as Decolonizing: Elders Albert Desjarlais, George McDermott, and Tom McCallum Share Understandings of Life in Healing Practices." *Decolonization: Indigeneity, Education & Society* 2(1) (2013): 35–54.

Owen, Suzanne. *The Appropriation of Native American Spirituality.* London: Bloomsbury Academic, 2008.

71
What is the Ghost Dance?

Tiffany Hale

The term "Ghost Dance" has been used by journalists, historians, and anthropologists to describe at least two Indigenous religious movements in the late nineteenth-century American West. The first, the 1870 Ghost Dance, refers to a movement that began in rural California, Nevada, and Oregon. The second and more famous Ghost Dance began in Nevada in 1889 and was carried throughout the Great Plains by messengers and emissaries. This iteration is known for its association with the Wounded Knee Massacre, where the US Army killed nearly three hundred unarmed Miniconjou people in South Dakota. The term has also been used retroactively to name various expressions of Native American religious activity in different places, including among Cherokees and Creeks in the early nineteenth century.

Ghost Dancing varies depending on linguistic and historical context. Each group that adopted it created their own unique version, but it tended to consist of some common elements, including a round dance style in which participants stood in a circle while moving and stomping their feet. This movement took place in coordination with song and the guidance of community-sanctioned religious leaders. Like other Indigenous religions, the distinction between prayer, song, and dance in this context is blurred or irrelevant. The purpose of the songs is to create and reaffirm ties between dancers and other participants, including passive observers. Ghost Dance songs give voice to particular states of consciousness, whether those are of reflection or the release of anger, sadness, or joy. These songs enable people to listen and to be heard at the same time, to focus, or to simply observe their own perceptions. Rhythmic concentration can also enable shifts of consciousness, including dreamlike states and euphoria. Nineteenth-century Ghost Dancers occasionally folded elements of Christian millenarian or prophetic tradition into their practice, although this aspect is sometimes overstated by historians. Regardless of the degree of Christian influence, Native peoples of the reservation era were resourceful in drawing upon numerous streams of inspiration in reacting to the hardships they faced.

Beyond simply responding to harrowing circumstances, Ghost Dancing carried a sense of newness at its core: it enabled Native American people to actualize and enact a different state of mind and social situation for themselves. This newness involved the adjustment and, in some cases, the dissolution of older ethnic boundaries in favor of a broader sense of Indianness. Some scholars have used the term "cultural revitalization" to refer to this adoption of pan-Indian identity, but they tend to overlook that this new selfhood was constructed and distinctly tied to broader patterns of racial consolidation in the post–Civil War era—namely, the assertion of normative whiteness. The Ghost Dance enabled Indigenous people from a wide range of backgrounds to begin seeing themselves as racially distinct from Europeans and their descendants, who had begun flowing into the Great Plains in unprecedented numbers.

Born from the social chaos unleashed by the Indian Wars and the waves of new immigrants in the West, the Ghost Dances of the nineteenth century sometimes implemented and inverted the racial binarism of the day. This is evident through future-oriented proclamations about the disappearance of White settlers through natural phenomena like floods or avalanches of soil. In this sense, Ghost Dancing presents an important yet underappreciated lens through which to consider rural Indigenous opposition to White supremacy and the logic of assimilation that prevailed in the 1870s and 1880s. Considered from this vantage point, Ghost Dance movements might be thought of as cousins to Blues traditions rooted in the Mississippi Delta, which emerged around the same time.

As was true of Black music and dance during this time period, Ghost Dancing was associated with criminality and being an outlaw. Today, however, it is often the subject of fascination and fetish by non-Indian people. Native American religion was formally banned by Congress in 1883, and anyone caught taking part in Indigenous religious ceremonies was subject to a fine or imprisonment. By 1890, White settlers began noticing that this new religious movement was inspiring Native people to come together in unprecedented ways and panicked. This panic ricocheted through the press and eventually inspired President Benjamin Harrison to deploy the US Army to Pine Ridge Reservation in the fall of 1890. The Wounded Knee Massacre resulted from this hysteria, and since that time, the Ghost Dance has become a moral touchstone in the American consciousness. The "outlaws" of the past may be considered heroes today, but because Ghost Dancing belongs to such a deeply fraught chapter of

American history, its meaning can be evasive. It meant—and continues to mean—different things to different people, and we should not allow false binaries or artificial categories to overdetermine its story.

About the author

Tiffany Hale is an assistant professor in the Department of Religion at Barnard College of Columbia University. She is a scholar of Indigenous religious traditions whose work focuses on nineteenth-century Native American history and US race relations. Professor Hale teaches courses in global Indigenous religious traditions, Native history, and religion in the Americas. Her current book project, *Fugitive Religion: The Ghost Dance and Native American Resistance after the Civil War*, is under contract with Yale University Press.

Suggestions for further reading

In this book
See also chapters 49 (What is the Idle No More movement, and what's a round dance?), 53 (Why is the public expression of Indigenous religion political?), and 54 (Why were Native American religious traditions outlawed?).

Elsewhere
Andersson, Rani-Henrik. *A Whirlwind Passed through Our Country: Lakota Voices of the Ghost Dance*. Norman: University of Oklahoma Press, 2018.

Gage, Justin. *We Do Not Want the Gates Closed between Us: Native Networks and the Spread of the Ghost Dance*. Norman: University of Oklahoma Press, 2020.

Warren, Louis. *God's Red Son: The Ghost Dance Religion and the Making of Modern America*. New York: Basic, 2017.

72

How are Indigenous narratives and oral traditions like "texts"?

Dennis Kelley

It is important to first establish what a "text" is. Many people tend to think of "texts" as only written or printed materials that need to be decoded into something that approximates spoken language, such as "reading" the "text" of a novel. In the analysis of human cultural production, however, any collection of symbolically meaningful things can be a "text," such as a dance, a painting, a film, or even things like buildings or vehicles. So let's think about texts as a collection of symbols that can communicate. In this way, orally transmitted materials that form the foundation of Indigenous cultural transmission are just as much a text as the Hindu Vedas, the Qu'ran, or the Bible. So the question can be reframed as, How can we view Indigenous narratives and oral traditions as *religious* texts?

Religious texts are somewhat unique, as they both tell the mythical stories of the traditions they belong to and establish the structures of reality in which that tradition exists. In other words, the stories found in religious narratives are about both the stories themselves and the world those stories are relevant to. This of course is the role of myths. Myths are stories of the *truly* true, the *really* real, ones that address the deeper meanings associated with particular traditions. These stories continue to reconstitute the universe in their telling, reestablishing the sacred by drawing on these deeper meanings. So religious stories in general—written or otherwise—are myths that communicate, affirm, and make real the foundational truths of the religious system.

Creation narratives provide a context for using mythic tales to determine the key ideas and values for the cultures that produce them. For example, the well-known story of creation in the Hebrew Bible—which is also relevant to both Christianity and Islam—from Genesis 1:1 to 2:3 begins with nothing but Yahweh, who then creates the entire universe and everything in it, including humans. The story emphasizes God as the author of the universe having universal control over everything in it, with humans acting as stewards of His creation. We can contrast this to the place-based Indigenous creation narrative of the Navajo, which begins in an already existing world below Navajo land. The story tells of collections of sacred beings interacting in each of four worlds, beginning with the First World and moving up the subsequent worlds until reaching the Fourth World, which is the Navajo lands in the southwestern United States. Once in the Fourth World, the beings organize the world, setting everything in place, before an earth goddess figure known as Changing Woman makes the Navajo people out of natural elements such as ground corn and minerals from the land.

The Genesis creation narrative sets up a relationship between Israel and Yahweh that is totally separate and subservient, while the Navajos are literally *of* the land and part of the natural order. These differences produce very different sorts of societies, or rather, these very different societies produce different creation stories. Nonetheless, they function in the same way in terms of giving their respective religious cultures a model to follow for living in the world.

The key difference between oral cultures and cultures of the book is the performative nature of sacred narratives. While certainly many religions that emphasize written texts also recite, sing, and often dance these stories as well as read them, oral cultures rely on proper physical proximity for the sacred tales to be transmitted. Communal knowledge and dedicated storytellers play important roles in the maintenance of the Indigenous nation's collective identity as well as the ethical systems the narratives encode.

Stories are at the heart of religious traditions in general, with the characters, scenes, and events illustrating the deepest truths that knit communities into a common world view. Religious texts, regardless of how they are told, heard, and remembered, are essential for maintaining the religious community and its connections to the foundational narrative. Indigenous stories, though they are orally transmitted, do the same work as written ones and so can be truly thought of as "texts."

About the author

Dennis Kelley is an associate professor of religious studies at the University of Missouri, Columbia. His research area is the intersection between religious, ethnic, and national identities, specifically in how they are negotiated and maintained through embodied practice in contemporary American Indian communities.

Suggestions for further reading

In this book

See also chapters 73 (What do trickster tales tell us about human beings, and why are they important in Indigenous cultures?), 74 (Why do so many Indigenous religions include trickster figures or ceremonial clowns?), and 75 (What is the Popol Vuh [and why is it not a Maya bible]?).

Elsewhere

Basso, Keith. *Wisdom Sits in Places*. Santa Fe: University of New Mexico Press, 1996.

Draper, Jonathan A., and Kenneth Mtata. "Orality, Literature, and African Religions." In *The Wiley-Blackwell Companion to African Religions*, 97–111. Malden, MA: Wiley-Blackwell, 2012.

Kunnie, Julian, and Nomalungelo Ivy Goduka. *Indigenous Peoples' Wisdom and Power: Affirming Our Knowledge through Narrative*. New York: Routledge, 1996.

73

What do trickster tales tell us about human beings, and why are they important in Indigenous cultures?

Davíd Carrasco

My first course at the University of Chicago Divinity School, Introduction to the History of Religion, taught me about trickster tales from Native America, Africa, and elsewhere. These tales told of a wandering rebel figure, part creator, part clown, sometimes thief, whose prodigious biological drives and exaggerated bodily parts brought mirth, examples of human limits, and lessons about creativity to the community. Tricksters are often animals like the wily coyote, the sly fox, the clever spider, and the cunning raven who challenge gods, insult shamans, undermine chiefs, and may become a cultural hero even when caught in the act. In some traditions, tricksters can change shapes and gender.

Stories my father told me about a Chicano trickster on the US-Mexico border came back to me. I wrote out the stories of the two-named "El Tortolo / Dusty Hobo," whose border adventures about police, thefts, sex, jokes, and death fascinated my professor. News of my trickster cycle passed through the faculty, and I became valued as akin to a primary source about tricksters in the US-Mexico borderlands.

One folktale mirroring some of these lessons tells about the trickster San Pedro and Jesucristo walking the countryside when Jesucristo sends San Pedro up to a nearby house to get a cooked chicken. On the way back, San Pedro ate one leg of the chicken, leading Jesucristo to ask, "Why has this chicken but one leg?" San Pedro says all the chickens in this area have "but one leg, sir."

Soon they see many sleeping chickens under a tree, all with one leg tucked up out of sight under their feathers. San Pedro, unable to restrain

230 INDIGENOUS RELIGIOUS TRADITIONS IN FIVE MINUTES

himself, tells Jesucristo proudly, "You see? All of the chickens have but one leg apiece." Then Jesucristo throws a rock at one chicken, and it stands up on both feet. Caught in his lie, San Pedro exclaims, "A miracle!" He quickly throws a rock at the other chickens, who all jump up on two feet. Pedro quickly turns to Jesucristo and says, "See? I can perform miracles, too."

Well-studied trickster tales, including the Yoruba deity Eshu-Elegba, the Greek god Hermes, the Norse god Loki, the Navajo Raven, and Coyote of the Great Plains, narrate how tricksters help prepare the world, with its conflicts and potentials, tragedies and comedies, for human habitation and culture. Tricksters have powers to create agriculture, free the animals for hunting, level mountains, create waterfalls, kill monsters, and yet bring social havoc through sexual misconduct. Sometimes they bring death into the world through carelessness.

One North American Indigenous tale making fun of male vanity tells of the Winnebago Trickster, whose enormous phallus is gnawed into fragments by a clever chipmunk. Humiliated, the trickster takes the fragments and transforms them, "for the people," into potatoes, turnips, artichokes, and ground beans. The story concludes that males in the future will have penises that are "a little long."

Tricksters have usually been considered male, though some change gender during the tale. More recent research shows that there are ample female trickster tales, such as the Japanese *kitsune*, fox tricksters who have paranormal abilities to trick samurai, merchants, and Buddhist monks. An example of a female trickster's combative power is told by the Desana people in southern Colombia. Turtle uses her wit to outsmart monkeys, foxes, deer, and other animals who threaten her. In one case, she helps invent music when she uses the leg bone of a jaguar as a flute.

Some tricksters steal from authority figures to benefit humankind. In the Navajo tradition, a powerful chief stashed the sun in a box. Raven turned himself into a tiny particle of drinking water that the chief's daughter drank and became pregnant. Raven was reborn as a baby in the chief's house, and when the baby cried for the box, it was given to him. Raven resumed his bird form and flew away, bringing the sun into the sky.

Among the Sanuma of Venezuela, a primordial alligator stores fire in its mouth, keeping it from humans. Hasimo, the bird man, shoots excrement into the alligator's face, causing it to laugh. Hasimo swoops in and steals the fire from the open mouth for humankind.

Enslaved Africans in the United States continued their ancestral traditions of telling animal trickster stories, such as Brer Rabbit tales, as moral education about the use of powers of cleverness, wit, and imagination to undermine the domination of slave masters and their cruelty.

Tricksters can create, educate, and challenge authorities, and they often undergo an ordeal.

A question for you the reader, Where do you find trickster tales in contemporary literature, films, and music?

About the author

Davíd Carrasco, Neil L. Rudenstine Professor of the Study of Latin America, is a Mexican American historian of religions with a particular interest in Mesoamerican cities as symbols and the US-Mexico borderlands. Working with Mexican archaeologists, he has carried out research in the excavations and archives associated with the sites of Teotihuacan and Mexico-Tenochtitlan, resulting in *Religions of Mesoamerica* and *City of Sacrifice*. Carrasco has received the Mexican Order of the Aztec Eagle, the highest honor the Mexican government gives to foreign nationals, and was recognized as the University of Chicago Alumnus of the Year in 2014.

Suggestions for further reading

In this book
See also chapters 72 (How are Indigenous narratives and oral traditions like "texts"?) and 74 (Why do so many Indigenous religions include trickster figures or ceremonial clowns?).

Elsewhere
Radin, P. *The Trickster: A Study in American Indian Mythology*. London: Routledge and Paul, 1956.

Sullivan, Lawrence. "Tricksters: An Overview." *Encyclopedia of Religion* 14 (2005): 9350–9352.

Sullivan, Lawrence. "Tricksters: Mesoamerican and South American Tricksters." *Encyclopedia of Religion* 14 (2005): 9357–9359.

Turner, Victor Witter. "Myth and Symbol." *International Encyclopedia of the Social Sciences* 10 (1968): 575–581.

74

Why do so many Indigenous religions include trickster figures or ceremonial clowns?

Chris Jocks

Much of what we recognize today as religion is serious business—deadly serious. Joking seems out of place when the orders of the day include converting the nations, avoiding eternal hellfire, vanquishing the forces of godlessness, or inching toward liberation from the cycle of samsara. Talmud and Zen are wonderful exceptions, but in our time, grimness is the rule. This means that humor, which psychologists insist is vital for human resilience, has no choice but to grow outside the walls of organized religion, in comedy clubs, in the break room, at home, in the woods, or in films. European-descended religions seem especially determined to condemn sexual humor, perennially the most popular variety of all.

Case in point, dateline 1921, Washington, DC: Commissioner of Indian Affairs Charles Burke issues "Circular No. 1665: Indian Dancing," authorizing and encouraging government Indian agents in New Mexico and Arizona to detain and punish Pueblo and Hopi Indians for engaging in their ceremonial dances. Burke was responding to years of complaints from missionaries in the field who were invited to Hopi and Pueblo ceremonial dances but were horrified at what they witnessed. Colorful, dignified dancers moving in complex, choreographed patterns while a chorus of men sing and keep time with deep, baritone drums. Then the clowns appear. Known by many names, they move freely amid the disciplined dancers until commencing one of their skits, full of gestures and jokes that draw embarrassed smiles and deep laughter from the spectators. And yes, some of the skits were clearly, unabashedly sexual.

Commissioner Burke's edict was only sporadically enforced and was finally voided in 1934, but the episode reveals a profound disconnect about these sacred clowns. In Hopi and Pueblo worlds, clown work is powerful.

It supports the community's life in a surprising variety of ways. To begin with, yes, on the surface, their antics remind people of what they should not be doing by doing it. Their skits parody broad categories of misbehavior, but they can also take sharper aim at specific individuals, delivering a dose of humility to someone who might need it. But that's not all. Sexual antics have a special place here because these are worlds that cherish the connection between human sexuality and the fertility of all life, on which the human community depends. Ultimately, these clowns are figures of liminality, purposefully leavening the strict and necessary structure of the dance. They hear and see everything. They improvise gestures of lighting that invite the rain, even while they step in between the lines to help a dancer whose regalia need adjustment. By the end of the hot day, the laughter, the gestures, and the smiles invite the cloud spirits with their gifts of life-giving rain. The cloud spirits were once ancestors, now at home again, happy that their descendants are full of life.

Other Indigenous peoples in North America have their own versions of this interplay of structure and spontaneity. Think of the Heyoka societies on the northern plains, or among the Diné, the Water Sprinkler of the Yei bichei ceremony. Such figures are even more abundant in stories—for instance, the ubiquitous coyote stories or, along the Pacific Northwest Coast, tales of the raven. Something worth pondering is that this raven is recognized not only as a trickster but as the Creator! Levity, like leavening, opens pockets of creativity that break the heaviness of structure. In a similar way, in spring in the longhouse where I come from, men perform a dance to welcome back the thunder beings. Their energy revitalizes our Mother Earth and wakes up the soil after her long winter sleep under heavy blankets. It's a dance full of spontaneous gestures. The singers suddenly stop, and the dancers freeze, usually in awkward positions. The people laugh. The gardens grow.

About the author

Chris Jocks, Kahnawà:ke Mohawk, is senior lecturer in Applied Indigenous Studies at Northern Arizona University. He earned his PhD in Religious Studies under the direction of Inés Talamantez at the University of California, Santa Barbara, in 1994. His work includes publications on the conceptual incongruity between Indigenous and settler state societies and nations, as manifest in law, religion, and social practices. He is also engaged with local Indigenous community advocacy in northern Arizona.

Suggestions for further reading

In this book
See also chapters 72 (How are Indigenous narratives and oral traditions like "texts"?) and 73 (What do trickster tales tell us about human beings, and why are they important in Indigenous cultures?).

Elsewhere

Beck, Peggy V., Anna Lee Walters, and Nia Francisco. *The Sacred: Ways of Knowledge, Sources of Life* (redesigned edition). Tsaile, AZ: Navajo Community College Press, 1992.

Nelson, Melissa K. "Mending the Split-Head Society with Trickster Consciousness." In *Original Instructions: Indigenous Teachings for a Sustainable Future*, edited by Melissa K. Nelson, 288–298. Rochester, VT: Bear, 2008.

Talayesva, Don. *Sun Chief: The Autobiography of a Hopi Indian.* Edited by Leo W. Simmons. New York: Yale University Press, 1942.

"The Trickster." *Parabola: Myth and the Quest for Meaning* 4(1) (1979).

Wenger, Tisa. *We Have a Religion: The 1920s Pueblo Indian Dance Controversy and American Religious Freedom.* Chapel Hill: University of North Carolina Press, 2009.

75

What is the Popol Vuh
(and why is it not a Maya bible)?

Mallory E. Matsumoto

Composed in the K'iche' Mayan language on fifty-six handwritten folios, the Popol Vuh or Popol Wuj is the most well-known colonial document from the Indigenous Americas. The oldest surviving version, now housed in the Newberry Library in Chicago, was copied in the early eighteenth century by the Dominican friar Francisco Ximénez in the Guatemalan town of Chichicastenango. The manuscript is structured in two columns: the left-hand side contains the K'iche' text and on the right is Ximénez's Spanish-translation commentary. But the origins of the K'iche' contents were surely much earlier; Ximénez probably based his copy on a mid-sixteenth-century compilation by K'iche' elites who lived around the town of Santa Cruz del Quiché in Guatemala, who had in turn drawn on narratives from precolonial times.

One of the Popol Vuh's most outstanding features is the K'iche' text's rich, poetic language, a testament to a centuries-long rhetorical tradition. Its contents span themes in mythology, cosmology, history, and genealogy. The creation account describes two unsuccessful creations inhabited first by mud people and then wooden people; not until the third, current generation of humans shaped from corn dough were the gods satisfied. A significant portion of the mythological narrative follows the so-called Hero Twins named Xbalanque and Junajpu', whose exploits established key components of the world order as it exists today, including relations with the underworld, or Xibalba. The final section addresses more recent history, including the origin of the K'iche' people and the genealogy of one K'iche' lineage known as the Kaweq.

As the earliest and most extensive manuscript known from the colonial Americas that was written by Indigenous authors in their native language, the Popol Vuh has been fundamental to Mesoamericanist scholarship, with researchers often using (and sometimes misusing) it to interpret precontact cosmology, religion, and history. Yet it has also achieved wide popular appeal. Since 1861, translations based on some combination of the Spanish and K'iche' texts in the Ximénez manuscript have been published in French, German, English, Hungarian, Japanese, and Turkish, among other languages. The K'iche' title literally translates to something like "mat book" or "book related to the mat" and has received many different glosses in English—the Sacred Book, the Book of the Council, the Book of the People—but perhaps its most widespread nickname is the Maya bible.

The most obvious explanation for the "Maya bible" epithet is that sections of the K'iche' text closely parallel parts of the Christian Bible—a resemblance that Garry Sparks argues was the K'iche' authors' intentional response to Spanish friars' attempts to translate the tenets of Catholicism into Maya terms. But this very limited resemblance does not make the Popol Vuh the Maya bible. Unlike the Christian Bible, the Jewish Torah, or the Muslim Qur'an, for that matter, the Popol Vuh was not venerated as a compendium of divine revelations or the product of heavenly inspiration; it recorded K'iche' beliefs and history, including accounts of their gods, but not the words of those gods themselves. The text was compiled for a specific audience and not widely disseminated; indeed, during the colonial era, its circulation was intentionally restricted to avoid the potentially violent consequences of discovery by Spanish clergy. Moreover, there is no evidence that the Popol Vuh narratives were considered "canonical" in the sense of being exclusively genuine or authoritative. On the contrary, comparing them with other colonial-era Maya accounts of mythology, cosmology, and history indicates that although authors may have disagreed with one another on some points, they did not strive to suppress or demean competing narratives as did those who canonized the Christian Bible.

Instead, the "Maya bible" moniker says more about those who use it than it does about the K'iche' text. Some would say that it provides non-Maya readers an easy point of entry for understanding the text's mythological and cosmological contents. After all, the Bible itself also integrates those themes with genealogical and historical information. Others may argue that comparison with the Christian Bible underscores the Popol Vuh's value as a piece of cultural patrimony—overlooking the irony that the efforts of Catholic missionaries are the very reason why the Popol Vuh is so precious today as a unique record of knowledge that was suppressed under Spanish colonialism. But why the need to find an analog at all? On its own terms, the Popol Vuh is a complex treatise on cosmology and mythology, a community response to a changing political and religious landscape, and a historical record of a culture that remains central to K'iche' identity today.

About the author

Mallory E. Matsumoto is assistant professor in the Department of Religious Studies at the University of Texas at Austin. Her research addresses the interface between language, material culture, and religion in precolonial and colonial Maya communities of Mesoamerica. She has conducted archaeological fieldwork and archival research in Guatemala, Mexico, Hungary, Peru, and the United States.

Suggestions for further reading

In this book
See also chapter 72 (How are Indigenous narratives and oral traditions like "texts"?).

Elsewhere
Christenson, Allen J., ed. and trans. *Popol Vuh: The Sacred Book of the Maya.* Norman: University of Oklahoma Press, 2007.

Quiroa, Néstor. "The Popol Vuh and the Dominican Religious Extirpation in Highland Guatemala: Prologues and Annotations of Fr. Francisco Ximénez." *Americas* 67(4) (2011): 467–494.

Sparks, Garry. "The Use of Mayan Scripture in the Americas' First Christian Theology." *Numen* 61(4) (2014): 396–429.

van Akkeren, Ruud W. "Authors of the Popol Wuj." *Ancient Mesoamerica* 14(2) (2003): 237–256.

76
Did colonial missions destroy Indigenous religions?

Brandon Bayne

European colonization in the Americas dramatically impacted precontact Indigenous lifeways. In their work of territorial dispossession, monarchs employed missionaries to either extirpate or convert Indigenous spaces, bodies, and customs. Extirpation campaigns set out to discover and destroy powerful objects as well as challenge the authority of Indigenous ritual leaders. When Native practices and peoples could not be altogether removed—because they were too prevalent, potent, or planted in the land—colonial missionaries worked to reorient them toward the worship of the Christian god. Strategies varied, depending on the empire, the denomination, the moment, and the mood. Still, pastors and priests of all persuasions consistently drew upon shared conceptions of "civilization" to determine their approach to Indigenous religions.

The Spanish Jesuit José de Acosta, for instance, developed a guide for "procuring the salvation of the Indians" that relied on his evaluation of their relative cultural sophistication in relation to Western Christendom's cities, political governance, alphabetic literacy, and Catholic religion. Believing Europe represented civilization's full fluorescence, Acosta measured all other cultures—from Asia to Africa to the Americas—by their perceived deviation from these fourfold criteria. Though he had not visited Asia, Acosta relied on reports from fellow Jesuits to rank China closest to this ideal and counted it fully civilized in all but its lack of alphabetic spelling and knowledge of the Christian deity. Likewise, Jesuits believed they could "accommodate" Catholicism to other Asian societies like Japan and India without dramatically reorienting their social, political, and linguistic practices.

In contrast, Acosta cited his own direct observation in the Americas to judge its Indigenous communities as mostly deficient. The Jesuit conceded that city-states like Tenochtitlan in Mesoamerica and Tawantinsuyu in the Andes came nearest to his archetype, as he begrudgingly praised their sophisticated urban, legal, and literary cultures. Nevertheless, he and fellow priests classified Aztec and Inka religious practices as "idolatrous" perversions that must be redirected to Christian worship. Following a practice that dated back to the sixth-century Pope Gregory I, missionaries decided that sacred places like Mexican temples or Andean *huacas* (monuments) could be "converted," toppling and repurposing them for Christian shrines and feasts dedicated to Jesus, the Virgin, or the saints. In this way, important Indigenous locations, objects, and ceremonies continued in Catholic translation.

From California to Paraguay, other Native peoples employed strategic mobility, oral memory, diffuse leadership, and permeable notions of sacred power according to their environment. Europeans concluded that these communities operated "*sin ley, sin rey, sin fe*" (without law, king, or religion) and attempted to thoroughly reconfigure Indigenous life through coerced movement and consolidation into *reducciones* (mission farms) focused on inculcating European languages, sedentary agriculture, and Christian sacraments. The Puritan pastor John Eliot attempted something similar in colonial Massachusetts, creating "praying towns" to school Algonquian converts in English customs and pastoral labors to accompany the intimate narrations of faith demanded by his rigorous form of Protestantism.

Even in the most thorough efforts of assimilation, however, missionaries rarely succeeded in destroying Indigenous religions. Andean huacas could not be removed from their landscapes. Story and medicine were passed down in homes and beyond surveillance in the *monte* (wild). In 1680s New Mexico, *katsina* (spirit beings) inspired diverse Pueblo to revolt, kill missionaries, and take up both traditional and Christian symbols as "signs of power and resistance." Farther north, Wendat communities moved into Catholic spaces and just as often moved back out in pursuit of more powerful *manitou* (life force) that would help them navigate escalating warfare and disease. Alongside resistance, many found ways of weaving their practices and positionalities into Christianity. The 1531 apparition and ensuing veneration of the Virgin of Guadalupe at Tepeyac in Mexico represents one prominent hybrid production. While priests hailed her as Mary and promoted her as patroness of Mexico, Nahuas recognized *tonantzin*, "our mother," to whom they had made pilgrimage and sacrifice long before Franciscan "fathers" arrived.

Native engagements with colonial missions were diverse and strategic. Many communities adopted Christian objects and rituals for a time, then rejected them according to seasonal demands or shifting necessities. Some found it best to integrate their beliefs and practices into the colonists' religion and freshly articulate them as a means of "survivance," a term employed by Gerald Vizenor (Minnesota Chippewa Tribe) to describe how Indigenous communities not only have survived colonial pressures but creatively repurpose practices as a way of transcending victimization and thriving in the present. Others resisted outright, as they revitalized tradition and resourced spiritual and material power to protect their territorial and cultural sovereignty. While missionaries may have desired the reconfiguration and even destruction of their religions, these dynamic responses helped Indigenous people navigate asymmetrical encounters, secure significant continuities, and strategically adapt in the midst of calamitous change.

About the author

Brandon Bayne is an associate professor in the Department of Religious Studies at the University of North Carolina at Chapel Hill. His first book, *Missions Begin with Blood: Suffering and Salvation in the Borderlands of New Spain* (Fordham University Press, 2021), argues that Catholic priests invoked the rhetoric of redemptive sacrifice to justify epidemic disease, colonial dislocation, and the territorial dispossession of Indigenous communities. His current research focuses on race, religion, and erasure in the modern memorialization of colonial missionaries in the US-Mexico borderlands.

Suggestions for further reading

In this book
See also chapters 77 (Why would Indigenous people venerate Roman Catholic saints?) and 79 (Did Indigenous children lose their religion in US residential boarding schools?).

Elsewhere
Anderson, Emma. *Betrayal of Faith: The Tragic Journey of a Colonial Native Convert.* Cambridge, MA: Harvard University Press, 2007.

Liebmann, Matthew. *Revolt: An Archaeological History of Pueblo Resistance and Revitalization in 17th Century New Mexico.* Tucson: University of Arizona Press, 2014.

Martin, Joel, and Mark A. Nicholas, eds. *Native Americans, Christianity, and the Reshaping of the American Religious Landscape.* Chapel Hill: University of North Carolina Press, 2010.

Mills, Kenneth. *Idolatry and Its Enemies: Colonial Andean Religion and Extirpation, 1640–1750.* Princeton, NJ: Princeton University Press, 2012.

Mt. Pleasant, Alyssa, Caroline Wigginton, and Kelly Wisecup, eds. "Materials and Methods in Native American and Indigenous Studies Forum." Part 1, *William and Mary Quarterly* 75(2) (2018): 207–236.

Mt. Pleasant, Alyssa, Caroline Wigginton, and Kelly Wisecup, eds. "Materials and Methods in Native American and Indigenous Studies Forum." Part 2, *Early American Literature* 53(2) (2018): 407–444.

77

Why would Indigenous people venerate Roman Catholic saints?

Daniel E. Nourry Burgos

For the Roman Catholic faithful, the lives of the saints stand as historical examples of exceptional lives of faith—that is to say, of lives lived within the secular world but without having compromised the virtues the Roman Catholic church extols. To the faithful, the saints provide proof of miracles and offer lived examples from which to draw inspiration and models to imitate as they live their own lives of faith. It is well known that the Catholic faith arrived upon the shores of the Americas hand in hand with colonization, and so the question is, Why would Indigenous people venerate Roman Catholic saints? A deceptively simple answer might be because within the history of saints, we find quite a few Indigenous people. Let's briefly meet a few of them.

In October 2017, Pope Francis declared three Tlaxcalan Indigenous children—known only by their Christian names as Cristobalito, Antonio, and Juan—to be saints. These young Indigenous boys were said to have been murdered in what is now Mexico at the very beginning of the Spanish evangelization and colonization of Abiayala. Cristobalito, who was the firstborn son of Ayoxtecatl, a prominent Tlaxcalan noble and ally of Hernando Cortés in the battle for Tenochtitlan, was killed by his father in 1527 for attempting to convert his own family and their many vassals to this newly arrived religion of Christianity. Two years later, in 1529, Antonio—grandson to Xiochtenactl, also a prominent Indigenous noble—and Juan, his servant, volunteered to accompany a Dominican missionary on an evangelization mission to Oaxaca, Mexico. It was during this mission that both were beaten to death and thrown into a ravine by the townspeople who had discovered them removing stone Indigenous religious relics from local households.

Juan Diego Cuāuhtlahtoātzin was an Indigenous person of the Chichimeca people. In 1531, he was reported to have experienced between four and five apparitions or visitations by the Virgin Mary. The reason for the visitations was that the Virgin Mary was selecting him to deliver a message to Juan Zumarraga, bishop of Mexico. The message, in simple terms, was that he should build a chapel in her name so that those who have need of her help can find a place from which to pray for her intervention. The bishop needed quite some convincing, and a now famous "miracle" finally persuaded him to do the Virgin's bidding. The miracle in question occurred during Juan Diego's fourth visit with the bishop, where he was to deliver some wild flowers on behalf of Mary. When Juan Diego laid the flowers at the bishop's feet, Zumarraga noticed that these flowers had left a clear and distinct image of the Virgin pressed into the fabric of Juan Diego's mantle. The bishop, of course, immediately acquiesced to the Virgin's demands. In 2002, some 471 years later, Pope John Paul II declared Juan Diego a saint in a ceremony held in Mexico City's cathedral.

Kateri Tekakwitha—an Indigenous woman of Algonquin-Mohawk descent—was born in 1656 to the Mohawk chief Kenneronkwa. Tekakwitha was the firstborn child of the union between Kenneronkwa and Kahenta, her mother, who was an Algonquin woman captured by Kenneronkwa's people during a raid and taken back to Mohawk lands. Tekakwitha was orphaned by a smallpox epidemic when she was approximately four years old. The same plague left her face visibly scarred and seriously damaged her vision. By the age of nineteen, she had converted to Catholicism and taken up the name Kateri. At the time of her conversion, Kateri took a vow of perpetual virginity, which she maintained for the rest of her short life. Kateri died five years later at the age of twenty-four. The Roman Catholic Church recognized the exceptional nature of her Christian life as an example of saintly virtues. She was canonized in a ceremony held in St. Peter's Basilica in October 2012 by Pope Benedict XVI. Her mother, Kahenta, had been baptized Catholic prior to having been taken from her people.

There are of course others I could mention, but I chose these three examples carefully in the hope that they might allow me to muddy the water, so to speak, by offering you a small sample of the questions raised by our original query. Saint making is an official process and one conducted by the Vatican. Saints are declared to be so after a long process of investigation. You will have noticed the difference in time between when these Indigenous people lived and when they were declared saints. Are there no contemporary Indigenous saints? What is Indigenous about these saints? There are many contemporary Indigenous communities who practice

Catholicism and Christianity, and the veneration of saints, Indigenous or otherwise, is a core aspect of this faith practice. If we remember that Catholicism came to the Americas as part of a colonial enterprise, then it seems legitimate to ask what might an Indigenous community find to venerate in the figure of a non-Indigenous saint like Michael the Archangel, St. Jude, or Santa Rosa de Lima? In what ways have Indigenous peoples contributed to the history of this faith?

These are preliminary questions, certainly. However, they are important, and I am hoping you will join me in believing that it is very important to pursue these lines of inquiry.

About the author

Daniel E. Nourry Burgos is PhD candidate in Iberian and Latin American literatures and cultures at the University of Texas at Austin in the Department of Spanish and Portuguese. He is also a graduate portfolio candidate in both the Native American and Indigenous Studies Program and the Study of Religion Graduate Portfolio Program. His research draws methodologically on the disciplines of religious studies, Latin American literature and cultural studies, ethnohistory, and critical Indigenous studies in order to analyze the processes that bring into existence the notion of an Indigenous Catholic martyr-saint.

Suggestions for further reading

In this book
See also chapters 56 (Do Indigenous people have churches?) and 76 (Did colonial missions destroy Indigenous religions?).

Elsewhere
Brading, D. A. *Mexican Phoenix, Our Lady of Guadalupe: Image and Tradition across Five Centuries.* Cambridge: Cambridge University Press, 2001.

Greer, Allan. *Mohawk Saint: Catherine Tekakwitha and the Jesuits.* Oxford: Oxford University Press, 2005.

Hamann, Byron Ellsworth. "Child Martyrs and Murderous Children: Age and Agency in Sixteenth-Century Transatlantic Religious Conflicts." In *The Social Experience of Childhood in Ancient Mesoamerica*, edited by Traci Ardren and Scott Hutson, 203–231. Boulder: University Press of Colorado, 2006.

Haskett, Robert. "Dying for Conversion: Faith, Obedience, and the Tlax-calan Boy Martyrs in New Spain." *Colonial Latin American Review* 17(2) (2008): 185–212.

Trexler, Richard C. "From the Mouths of Babes: Christianization by Children in 16th Century New Spain." In *Church and Community, 1200–1600: Studies in the History of Florence and New Spain*, 549–573. Rome: Edizioni di storia e letteratura, 1987.

78

How might we talk about Indigeneity and Catholicism in the Andes?

Sierra L. Lawson

When we think of or discuss religion in the Andes, it is important to keep in mind how, following the conquest of Peru, categories of European Catholicism and Andean Indigeneity were not mutually exclusive. A significant number of Indigenous communities today as well as the descendants of Indigenous Andeans—sometimes classified as mestizos or Creoles—identify as Catholic. Throughout the pan-Andean region, from the islands of Chiloe to the Pacific Lowlands cradled by the Cordillera Occidental in modern-day Colombia, Catholic saints are venerated, and Catholic festivals are coordinated. Andean Catholicism involves regionally specific traditions where practitioners integrate elements of Christianity as well as Indigenous Andean beliefs and practices in different ways according to their respective local histories. It is therefore necessary to more carefully consider the particulars of processes involved in interactions between European and Andean genealogies of religion while remaining mindful that neither operated as discrete entities and, instead, produced multiple variations of religious beliefs and practices across the Americas.

Local festivals, juridical procedures, rites of passage, and rituals related to the agriculture-based calendar continue to draw on the oral histories and materials that were popular in the vast Inca Empire prior to the arrival of Spanish conquistadors. For example, Corpus Christi festivals in Cuzco—which was the capital of Tawantinsuyu (the Inca Empire) in precontact times—continue to occur on the same timeline as the Inca's harvest cycles, which culminated in their celebration of the winter solstice. While the category of religion certainly is tainted with a European foundation, we can reasonably describe the continuation of the Inca calendar through Catholic rituals as one site where Indigenous Andeans are participating in something they themselves identify as religious.

In addition to contemporary forms of religion that Indigenous Andeans engage in today, there are historical examples of Inca elite educated in the Andean Highlands who produced materials that speak to the influence both Catholic and Indigenous elements had on Indigenous systems of belief. One example is Felipe Guaman Poma de Ayala, a chronicler well known for his illustrated chronicle written with the audience of King Phillip III of Spain in mind. While the chronicle was finished in the early seventeenth century, Guaman Poma was highly influenced by the conquest of Tawantinsuyu during the mid- to late sixteenth century. Guaman Poma's native language was Quechua, but he became fluent in Spanish during his education among communities of Iberian-born religious men. For when the Pizarro brothers made their voyage from their homeland in the south of Spain to the coast of South America in the early sixteenth century, they brought with them their own local practices and notions of religion. Being from Extremadura, they were especially acquainted with the Virgin of Guadalupe—a black Madonna in Cáceres popular among Iberian devotees since the late Middle Ages, not to be confused with the Mexican apparition from the early sixteenth century. While Marian devotion remains a prominent element of the Catholicism practiced throughout the Americas today, we can also see a variety of sites wherein Indigenous Andeans continue to draw on strategies from moments of early contact that their predecessors used to maintain Indigenous devotional practices.

Like many other descendants of Inca elite such as his contemporary Don Diego de Castro Titu Cusi Yupanqui, Guaman Poma used his Spanish education to make land rights claims on behalf of Indigenous Andeans as well as depict the many ways that his community had come to interact with elements of Catholicism introduced by the Pizarros and their entourage. The first portion of his chronicle depicts a series of scenes from Genesis. These illustrations reimagine each scene as distinctly Andean—Adam is portrayed as working the arid soil specific to high-altitude mountain peaks using the traditional *taki chaclla* (Andean digging device) in a scene Guaman Poma labels *El Primer Mundo*, or "the first world." His chronicle continues with drawings of Hebrew Bible patriarchs in succession (Noah, Abraham, and David) as well as key Christian figures such as the Virgin Mary and her corresponding miracles. All while depicting these scenes and reimagining them according to his understanding of the conquest, Guaman Poma also draws and describes Indigenous Andean beliefs, such as their worship of *huacas* (sometimes spelled *waqas*); their division of Tawantinsuyu into four provinces (Chinchaysuyu, Collasuyu, Antisuyu, and Cuntisuyu), with the capital city Cuzco at the center; and other pre-conquest practices he positions as interacting with Catholicism following Spanish contact.

As Guaman Poma and Indigenous Andeans today demonstrate, the interaction of Catholicism and Indigenous traditions in South America is not a simple matter. The history of Catholicism and Indigenous traditions in the Andes in particular has been framed in a number of ways today. Such interactions—whether coined as hybridity, syncretism, or any other name—were the result of complex power dynamics and Iberian under-standings of religion specific to the early contact and colonial period.

About the author

Sierra L. Lawson is a doctoral student in the religion and culture track in the Department of Religious Studies at the University of North Caro-lina at Chapel Hill. Sierra's current work examines competing transat-lantic discourses on maternal health within visual and textual archives. She is specifically interested in the devotional labor of "Morisca" women in the Ebro region and women in early Andean colonies as mutu-ally influenced by and influencing imperial grammars for classifying "religion." In studying rhetorics of devotion, she has previously focused on communities who describe themselves as Marian—and, specifically, Guadalupan—devotees.

Suggestions for further reading

In this book
See also chapters 76 (Did colonial missions destroy Indigenous religions?) and 77 (Why would Indigenous people venerate Roman Catholic saints?).

Elsewhere
Adorno, Rolena, ed. *From Oral to Written Expression: Native Andean Chronicles of the Early Colonial Period.* Syracuse, NY: Maxwell School of Citizenship and Public Affairs, 1982.

Burns, Kathryn. "Making Indigenous Archives: The Quilcaycamayoc of Colonial Cuzco." *Hispanic American Historical Review* 91(4) (2011): 665–689.

Dean, Carolyn. *Inka Bodies and the Body of Christ: Corpus Christi in Colonial Cuzco, Peru.* Durham, NC: Duke University Press, 1999.

Dueñas, Alcira. *Indians and Mestizos in the "Lettered City": Reshaping Justice, Social Hierarchy, and Political Culture in Colonial Peru.* Boulder: University Press of Colorado, 2010.

Ramos, Gabriela, and Yanna Yannakakis. *Indigenous Intellectuals: Knowledge, Power, and Colonial Culture in Mexico and the Andes.* Durham, NC: Duke University Press, 2014.

79
Did Indigenous children lose their religion in US residential boarding schools?

Zara Surratt

Residential boarding schools were a central component of federal Indian policy after the Civil War. Although they predated it, they were intended to complement the Dawes General Allotment Act of 1887, which authorized the subdivision of land owned by tribes into portions deemed appropriate for agriculture. Policymakers envisioned that this process would separate communities into nuclear family units. Meanwhile, boarding school education would eliminate the transmission of Indigenous cultural knowledge through separation. Through political, cultural, and religious education, reformers aimed to bring students into compliance with prescribed social norms. There is no single way to describe students' religious experiences at these institutions, but it is clear that Indian education policy failed to annihilate Indigenous religions, and students creatively responded to their new situations in diverse ways.

While schools varied in location, religious denomination, and day-to-day operation, they were all militaristically organized. Students were transported, sometimes thousands of miles, from their homes and instructed in military drills and industrial training—agricultural for boys, domestic for girls. Surveillance was the order of the day (though institutions varied in their leniency), and staff monitored students constantly. Daily schedules allocated half the day to classroom and chapel activities and the remainder to industrial work, which schools depended on for revenue. Some survivors report that despite moments of useful instruction, the work was largely repetitive and extremely tiring.

These institutions ultimately sought the destruction of their pupils' religious identities. The founder of Carlisle Indian Industrial Institute stated this goal in chilling fashion: "All the Indian there is in the race should be dead. Kill the Indian in him and save the man." Proponents believed the separation of Natives from their traditions was a necessary part of a providential Christian mission. Ulysses S. Grant endorsed hiring "godly men and women," who would instruct students in a Protestant-Republican ideology advocating reverence for private property, personal industry, and obedient patriotism.

Federal policymakers recognized the broad diversity of Indigenous religions and hoped to supplant it. Institutions separated students from their communities and land to break connections and keep them from learning traditional ways of being. They separated kin members across institutions when budget and circumstance allowed and cut students off from religious celebrations that were locational and seasonal. Some of the first actions administrators would take when receiving a student were renaming them according to Christian standards, cutting their hair, and replacing their traditional clothing with a school uniform. Yankton Dakota activist Zitkála-Šá remembers this process as one of a series of "extreme indignities" she was forced to suffer. Through surveillance and discipline, students were forbidden from using their tribal languages and expressing their oral cultures. This all occurred within a larger framework that denigrated Indigeneity as heathenish and backward. Schools emphasized assimilation into American Christianity, which was presented as culturally and universally superior.

There is no singular residential boarding school experience. Institutions varied in method and strictness. Students came from various backgrounds, with different ideas of themselves and the world, which affected how they responded to their circumstances. Some students reacted with confusion to the religious instruction they received. Others were torn between what they knew from home and what they heard at school. Some found deep meaning in the Christianity they encountered. Many of the students came from communities with centuries of missionization history and may have found the instruction and tactics familiar, perhaps even comforting or irritating.

Many students certainly drew upon the religious resources of their homes as they survived. Hopi Don C. Talayesva shares an account of being hospitalized at Sherman Institute and making a journey back home in his sleep. His experience begs the question of how many other students may have been in connection with their community's religious traditions unconsciously, whether in resistance to or creatively alongside the Christianity they were being taught. Some experienced linguistic and cultural exchange, which set the groundwork for a pan-Indian consciousness. Others deepened their commitment to particular tribal identities.

A consistent theme of survivor accounts is the pain and trauma associated with removal that ruptured relationships, made children wildly vulnerable to abuse, and decreased opportunities for cultural transmission. Survivors, descendants, and their communities still grapple with the aftermath of these institutions and the policies that created them. And in that struggle, many individuals and communities are finding the recovery and renewal of traditional ways of being to be at the core of intergenerational healing and communal revitalization.

About the author

Zara Surratt is a doctoral candidate in the Department of Religious Studies at the University of North Carolina at Chapel Hill. Her research interests include the religious history of the American West; the intersections of race, disability, and religion; ideas of embodied difference; and religion and children.

Suggestions for further reading

In this book
See also chapters 56 (Do Indigenous people have churches?) and 76 (Did colonial missions destroy Indigenous religions?).

Elsewhere
Adams, David Wallace. *Education for Extinction: American Indians and the Boarding School Experience, 1875–1928.* Lawrence: University Press of Kansas, 1995.

Lajimodiere, Denise K. *Stringing Rosaries: The History, the Unforgivable, and the Healing of Northern Plains American Indian Boarding School Survivors.* Fargo: North Dakota State University Press, 2019.

Lomawaima, K. Tsianina. *They Called It Prairie Light: The Story of Chilocco Indian School.* Lincoln: University of Nebraska Press, 1995.

80
How do Indigenous religions approach disability?

Zara Surratt

While everyone has an idea of what constitutes disability, people continue to dispute what disability is, what it means, and how it should be approached. Experts in Western medicine identify health and wellness as pertaining to individual bodies, but Indigenous models understand it to be connected to something larger, involving a balance associated with proper relationship to land, kin, ceremony, and tradition. Indigenous religions have no singular approach to bodily and cognitive differences but are universally more concerned with ideas of connection and disconnection than ability or disability.

Bodily differences and the meanings they hold are affected by cultural context. For example, a deaf girl in early twentieth-century New York would undoubtedly experience issues of unequal access and discrimination. They would affect who she could marry, where she could work, who could teach her, and other legal and social obstacles. Meanwhile, a Lakota girl with the same impairment might not consider herself "disabled" at all. In addition to spoken language, her people would have used Plains Indian Sign Language regularly in conversation, trade, and ceremony. In these differing contexts, the experience of deafness is shaped by issues of access and cultural understanding—for the girl in New York, her deafness is an inherent attribute that requires policing. For the Lakota girl, her impairment has little, if any, social relevance.

Indigenous world views do not acknowledge the same fixity that Western societies assign to the phenomenon of impairment. Ethnographer Cruz Begay (Tohono O'odham) shares, "This is the way that we are taught to be in the world: to feel in harmony with the world around us. Using the words *disabled* or *disability* seemed like there was a permanent disharmony in the world of a person with disabilities." The founding story of the Confederacy of the Five Nations tells of an Onondaga named Hiawatha who becomes sad, aimless, and distracted when an evil sorcerer kills his family and leaves him isolated. A fateful visit to Mohawk land introduces him to Deganawidah, a peacemaker who cannot relay his unifying message due to a speech impediment. The two men conduct a ceremony of healing with wampum and produce a speech that unites the Five Nations. Through intimacy and relationality, they are restored to a state of balance that enables their unique gifts to benefit their communities.

In this story, imbalance is the result of disconnection from their people, not the impairments themselves. Similar ideas abound in other American Indian cosmologies. According to some Navajo world views, differences visible at birth, such as a cleft palate, were a sign of taboo parental actions such as performing incest or being struck by lightning. Balance could be restored through ceremony, but the visible difference would remain. Disconnection was not the difference itself but the rupture in relationality or ceremonial correctness that was associated with it. Fascinatingly, some Navajo traditions understood transverse births to be the result of a spiritually powerful being trying to bypass corporeal life. Children that survived were expected to become shamans, revealing an association of bodily difference with dangerous but vital spiritual power.

Indigenous religions have complex views on life, death, and lethal harm. Popular stereotypes depict the abandonment of elders, youth, and the disabled as commonplace, but this actually occurred rarely. It was likely in times of extreme deprivation, such as wartime or drought. Arapaho accounts portray elderly people choosing to stay behind when a migratory group moved on, likely to avoid a difficult journey and death in an unfamiliar place. This suggests that in at least some cases, subjects had agency in determining whether and how their lives ended. Native cosmologies generally disapproved of suicide, associating it with alterations in the afterlife, but at least some acknowledged a right to die. Some Iroquois committed suicide to avoid suffering in captivity. A group of Cherokees in the eighteenth century were afflicted with smallpox and associated it with ritual pollution. When traditional medicine failed to cure it, they chose suicide. These cases defy simplification and demonstrate complex valuations of the meaning of pain and illness.

Indigenous religions emphasize connectivity. They complexly and diversely valuate physical and cognitive differences within communities. These frameworks preclude the establishment of a systemic approach to disability as inherently deviant, such as twentieth-century eugenics, which viewed the sterilization and eventual elimination of the "unfit" as socially imperative. Instead, responses to bodily variation are fluidic and dynamic but circulate around the restoration of balance and proper relationality.

About the author

Zara Surratt is a doctoral candidate in the Department of Religious Studies at the University of North Carolina at Chapel Hill. Her research interests include the religious history of the American West; the intersections of race, disability, and religion; ideas of embodied difference; and religion and children.

Suggestions for further reading

In this book
See also chapter 61 (What role does healing play in Native American and Indigenous religious traditions?).

Elsewhere
Kelsey, Penelope. "Disability and Native North American Boarding School Narratives: Madonna Swan and Sioux Sanitorium." *Journal of Literary & Cultural Disability Studies* 7(2) (2013): 195–211. https://search-proquest-com.libproxy.lib.unc.edu/docview/1426059396?pq-origsite=summon.

Nielsen, Kim E. *A Disability History of the United States*. Boston: Beacon, 2012.

Weaver, Hilary N. "Disability through a Native American Lens: Examining Influences of Culture and Colonization." *Journal of Social Work in Disability and Rehabilitation* 14(3–4) (2015): 148–162. https://pubmed.ncbi.nlm.nih.gov/26288090/.

81

Are Indigenous religious traditions patriarchal?

Donnie Begay

(Thanks to Renee Begay, Zuni, and Kristen Riley, Laguna, for contributing.)

Outsiders who are peering into the Native American Southwest religious traditions may perceive them as patriarchal. "Outsiders" refers to non-Indigenous people who understand what "patriarchal" means, but the term "patriarchal" and its concept may not be part of the Indigenous people's lexicon. Insiders, or Indigenous people, can decipher the concepts of patriarchy, but it is a foreign concept because of how most, if not all, Indigenous people come from matrilineal societies.

For most, if not all, Native American tribes, the word "religion" fails to grasp the interconnected and interrelatedness of all of life, creation, spirituality, traditions, and culture. This interconnectedness and interrelation within Indigenous religious traditions are not predicated on a hierarchy in which men are on top over everyone else. From *Cherokee Women: Gender and Culture Change, 1700–1835*, traditional Cherokee societies were matrilineal, probably more than today, but a person is deemed Cherokee if they are related biologically or by adoption to a Cherokee woman. White men who intermarried with the Cherokee would be considered Cherokee due to their connection to a Cherokee woman. Matrilineal societies are usually governed culturally, socially, economically (up until colonizers arrived and dealt and traded only with other Indigenous men), and politically by women, while religious life was left to the men. The Pueblo people of the American Southwest have been initiating only the young men into their religious societies, where they learn the prayers used in ceremonies that keep the balance and peace of their communities. Most of the nineteen Pueblos utilize kivas, a sort of religious center where initiated men gather to discuss issues pertaining to their people and often include religious matters. Outsiders who are unfamiliar with Pueblo traditions could be perceived as patriarchal—controlled and monitored by men. Yet when feasts happen or certain ceremonies are conducted, the women play a major role. Their roles include but are not limited to cooking the food, grinding the corn (for ceremonial use), and caring for the men who make pilgrimages. Many of these roles are necessary for feasts and carrying out the duties of ceremonies. Women are also responsible for donating foods to families or plazas where dances occur, and they usually have to recite a specific greeting or prayer. When these feasts or ceremonies occur, all people play a role and are responsible to teach the next generation their Indigenous religious traditions.

The normativity of the gender binary is generally accepted by most of American society and by plenty of Native Americans, but gender binaries are not the norm in traditional oral narratives. In the Navajo creation narrative, two of the first created beings, not exactly the same as the human beings of today, were intersex and skilled with earthenware. Eventually, the two intersex persons, who are considered sacred beings, became the sun and the moon. In Zuni, one of the nineteen Pueblos, Weiwha is revered for his/her many contributions to the life of her/his people by carrying out the duties of men and women. Weiwha is still revered and celebrated among the Zuni today. The strict distinction between male and female is weakened in Indigenous thought and world view. The interrelatedness and interconnection of all creation are essential to maintain and/or restore harmony and balance. Being intersex or other nonbinary gender does not exclude them from their people or the journey to personhood.

To think of Indigenous religious traditions as patriarchal is to assume Indigenous people fully adopt Western concepts like "patriarchal" gender binaries. It is possible to argue Indigenous religious traditions are patriarchal due to the fact that many sacred teachings of tribes are often reserved to be learned and taught by men only. But through an Indigenous lens, the concept of male and female is only part of the whole where everyone—male, female, neither, both—plays a major role in daily life, feasts, and ceremonies. They all have a responsibility to teach the next generation their Indigenous religious traditions.

About the author

Yáʼátʼééh, **Donnie Begay** lives in Albuquerque, New Mexico, and is married to Renee, who is from Zuni Pueblo. They have three daughters: Natalia, Kaya, and Peri. Donnie is Navajo and grew up on the Navajo reservation. He is born into his mother's clan, Honágháahnii (One-Who-Walks-Around), and born for his father's clan, Kinyaaʼáanii (Towering House People).

He graduated from New Mexico State University with a BA in business administration, graduated from George Fox University (now Portland Seminary) with an MA in intercultural studies, and is working on his PhD from the University of Divinity in Australia.

Suggestions for further reading

In this book
See also chapters 63 (Why is distinguishing a Native American world view from a eurochristian one important?) and 82 (Did Indigenous people really honor LGBT/two-spirit people?).

Elsewhere
Perdue, Theda. *Cherokee Women: Gender and Culture Change, 1700–1835.* Indians of the Southeast. Lincoln: University of Nebraska Press, 1999.

Smith, Andrea. *Conquest: Sexual Violence and American Indian Genocide.* Boston: South End, 2005.

82

Did Indigenous people really honor LGBT/two-spirit people?

Lisa Poirier

The short answer is yes, but the better answer is a bit more complicated. The term "two-spirit" is relatively new. Dr. Myra Laramee (Fisher River Cree Nation) first shared the term with others at a conference for LGBT First Nations people that was held in Winnipeg in 1990. Before the conference, she had a vision in which she learned that her Anishinaabemowin name, *niizh manidoowag*, signified two spirits, energies, or sacred powers, one masculine and one feminine, that resided together inside herself. The term "two-spirit" was subsequently adopted and used by growing numbers of Indigenous people from many different Native nations across North America.

Some Indigenous people who use the term "two-spirit" claim identities that fit within the LGBTQIA spectrum and are comfortable naming themselves as lesbian, gay, bisexual, trans, queer, intersex, or asexual. Others identify with and intentionally reclaim Indigenous gender identities that existed prior to European colonization and are not adequately represented in the LGBTQIA acronym. This is the reason for the expanded acronym used by many activist groups today: LGBTQIA2S+, which specifically includes the two-spirit (2S) and other gender identities that Euro-American categories have historically excluded and erased.

This erasure began with the European colonization of the Americas. Many European explorers, missionaries, and settlers observed Indigenous people who did not conform to European binary notions of gender or who did not adhere to European heteronormative expectations in regard to sexuality. Colonial documents are filled with examples. French explorers in Florida in the sixteenth century who identified some Timucua people as "hermaphrodites" because their appearance and their cultural roles (which included acting as emissaries, giving aid to warriors, and supplying war parties with provisions) differed from those that the French—and evidently the Timucua—classified as men or women. In the seventeenth and eighteenth centuries, French missionaries and explorers recorded seeing among the Illinois Confederacy and the Natchez male-bodied people who did women's work and had ritual responsibilities as singers. In the sixteenth century, Spanish conquistadors, missionaries, and administrators noted the presence of noncisgender and nonheterosexual Indigenous people as far south as today's Brazil and as far north as the Colorado River. Colonial documents include accounts of horrific tortures and murders of Indigenous people by both Spanish and French colonizers as punishment. Murder for the crime of "sodomy" or for being otherwise "unnatural" illustrates the extent of European intolerance of Indigenous gender identities and sexual practices that did not strictly conform to European norms.

Today, scholars and two-spirit people alike often look to Indigenous languages for terms for people whose genders transcend the male/female binary. In North America alone, over 150 Native nations have words for these genders. The biographies of particularly outstanding people who are remembered by these nations in their oral histories are also of significant interest. The Stones of Kapemahu are monuments in Waikiki commemorating four *māhū* (third-gender) religious specialists, known for their healing powers. Qánqon-kamek-klaúlha (Sitting-in-the-water-grizzly) was a Kutenai person assigned female gender at birth who later in life claimed a male gender identity. The Kutenai descriptor is *titqattek*. He had visions, fought in battle, took a wife, and was known for healing a chief. The Absalooke (Crow) tell stories about Woman Chief, who identified as male and eventually married four women. He was an accomplished horseman, hunter, and leader in both wartime and peacetime. The Absalooke also remember Ochiish, whose skills in warfare earned him the name "He-finds-them-and-kills-them." Ochiish was a *badé* (third-gender) who made and wore women's garments and was skilled at leatherwork and beading. She and a few others like her were punished by US government Indian agents by being made to wear men's clothing and perform manual labor under their supervision. We'wha was a highly regarded A:shiwi (Zuni) potter and weaver *lha'mana* (third-gender). She became an ambassador for her people, visiting Washington, DC, and charming officials there. However, she was later unjustly imprisoned for preventing a US soldier from arresting the governor of Zuni Pueblo.

Two-spirit, third-gender (or fourth- or fifth-gender) people have always been present in Indigenous societies. Their roles have differed from culture to culture; each person's identity falls somewhere along the spectrum of gender known to their particular nation. Some have been warriors, some have been peacemakers, some have been potters, some have been singers, some have been leaders, and some have been religious specialists. While their gender identities have made them worthy of note, their special contributions to their societies are ultimately what have kept them alive in the memories of their people. American Indian Movement (AIM) leader Russell Means was quoted by Duane Brayboy as saying, "In my culture we have people who dress half-man, half-woman. Winkte, we call them in our language. If you are Winkte, that is an honorable term and you are a special human being and among my nation and all Plains people, we consider you a teacher of our children and are proud of what and who you are."

About the author

Lisa Poirier is an associate professor in the Department of Religious Studies at DePaul University in Chicago. She lives and works on the traditional lands of the Council of the Three Fires—the Ojibwe, Odawa, and Potawatomi Nations. At DePaul, she teaches classes about Native American religions, theory and method in the study of religion, new religious movements, and gender and sexuality in religion.

Suggestions for further reading

In this book
See also chapter 81 (Are Indigenous religious traditions patriarchal?).

Elsewhere
Brayboy, Duane. "Two Spirits, One Heart, Five Genders." *Indian Country Today*, September 13, 2018. https://indiancountrytoday.com/archive/two -spirits-one-heart-five-genders.

Jacobs, Sue-Ellen, Wesley Thomas, and Sabine Lang, eds. *Two-Spirit People: Native American Gender Identity, Sexuality, and Spirituality*. Urbana: University of Illinois Press, 1997.

Rifkin, Mark. *When Did Indians Become Straight? Kinship, the History of Sexuality, and Native Sovereignty*. Oxford: Oxford University Press, 2011.

Roscoe, Will. "Sexual and Gender Diversity in Native America and the Pacific Islands." In *LGBTQ America: A Theme Study of Lesbian, Gay, Bisexual, Transgender and Queer History*, edited by Megan E. Springate. Washington, DC: National Park Foundation, 2016. https://www.nps.gov/ subjects/lgbtqheritage/upload/lgbtqtheme-nativeamerica.pdf.

83
What is the relationship between Indigenous religion and sovereignty?

Stacie Swain

Sovereignty, like other key concepts, is subject to questions of meaning, translation, and application. Sovereignty serves as a language of power because—not unlike the category of religion—sovereignty relates to political community, boundaries, and authority. Since the concept originates within European law and politics, scholars hold a range of opinions on whether it is an inherently imperial or colonial term and its utility for Indigenous peoples. Does using the term "sovereignty" automatically recapture Indigenous peoples within the language and thus the ideas and structures of the colonizer? Or can Indigenous peoples take up and use the language of sovereignty strategically, grounded in their own world views, to assert authority and territorial rights or responsibilities? To understand sovereignty, we can look at the claims and contexts in which the concept gets used.

For example, consider the context presently known as "Canada." Before this place became known as such, explorers planted the flags and symbols of empires—France, Britain, Spain, and Russia—into the land. This was a recognized legal ritual within papal law called the Doctrine of Discovery. Through this ritual, Christian European nations acquired sovereignty in the so-called new world, which entailed both property rights and power over the non-Christian, non-European peoples living there, despite Indigenous peoples' own political identities and relationships to the land. State sovereignty is understood as supreme power or authority over a bounded territory and those within it; this power is exerted through the ability to dispose of property, a degree of external autonomy, the internal delegation of power, and a monopoly on legalized violence. In this context, explorers made sovereignty claims on behalf of empires, which saw their right to rule as God given and authorized by the pope.

Despite these conceptual origins, however, Indigenous peoples use the language of sovereignty to draw attention to their own authority and relationships to territory. For example, Indigenous peoples may assert their *inherent* sovereignty, meaning authority that is derived from their own legal orders; this can be contrasted against, for example, forms of delegated authority that get granted through the state's legal and legislative institutions. The language of sovereignty also gets applied to other domains of life: there are discourses on intellectual, bodily, sexual, spiritual, and food sovereignty. For some, sovereignty's reference to ultimate authority over an area of life can serve as potent language to claim one's rights or autonomy.

As opposed to how the concept is understood within Christian-derived law, however, when Indigenous peoples assert sovereignty, they rarely seem to claim absolute power over the land or the right to dispose of it as property. Rather, what *can* the concept mean if understood in relation to Indigenous peoples' own legal traditions? For example, some Indigenous creation stories express that a place has been given to members of an Indigenous nation for the nation to meet their needs, which then entails a responsibility to care for the land's needs. Here, the circulation of power operates through practices of reciprocity, where Indigenous people derive their power *from* the land and community that sustains them versus claiming power *over* a territory to fulfill Christian-derived ideas about the "use" of the land. These relationships of responsibility and accountability are articulated within oral traditions and transmitted through a range of activities that often get categorized as Indigenous religious tradition.

When it comes to scholarly analysis, some of the caveats that apply to the concept of "religion" also apply to "sovereignty." Both concepts share Christian origins and have legitimized claims of religious and racial supremacy but have also been used to contest colonization. Both concepts relate to the construction of political communities and the circulation of power within and between them. While neither scholars nor practitioners agree on whether Indigenous assertions of sovereignty will ultimately dismantle imperial and colonial power structures, any analysis of such must consider meaning, context, and what is happening within the territory in question.

When considering the concept of sovereignty in relation to Indigenous nationhood, it can be helpful to bracket assumptions about the concept's etymology and consider how the term is being applied. Sovereignty's applicability depends on who you ask and how the concept is being understood and made effective through, for example, practices of jurisdiction—how legal authority is actually established and enacted within a specific context. Despite colonial assertions of sovereignty, many Indigenous people and communities continue to maintain their relationships with the land and other relatives through such practices. It is worth asking why some assertions of sovereignty are recognized as political and others treated as "merely" religious, spiritual, or cultural.

About the author

Stacie Swain is a Ukrainian-British doctoral student in the Department of Political Science and the Indigenous Nationhood Program at the University of Victoria in lək̓ʷəŋən territories (Victoria, BC). Her research considers Indigenous ceremony and the categories of religion and politics, particularly in relation to settler colonialism, Indigenous legal orders, and the governance of public space.

Suggestions for further reading

In this book
See also chapters 1 (Why does the title of this book use the phrase "Indigenous religious traditions" rather than "Indigenous religions"?) and 84 (Indigenous futurism . . . is that like science fiction?).

Elsewhere
Barker, Joanne, ed. *Critically Sovereign: Indigenous Gender, Sexuality, and Feminist Studies*. Durham, NC: Duke University Press, 2017.

Barker, Joanne, ed. *Sovereignty Matters: Locations of Contestation and Possibility in Indigenous Struggles for Self-Determination*. Contemporary Indigenous Issues. Lincoln: University of Nebraska Press, 2005.

Klassen, Pamela E. "Fantasies of Sovereignty: Civic Secularism in Canada." *Critical Research on Religion* 3(1) (2015): 41–56. https://doi.org/10.1177/2050303215584230.

Miller, Robert J., Jacinta Ruru, Larissa Behrendt, and Tracey Lindberg, eds. *Discovering Indigenous Lands: The Doctrine of Discovery in the English Colonies*. Oxford: Oxford University Press, 2010.

Pasternak, Shiri. *Grounded Authority: The Algonquins of Barriere Lake against the State*. Minneapolis: University of Minnesota Press, 2017.

Stark, Heidi. "Nenabozho's Smart Berries: Rethinking Tribal Sovereignty and Accountability." *Michigan State Law Review* 2 (2013): 339. http://digitalcommons.law.msu.edu/lr/vol2013/iss2/6.

Indigenous Futurity

84
Indigenous futurism … is that like science fiction?

Matt Sheedy

The 2009 Hollywood film *2012* is loosely based on a Mayan prophecy that circulated for years in popular culture. A common interpretation of this prophecy was that the world would end in 2012, which the film reproduces in its own way, tapping into elements of Christian millenarianism, "New Age" prophecies (e.g., Mayanism), and fears of environmental collapse. Although the Mesoamerican Long Count calendar did come to an end in 2012, for most Mayan cultures, this signaled a time of transition and hope for renewal. This example is one of many appropriations of Indigenous traditions that reflect the concerns and interests of settler societies. Indigenous futurism (IF), by contrast, is a genre told by Indigenous people.

History of religions scholar Bruce Lincoln famously wrote about how societies are constructed on the basis of force and discourse. As Indigenous people were subject to tremendous force under colonialism and shaped by how settler discourse (mis)represented them (e.g., in art, education, media, etc.), IF can be thought of as a form of counterdiscourse that attempts to reclaim elements of Indigenous cultures, such as language, ceremony, and forms of knowledge.

In her introduction to *Walking the Clouds: An Anthology of Indigenous Science Fiction* (2012), Grace Dillion (Anishinaabe), who coined the term "Indigenous futurism," notes a variety of themes that are common to IF, including Native slipstream; Indigenous knowledge as a form of science; confronting themes of apocalypse, revolution, and sovereignty for Native peoples; and *biskaabiiyang*, an Anishinaabe term meaning "returning to ourselves."

Although IF often features pan-Indigenous experiences, such as boarding/residential schools in the United States and Canada, and (in)famous conflicts like the Battle of Little Bighorn, it is also a site for engaging with particular Indigenous cultures. In this way, IF reengages with distinct histories, customs, cosmologies, and so on from a tradition-specific point of view. For example, in the web series *Time Traveler*™, the main protagonist is a Mohawk man who explores a variety of pan-Indigenous colonial encounters and acts of resistance, such as the story of Pocahontas and the occupation of Alcatraz Island by members of the American Indian movement in 1969. At the same time, he grapples with particular elements of his own tradition while envisioning a thriving future for Indigenous communities.

The term "Native slipstream" is attributed to science fiction writer Gerald Vizenor (Chippewa), who uses it to describe stories that bend the space-time continuum (e.g., time travel) and links it to the concept of "survivance," which combines the words survival and resistance. Relatedly, Kyle Whyte (Potawatomi) draws upon the Anishinaabe expression *aanikoobijigan* as an example of "spiraling time" between the past and the future, where ancestors exist on the same intergenerational plane of existence as their descendants. Taken together, Vizenor and Whyte highlight the very clear link between certain types of Indigenous knowledge and IF—from dreamtime (commonly linked to Aborigines cultures) to cyclical understandings of the past, present, and future that depart from Western modes of temporality.

On the themes of apocalypse, revolution, and sovereignty for Native peoples, IF often foregrounds the continuing effects of colonialism, such as dispossession of land, forced relocation, loss of culture, and ecosystem collapse. This functions as a way of grappling with present dystopian realities while also pointing to forms of Indigenous knowledge as a way out of these predicaments. For example, Candis Callison (Tahltan) writes about how the climate crisis mimics experiences that Indigenous people have already gone through and thereby positions them as potential leaders in bringing forward possible solutions. A variation of this theme is taken up by Jeff Barnaby (Mi'kmaq) in his 2019 zombie film *Blood Quantum*, where Indigenous people are the only ones unaffected by a plague as settlers flee to them for safety. Relatedly, Danika Medak-Saltzman (Turtle Mountain Chippewa) points to the Anishinaabe Seven Fires prophecy as a future-oriented cosmology that blends seamlessly with IF. The seven fires reflect a time of Indigenous renewal, when the decisions that Native and non-Native people make will determine whether we reach the Eighth Fire.

In these and other ways, IF can be viewed as a popular medium that draws on the genre of science fiction to reengage the past and imagine a different and better future for Indigenous people. This genre blends seamlessly with many Indigenous cosmologies that present nonlinear modes of time and intergenerational relationships and has gained greater attention over the last decade or so through Indigenous activism, from the Idle No More movement to the campaign to change Native mascots.

About the author

Matt Sheedy holds a PhD in the study of religion and is visiting professor of North American studies at the University of Bonn, Germany. His research includes critical theories of secularism and religion and representations of atheism, Islam, Christianity, and Native American traditions in popular and political culture. His latest book is *Owning the Secular: Religious Symbols, Culture Wars, Western Fragility* (Routledge, 2021).

Suggestions for further reading

In this book
See also chapters 75 (What is the Popol Vuh [and why is it not a Maya bible]?) and 72 (How are Indigenous narratives and oral traditions like "texts"?).

Elsewhere
Dillon, Grace. *Walking the Clouds: An Anthology of Indigenous Science Fiction.* Tucson: University of Arizona Press, 2012.

Medak-Saltzman, Danika. "Coming to You from the Indigenous Future: Native Women, Speculative Short Films, and the Art of the Possible." *Studies in American Indian Literatures* 29(1) (Spring 2017): 139–171.

Whyte, Kyle. "Indigenous Science (Fiction) for the Anthropocene: Ancestral Dystopias and Fantasies of Climate Change Crisis." *Nature and Space* 1(1–2) (2018): 224–242.

Index